SPECTACLES AND SPECTERS

Spectacles and Specters

A PERFORMATIVE THEORY OF POLITICAL TRIALS

Başak Ertür

FORDHAM UNIVERSITY PRESS   NEW YORK   2022

Fordham University Press has no responsibility for the persistence or accuracy of URLs for external or third-party Internet websites referred to in this publication and does not guarantee that any content on such websites is, or will remain, accurate or appropriate.

Fordham University Press also publishes its books in a variety of electronic formats. Some content that appears in print may not be available in electronic books.

Visit us online at www.fordhampress.com.

Library of Congress Cataloging-in-Publication Data available online at https://catalog.loc.gov.

Printed in the United States of America

24 23 22   5 4 3 2 1

First edition

For my parents, Yaprak Zihnioğlu and Gürhan Ertür, and their comrades

Contents

    Armenian Genocide   131
    Legal Returns • Atemporal Histories of Terror • Process unto Oblivion •
    "Genocide" as Counter-Memory

6   Law of Denial: The Armenian Genocide before the
    European Court of Human Rights   156
    The Envoy • The Judge, The Historian, and the Politician •
    Judging the Presence of the Past

    Conclusion   175

    ACKNOWLEDGMENTS   187

    NOTES   191

    INDEX   223

Preface

It is the morning of 4 April 2019 and I'm in the labyrinthine new Palace of Justice in Istanbul. Completed in 2011, this mammoth structure now houses the courts that used to be strewn across eleven different courthouses around the city. The complex is made up of eighteen blocks of four- to nineteen-story buildings bunched up together right in the middle of a messy network of highways. It is difficult to make spatial sense of this thing even in aerial photographs, and it becomes increasingly impossible as one approaches it. Once inside, it is a maze: bewildering in its combination of senseless vastness and suffocating crampedness, disorienting in its lack of acoustic design, soul-sucking in its ghastly aesthetics. Compared to other monumental architectural structures of the city, it really is brand new, but it feels as if it has been in accelerated decay since the moment of its founding.

Up and down the seemingly non-consecutive floors, through the low ceilinged and arbitrarily barricaded corridors, I find my way to the Istanbul 32nd Heavy Penal Court. The name sounds grand, but it is just one of the hundreds of rooms here, with its resident panel of judges. Mine will be the first hearing in this courtroom this morning, but the three judges have yet to arrive, so I wait around. I am not alone, my lawyer, friends, and parents are with me. There is also a crowd of academics, some acquaintances, some not, who have turned up either for the solidarity shift, or to stand trial themselves as signatories of the Academics for Peace petition. They are all at different stages of their respective trials. Like me, all are charged with "terrorist propaganda," using the same copy-paste indictment, for the same act of adding our names to the same petition. But we are tried individually in different courts— "Mine's 25, yours?" I overhear in the corridors. I find out that Fadime, a close family friend, also has her hearing this morning, and hers is also 32, though it's her fifth or sixth hearing. I sit next to her on the hard bench outside the courtroom in the loving warmth of her smile, as we wait for the men of law to finish sipping their tea.

So far, the sentences have varied for each of the hundreds of academics convicted for signing the same petition. The judge that presides over 32 is not one of the most notorious ones, so if we play it right, my lawyer expects I will get the median: a fifteen-month prison sentence, suspended. But our strategy for this hearing is to try to postpone the verdict, and number 32 is known to hurry the cases to conclusion. My lawyer believes that the Constitutional Court may eventually put an end to this affair and says it would be good to avoid a conviction until then: It will be just so much more paperwork if I am convicted before the high court throws out the cases. Notably, one of the appellants in the case before the Constitutional Court is Professor Füsun Üstel who received a fifteen-month prison sentence and served two and half months of it, because she refused to ask for a suspension, as it amounts to accepting the attributed crime as committed. Hers was also 32. I am advised to ask for a suspension, and I will do so. I ask Fadime whether she has agreed to a suspension. She says she managed to delay her answer so far, but if she is forced to give an answer today, she will refuse to request it. She says it would not be appropriate for someone of her age and professional status to ask for a suspended sentence. I'm struck by the contrast between the weight of the meaning of her words, and the utter modesty and lightness with which she speaks.

Eventually we are allowed into the courtroom, I sit alone in the dock, right in the center of the space, facing an empty judicial bench. My lawyer sits at a distance, in the space dedicated to the defense team toward the front of the room on the right. She is behind a desk with her back to the right-hand side wall, facing toward the middle of the room. When the proceedings begin, she will shift her chair 45 degrees to her right so as to face the bench more directly. Straight across from her, on the left side of the room is a desk that mirrors the defense desk. I presume it must be where the prosecutor will sit. I turn around in my seat and see the public audience sitting in two columns behind me. My friends and family are on the left, and Fadime's friends are on the right; they are a fiery cohort of feminists in their sixties and seventies, some of whom I've been intimately familiar with all my life through my mother. I feel watched over and emboldened. There is the same frown on everybody's face, preparing for yet another episode of the senseless charade.

Finally, the panel of judges arrives. The chief judge makes a point of taking some time to scan and stare down the audience from his seat on the raised bench. I think of a pack of dogs on a hill, trying to intimidate those on the path below using the vertical advantage. I have my back to the audience, but I can feel that they are staring right back at him. As far as I can see, the prosecutor hasn't arrived, but I'm asked to stand up and approach the pulpit directly in front of the chief judge. I had already noticed in the hearings of other colleagues that this is an awkwardly designed item, too low and too wide to rest your hands on, but it prompts its utilization just by virtue of being there. I ignore the demand of the furniture so as to avoid taking a distorted posture in front of the judges. I stand upright and wait for the men to begin the proceedings. The first stage, my lawyer had advised, will be identification: I am to confirm that I am indeed the accused on file. The judge starts speaking, but I realize he has already gone off script, he is not asking me my name and date of birth, he is asking me to take my hands from my pockets. I look down and am amused to see that I have taken an unpremeditated cowboy posture: thumbs in pockets, fingers pointing towards my crotch, ready to go for my guns. I remove my thumbs from my pockets.

The judge asks for my defense, I ask for the charges. He says I should have received the indictment, I say I haven't. He looks at the computer screen in front of him, and says it was sent to Ankara. I am confused; my lawyer is based in Ankara but I have nothing to do with the capital: I'm from Istanbul, and I live and work in London. There is some shuffling below the bench, and one of the clerks hands me the indictment hot off the printer on the stenographer's desk. I know what's in the indictment; it is the same as everyone else's; and I've even written and published an analysis of it. But I scan the top page and see that the document identifies me as employed by Middle East Technical University in Ankara. Clearly a sloppy copy-paste error, as I've never been affiliated in any way with the institution. If this document is powerful enough to send me to prison, can I use it, I wonder, to claim my post there? After all, it is one of the top two universities in the country. How about some back pay?

The judge asks for my defense again. My lawyer intervenes to politely remind him of all the prior procedural steps that he has just attempted to skip, and also that I will not be offering my defense at this hearing, having just received the indictment. He can ask me, however, for my initial plea as required by criminal procedure. The judge rolls his eyes and rewinds to the beginning. He asks for my plea to the charge of terrorist propaganda. I speak a few sentences, slowly, explaining why I signed the petition and that it constitutes no crime. I make sure to avoid using the word "peace" as per my lawyer's advice: "It terrorizes them." The judge asks whether I agree to a suspension of the verdict. I say yes. He visibly relaxes: I have capitulated.

Then it is my lawyer's turn. She speaks eloquently of her astonishment that these trials are still going on, that hundreds of academics are being prosecuted individually for signing the same peace petition, with the same shabby indictment that represents a shameful blot on the legal profession. She then articulates a series of procedural requests, and I realize that in the course of her speech she has repeated the name of the capital several times: "In the discussions we've had with the Ministry of Justice in Ankara . . ."; "in the judiciary circles of Ankara"; "in the Academics for Peace hearings in Ankara." What she seems to be saying in between the lines is, you've gone rogue here in Istanbul, I have some news from the capital.

Then the prosecutor speaks, or rather, something starts speaking in the courtroom. I first think it is one of the Fujitsu computer screens on the high bench to the left of the three judges and then understand it is the prosecutor behind the screen. I never see his face, and he speaks in dictation mode, like an automated voice software, addressing only the stenographer. A lawyer friend later settles my architectural confusion: Initially this new court complex was designed with the idea that the prosecutors would sit across from the defense teams, on the same level with them, at the opposite desk, where I expected my prosecutor to sit. But later they decided to retain the old practice of seating the prosecutors at one end of the high bench, imperiously peering down alongside the judges: The new Palace of not so much Justice. The judge accepts everything Fujitsu says and by implication rejects all procedural requests by my lawyer. My trial is postponed to the next hearing in June. They make sure to schedule the hearing according to the preference of my lawyer, since their esteemed colleague will need to travel from Ankara. I'm amazed that she's managed to pull it off; we've got the Ankara-effect on our side, and I hadn't even realized it was a thing. But I will not appear before the court again; we will manage to postpone the trial to yet another hearing, and my lawyer will prove right: In late July 2019, the Constitutional Court in Ankara will rule that these trials are in breach of our right to freedom of expression. Eventually, along with hundreds of other signatories, I will be acquitted.

I step out of the courtroom with my supporters. We all pose for a souvenir picture in front of 32, me in the middle, with thumbs in pockets. My friend Billur keeps looking at me incredulously and shaking her head with a smile. When we finally sit down for tea, I get to ask her what she is thinking. She says, of all people, you going through this, it is just too absurd. I sincerely admire her ability to remain surprised; after all, mine was Academics for Peace trial number eight hundred and something, and I'm not her first close friend to face trial either. But I also know what she means, we were writing companions as we worked on our doctoral theses at the British Library, hers on the slow food movement in Turkey, mine on political trials. I think to myself, I really should get that work out and be done with all this.

SPECTACLES AND SPECTERS

Introduction

This is a book about political trials that draws on theories of performativity to conceptualize the entanglements of law and political violence. While political trials are most commonly accounted for in terms of the political instrumentalization of law, this book argues that making sense of the politics of a trial requires a shift of focus, or rather, a readjustment of our frame so that the focal point is no longer law's instrumentality but instead its performativity. It also argues the converse, that political trials are exceptionally illuminating occasions for grasping the performative workings of law.

In using the phrase "political trials" to describe the scope of this book, I do not limit it to its loose journalistic sense that is most common today. In this narrow usage, "political trials" refer to what are understood as "illiberal" recourses to legal procedure for sake of political expediency—for example, the use of criminal trials to persecute, undermine, or incapacitate a political opponent. The wider sense of political trials that I work with includes the more "liberal" political recourses to trials, such as the deployment of legal proceedings to hold former dictators to account or to achieve closure and consensus in the aftermath of mass atrocity. Today, these forms of political justice are widely celebrated, most notably by the contemporary discourses and industries of international criminal law, human rights, and transitional justice, for which the Nuremberg Trial of Major War Criminals of 1945–46 serves as origin and precedent. Such political utilizations of the legal form are thus rarely tainted with the epithet "political trial" other than by their critics; and when they are, the designation itself tends to exhaust the criticism. But this was not always the case. Early critical thinking on Nuremberg and other post-Holocaust trials addressed these proceedings indeed as "political trials" and analyzed them as

1

continuous with manifestly less lofty recourses to political justice. This usage did not automatically imply that such processes should be dismissed outright as "show trials" or as "victor's justice." Instead, it inscribed the necessity to think the politics of trials beyond questions of expediency and cynical instrumentalization, while nevertheless retaining the awareness of the potential violence of political justice. I thus revive this usage to emphasize the continuity between ostensibly liberal and illiberal uses of legal trials for political ends. Remaining alive to this continuity allows reflection on such proceedings with a certain clarity vis-à-vis the entanglements of law, politics, and violence, rather than conveniently disavowing the violence of the law where it serves seemingly liberal ends. It also allows us to pause on the politics of a political trial, rather than using the designation only to declare "case closed."

I should also note that the definition of "political trials" that I work with is not an all-encompassing one. We encounter this as a proposal in early critical legal literature: Every trial is a political trial, because any given legal system reflects the power dynamics and values of its particular political milieu. This is no doubt true, but it is also a truism that forecloses further analysis. For example, it prevents the question why certain seemingly ordinary legal proceedings come to have political resonances and lives beyond the courtroom, while the rest continue to disappear into its daily grind. This line of questioning is also preempted by the narrow definition of political trials that suffices with an instrumentalist understanding, limiting the "political" of political trials to matters of governmental expediency, and applying the rubric only to those proceedings where there is an explicit or perceived power investment in the prosecution itself. But as we know, sometimes trials become politicized due to defense strategy, sometimes due to their public reception, and sometimes by organized mobilization outside the courts. Often they become politicized in incalculable ways.

In most considerations of political trials, law's relationship to political violence, that which is deemed law's other, is conceived of in terms of instrumentality: Law is either seen to be reduced to an instrument of political violence (i.e., trials as convenient venues for persecuting political enemies), or it is seen as an instrument to contain political violence (i.e., trials as appropriate venues to come to terms with the transgressions of a previous regime, or to achieve closure and consensus in the aftermath of political violence). Yet the political meanings, effects, lives, and afterlives of trials frequently exceed or contravene the sovereign wills and intentions that the proceedings are meant to serve. This book argues that making sense of the often incalculable interpenetrations of law, politics, and violence requires looking away from law's instrumentality to its performativity. In addition to enabling us to capture the various modalities in which the political emerges in, through, and in relation to legal forms in the theater of the courtroom, such a shift also attunes us to the performative failures, contradictions, and excesses of law, allowing us to account for how sovereign schemes can misfire, how trials can come to have unintended political lives and afterlives, and how law entangles with and perpetuates certain histories of violence, rather than ever simply mastering these or providing closure. It allows us, in other words, to trace the specters in the spectacles.

The book is organized in two parts. In Part I, I present a theory of political trials by reconstructing a legacy of critical thought on Nuremberg in engagement with theories of performativity. I begin by revisiting a moment of creative theoretical production on the intersection of law and politics in the early 1960s by Otto Kirchheimer, Hannah Arendt, and Judith Shklar, who grappled with the question of what legal trials could mean and do in the aftermath of the Holocaust. What is particularly noteworthy in this literature is the critical urgency with which these scholars attempted to address a key tension between the perceived necessity of a legal response to atrocity as a form of repair on the one hand, and a keen awareness of law's incongruities and potentials for misfire on the other. It is in attempting to address that tension and grapple with legal violence that they go beyond a purely instrumentalist account of political trials and begin to tease out what we may conceptualize in terms of performativity: the world-making, constitutive, institutive effects of trials. Kirchheimer, for example, discerns the ability of law to enact its own foundations into being through a trial. Arendt invests in the legal substantiation of the newly coined category of "crimes against humanity" as a way to performatively produce humanity as legal community. Shklar's identification of the performative function of a trial is one that brings embodied practice into play: The performance of a trial as a legalistic ritual can performatively re-create a culture of legalism in the aftermath of the Nazi regime's destruction of Germany's legal culture. But unlike later literature that draws on their works to uncritically celebrate the performative potentials of political trials, Kirchheimer, Arendt, and Shklar are rather cautious about their own investments in legal violence. They remain cognizant of certain fundamental questions that have become too easily forgotten in contemporary discourses of human rights, transitional justice, and international criminal law: What does it mean to mobilize the law and to attempt to instrumentalize its violence to address political violence? What does it mean to do so in venues where a fantasy of the mutual autonomy of law and politics no longer holds, and therefore legal violence is no longer strictly separable from political violence?

The performative theory of political trials proposed in this book takes up the 1960s critical legacy, couching and further developing the incipient insights we encounter therein. In the trajectory of theories of performativity that I trace, a concept that was coined within the philosophy of language for capturing how speaking and doing coincide, or how speech can bring about its referent, blossoms into a valuable idiom for theorizing the interrelated operations of force, convention, and authority. In other words, we might do well to take Jacques Derrida's quip "the juridical is at work in the performative," seriously.[1] As a conceptual idiom, performativity proves helpful both for rethinking the role of performance in trials, and for understanding the various ways in which violence is addressed, negotiated, transformed, re-enacted, and perpetuated through legal proceedings. As opposed to readings that tend to approach political trials as scenes of mastery, that is, as convenient instruments of sovereign power through which political violence is wielded, say, for the sake of persecuting political adversaries, or contained through pedagogic spectacle or therapeutic working-through, a performative theory of political trials allows us to avoid such overdeterminations of the political.

In Part II, I offer close readings of a number of trials concerning the Armenian genocide, including the 1921 Berlin trial of Soghomon Tehlirian who assassinated Talat Pasha, the Ottoman statesman widely deemed the architect of the genocide; the Istanbul trial concerning the state-sponsored assassination of Armenian Turkish journalist Hrant Dink in 2007; and the 2015 European Court of Human Rights case concerning genocide denial, *Perinçek v. Switzerland*. In addition to grounding my proposals for a performative theory of political trials, these case studies introduce a shift of perspective by looking beyond the Holocaust and its trials, to the Armenian genocide and its fragmentary, oblique legal aftermaths. Nuremberg as precedent has come to dominate our ways of making sense of the potentials and limits of political justice in tending to political violence. In thus dislocating the meaning-making centrality of Nuremberg, this shift of perspective facilitates a reconsideration of various investments in political justice that have become all too habitual in the wake of Nuremberg, including the pedagogic, didactic, historiographic, therapeutic, and memorial functions attributed to legal trials in the aftermath of political violence.

Performativity and Performance

You will have probably already noted that I use the term "performative" not in its increasingly common contemporary sense as an adjective derived from "performance." Instead, my usage refers to the sense of the term as coined by J. L. Austin, a key figure in ordinary language philosophy, and the various inflections that the term has taken on in critical theory. My engagement in this book with the conceptual apparatus of performativity for understanding how law operates in general, and theorizing political trials in particular, is mainly indebted to Jacques Derrida's and Judith Butler's insights on the intersection between law and performativity. In these renditions, the conceptual apparatus of performativity goes beyond the immediate question of how legal language works, to serve as part of a wider analytic frame for legal thought, including for theorizing normativity, conventionality, and law's relationship to its origins and its historicity. The suggestion that performativity can explain not only how legal language works but also how law works is perhaps an obvious point for legal scholars who propose that we must study law *as* language. Further, the genre of deconstructive analysis that I draw on is often interpreted to render linguistic whatever its object is. But my orientation here is somewhat different. While some of the work that "performativity" does in this book can indeed be understood as pertaining to a linguistic or language-based model of interpreting law, I also demand more of the concept in drawing on Derrida's and Butler's work. I engage with it to address what in the final instance is not reducible to language and its forms: the question of the force/violence that posits and preserves law, and the operations and effects of the historical sedimentation of legal conventions and forms. Thus to inquire into the workings of legal performativity is not necessarily to remain within a linguistic model. To the contrary, in facilitating the conceptualization of law's relationship to its historicity, legal performativity provides a lens with which to interpret how this relationship is structurally sustained within legal forms that are often embodied and material.

While I do not mean "performative" in the sense of "pertaining to performance," I also do not mean to occlude the critical significance of performance for legal performativity. Insofar as force, convention, and authority involve embodied practices in addition to linguistic ones, the thinking of legal performativity necessitates addressing matters of legal performance. For example, it is worthwhile to consider the questions raised by the strange conflation of legal performance and performativity in the opening passages of Hannah Arendt's *Eichmann in Jerusalem.* Arendt begins her report on the Eichmann trial by offering a vivid visual description of the courtroom. She claims with some disdain that the architect of the courtroom must have "had a theater in mind,"[2] curiously omitting the detail that the site was indeed purpose-built as a public hall for concerts and plays, and converted into an improvised courtroom for the event simply because there were no courts large enough to accommodate the numbers that were expected at the historic trial.[3] "Clearly," Arendt adds, "this courtroom is not a bad place for the show trial David Ben-Gurion, Prime Minister of Israel, had in mind when he decided to have Eichmann kidnapped in Argentina and brought to the District Court of Jerusalem to stand trial for his role in the 'final solution of the Jewish question.'"[4] Seemingly unable to resist the dramatic flair that she criticizes, Arendt places her narrative's dramatis personae on this theatrical stage through a rhetoric of stark opposition. This is not an opposition of the typical adversarial variety between the prosecution and the defense, but between the prosecution and the bench, and notably, it pertains to their performance. Arendt lauds the judges for not being theatrical in their conduct at any point during the proceedings, and for trying "to prevent the trial from becoming a show trial under the influence of the prosecutor's love of showmanship" (5). She notes that the odds were high against this effort due to the political origins of the trial—it was made possible by Prime Minister David Ben-Gurion's technically illegal but politically expedient decision to kidnap Eichmann to stage this trial for various ideological and pedagogical ends. Arendt writes:

> And Ben-Gurion, rightly called the "architect of the state," remains the invisible stage manager of the proceedings. Not once does he attend a session; in the courtroom he speaks with the voice of Gideon Hausner, the Attorney General, who, representing the government, does his best, his very best, to obey his master. . . . The latter's rule, as Mr. Hausner is not slow in demonstrating, is permissive; it permits the prosecutor to give press-conferences and interviews for televisions during the trial, and even "spontaneous" outbursts to reporters in the court building. . . . It permits frequent side glances into the audience, and the theatrics characteristic of a more than ordinary vanity. (5–6)

Mr. Hausner is said to fully indulge in "all the nice pleasures of putting oneself in the limelight" (6). Compare this to Arendt's description of the conduct of the judges, in which,

> At no time is there anything theatrical. . . . Their walk is unstudied, their sober and intense attention, visibly stiffening under the impact of grief as they listen to the tales of suffering, is natural, their impatience with the prosecutor's attempt to drag out these hearings forever is spontaneous and refreshing, their attitude to the defense perhaps a shade over-polite. . . . Their manner toward the accused always beyond reproach. They are so obviously three good and honest men that one is not surprised that none of them yields to the greatest temptation to playact in this setting. (4)

It is often conceded that the Eichmann trial had the trappings of a show trial,[5] yet these opening passages in Arendt's account are nevertheless curious.

She regards the prosecutor's portrayal of his sense of justice as "showmanship," and yet the judges' portrayal of their sense of justice is regarded as a token of their honesty. The setting is that of a theater, the prosecutor playacts, but somehow the judges manage not to. She understands the judges' performance to be a non-performance; it is, apparently, "natural"—an odd word choice for Arendt. The judges, according to Arendt, are unstudied, spontaneous, sober, attentive, able to grieve, impatient with twaddle, polite, and beyond reproach. But the spontaneity of the prosecutor is doubtful, with scare-quotes around the adjective when she refers to his "outbursts." In her criticism of the prosecutor's conduct, there is an implicit suggestion that justice requires a certain kind of performance, and her appraisal of the judges' conduct implies that the kind of performance that justice requires is something that passes as non-performance, that is to say, non-theatrical. But why assume that the performance of the judges in this case is unstudied and unprescribed? May it not be that the judges, too, were aware that there is a certain protocol for displaying justness, for posing as just, a certain attitude that is deemed becoming of doing justice? When it comes to the formal instance of doing justice in the formal setting of a court, why should the sobriety and solemnity of the authorities that judge be necessarily deemed "natural"? May it not rather be that the common-sense expectation of how justice should be performed is at the basis of that particular kind of performance? Hence, may it not be that this particular kind of performance is indeed studied and prescribed?

Arendt's investments in how this trial was performed had to do with what we may retrospectively conceptualize as its performative aspects. Arendt wanted the Eichmann trial to be able to substantiate and give proper shape to the notion of crimes against humanity, which was only roughly moulded in Nuremberg. In this regard, the trial's dominant performance starring Gideon Hausner constituted a failure for Arendt, and mirrored or symptomized what we may understand as its infelicitous performativity, that is, its inability to offer the much needed legal innovation with regard to this new category of crimes. In presenting what Arendt read as a rehearsed performance, based on an obsession with both legal and historic precedents, Hausner failed to help build a judicial space that could be alive to the actual significance of the crime. Arendt's conviction that this was not an innocent failure, a mere inability to cope with the enormity of the task, accounts for her brilliantly bitter polemic in her report. As I elaborate further in my discussion in Chapter 1, the failure was instead due to the prioritization of other investments, namely Ben-Gurion's own vision for the trial's performative outcomes such as state-sanctioned historiography, Zionist propaganda, and a veritable threat to Israel's potential and actual foes. According to Arendt, the trial failed in certain crucial respects because it was engineered to succeed in achieving this prioritized set of goals, which she understood to be parochial and misdirected. Importantly, in Arendt's response to the Eichmann trial we see the coincidence, if not the confounding, of questions of performance and performativity. What Arendt takes issue with is first and foremost the performative pretensions of the prosecution, but this critique is initially formulated in terms of disdain for the prosecutor's performance.[6]

There are two important matters here in this conflation of legal performance and legal performativity. The first has to do with the deep ambivalence of the significance of performance for law; and the second to do with the relationship between the form and the substance of doing justice. The first question, the ambivalence of the significance of performance for law, is to some extent captured by the importance attributed to live performance in trials especially in common law jurisdictions.[7] On the one hand, this importance is intimately related to the expectation we find in Arendt that a judgment ought to be responsive to the novelty and uniqueness of the matter to be judged. The very liveness of trial performance is supposed to signify a liveliness on the part of all participants to that which is on trial. But there is always a flip side to this: The strict conventions of live performance in the trial, the organization of space and the bodies in space, the authorization of speech, the rituals of conduct, the costumes, and so on, are also precisely what risk a perception of the rehearsedness of what transpires, which in turn may lead to the dismissal of proceedings as pure theater. Julie Stone Peters discusses this in terms of the historically ambivalent relation that law has had to its own theatricality: "Theater is law's twisted mirror, its funhouse double: ever-present, substantiating, mocking, reinforcing, undermining."[8]

The second question is even more pertinent to the tasks undertaken in this book: What is the relationship between the form and substance of doing justice? That legal performance and performativity are closely connected is idealized in the classic formulation of "not only must justice be done, it must also be seen to be done." Although at face value this seems to be a relatively unproblematic combination of the doing and showing of justice, it may be necessary to question to what extent the grammar of "not only, but also" does justice to the nature of the combination. Notably, this classic formulation originated in a judicial bias case where bias was not proven but suspected. It merely "appeared" that there may have been bias, yet the appearance was sufficient to quash the original conviction.[9] Unseen justice was justice undone. We may ask, then, is it possible to speak of two separate instances, one doing, the other showing, so that justice is "not only" done, "but also" shown; or do we instead have a strange conflation of the two whereby it is difficult to tell them apart? Peters writes of this in terms of the "ontologically ambiguous fusion" of performance and performativity in law,[10] and this is indeed a succinct way to capture the question. The attempt to conceptualize the dynamics of this ambiguous fusion by examining legal performativity and performance as distinct but related terms is one of the main undertakings of this book, as part of the project of formulating a performative theory of political trials. In studying how legal performatives take shape, it is particularly important to investigate the intersections and interstices of legal performativity and legal performance in the hyper-conventional space of the trial where speech acts and bodily enactments matter in unusually accentuated ways.

Performativity and Errancy

Particularly in the wake of Judith Butler's reworking of the term "performativity" for gender theory, there was a proliferation of what I will call for lack of a better description "theatrical misreadings" of the concept, in which it was understood to designate something primarily to do with performance, in the sense of "twice-behaved behavior." This may be because Butler brought what was essentially a linguistic theoretical scheme to bear on a reading of embodied practices, gestures, and indeed, performances of gender to explicate the ways in which the "truth" of gender is performatively constructed by the repeated reenactments of gendered conventions. To put it briefly, Butler's proposal was that it is not a "truth" or "essence" of gender that is naturally given and from which the conventions of gendered practices derive, but rather the other way around; the historical sedimentation, or the repetition over time, of embodied practices of gender creates the "truth," or rather the truth-effects of gender. In thus capturing the material and embodied dimensions of discursive formations, Butler's theorization of performativity offered a unique scheme for understanding how performance, or embodied practice more generally, relates to performativity, that is, the ways in which discursive practices bring their referents into being. It is difficult to pinpoint why exactly Butler's proposal was subject to such an onslaught of theatrical misreadings. It may be that the etymology of Austin's coinage came to dominate the meaning of the term, overpowering the sense in which Austin proposed and Butler and other philosophers used it. It may have to do with the fact that by the early nineties, when Butler formulated their theory of gender performativity, the word "performative" had already made its way to performance studies where it was used primarily as the adjectival form of performance. Or perhaps it had to do with the misreading of the status of drag (by definition a theatrically exaggerated and thus denaturalized gender performance) in Butler's discussion of gender performativity, so that what Butler offered as a *marginal* example, or a limit case that throws light on the norm, was taken up as the *paradigmatic* example of gender performativity.

No matter what exactly the cause is, the main effect of the theatrical misreadings of Butler's reworking of performativity was the misconceptualization of the status of agency in performative theory. The scene of performativity was either conceived of as the scene of an absolute and unfettered sovereign agency, where "actors" performed their "truth" according to their will or whim; or it was conceived of as the complete debunking of agency, a puppet show of sorts, where the strings were understood as pulled by "discourse" as a mystified matrix of power. What these forms of theatrical misreading missed was the important reconceptualization of agency that performative theory allows, which is somewhere between these two poles of absolute sovereign agency and the absolute lack thereof. Further, they tended to neglect the ways in which performative theory offers a crucial rethinking of normativity as a sedimented historicity that is constructed and sustained through the interplay of force, conventionality, and authority. The agent in performative theory is neither sovereign nor irredeemably bonded. The ties of conventionality that bind the subject owe their force to their repetition over time, their sedimented historicity. But it is also precisely this performative structure sustained over time by the interplay of force, conventionality, and authority that leaves room for failure, errancy, subversion, and resignification.

In one sense, performative theory is, and was from the outset, a theory of errancy and failure. This may well be one of the most fascinating aspects of J. L. Austin's tract *How to Do Things with Words*, in which he elaborates his theory of the performative utterances. In naming and conceptualizing the linguistic operation whereby speech acts, Austin also names and theorizes all the ways in which it fails in attempting to do so. In effect, a substantial portion of the book is dedicated to what Austin refers to as "the doctrine of the *Infelicities*,"[11] whereby he offers a full-fledged taxonomy of failure: misfires, misinvocations, misexecutions, misapplications, flaws, hitches, abuses, insincerities, and so on. As Butler suggests, it is possible to read Austin's book "as an amusing catalogue of such failed performatives."[12] In any case, as wonderfully demonstrated by Shoshana Felman in *The Scandal of the Speaking Body*, it is actually important to take seriously the status of (often comical) failure in Austin's performative theory. In this book, originally published in French in 1980, Felman importantly brings the body, and with it the unconscious, to bear on conceptualizing performativity, thus paving the way for Judith Butler's work on the intersection of embodied practices, psychoanalysis, and performative theory.

What does all this have to do with political trials? In offering a unique lens for understanding not only the workings but also the vicissitudes of force, authority, convention, and agency, theories of performativity allow us to rethink the political in political trials beyond the sovereign schemes that they are designed or meant to serve. As instances in which sovereign power attempts to mediate its will through legal procedure, political trials always carry what Kirchheimer refers to as an "irreducible element of risk." Indeed, much like Austin and others who heed his emphasis on infelicities for conceptualizing performativity, Kirchheimer, in theorizing trials, understood the potential for failure as a defining feature of political justice. For Kirchheimer the irreducible risk emerges from various sources, including the political commitments of witnesses who may not play along with the sovereign vision for the trial and the interpretation of defendants who may effectively hijack the proceedings. But most important for a performative theory of political trials, Kirchheimer identifies legal procedure and the conventions of trial performance as key sources of risk. This effectively corresponds to the infelicities of conventionality in performative theory. On the one hand, the hyper-conventionality of legal proceedings bestows significant performative power on political agents who seek to use the courts for their sovereign schemes. On the other hand, in most political trials, there are also many counterforces involved, often precisely owing to uncertainties stemming from legal procedure itself. As I explore over the course of Chapters 3 to 6, the counterforces that militate against sovereign investments in a political trial include counter-narratives that find an effective platform in the hearings, the scandals of the speaking body, and literal and figurative hauntings. In short, political trials, even when they have an explicit agenda, are never fully directed by the sovereign investments that they are burdened with. A performative perspective on political trials sharpens our awareness as to the ways in which trials can fail to serve sovereign schemes, how law's structural unconscious may play out in a trial, manifesting the violence at its origin, and how embodied practices bring fears, desires, anxieties, fantasies, and hauntings into the scene of the trial to unsettle and recast its political meaning and effects.

Rethinking the Politics of Trials

The literature on political trials is, in one sense, vast. For well-known early instances we could easily go as far back as the 4th century BCE to the two Apologies, namely, Plato's and Xenophon's respective accounts of Socrates' defense in his trial for impiety.[13] Curiously, this trial from 399 BCE often crops up in contemporary works on political trials. This is true not only for works intended for a wide readership[14] but also for the more systematic studies that aim to provide a genre definition of sorts by presenting an encyclopaedic compilation of accounts of various trials,[15] as well as for the more analytic treatments, including Kirchheimer's *Political Justice*. The persistence of this fascination with a trial that is twenty-four centuries old could perhaps be explained by the lively intellectual legacy of Ancient Greece and its philosophers, if not by a hint of nostalgic envy on the part of the contemporary scholar who gazes with awe upon the philosopher whose philosophizing was deemed so influential as to be worthy of a public trial and capital punishment.

Another explanation for the untimely contemporaneity of Socrates' trial would be that his defense involved quintessential elements of what today would generally be recognized as a political defense. We encounter in many contemporary political trials something akin to Socrates' attempt to ridicule his prosecutor Meletus[16] with the charge of "playfulness"[17] and of "contradicting himself in the indictment."[18] Similarly, it is quite common for political defendants to attempt to turn the trial on its head so as to accuse the accusers, like Socrates does when he tells Meletus "You have cared nothing about the things for which you bring me in here" (25c), and condemn the condemners: "this brings disgrace not on me but on those who condemned me."[19] Or consider the immense drama of Socrates' refusal to repent to avail himself of a lesser sentence—could we not say that something of that drama was replayed in the 1951 trial of American communists Julius and Ethel Rosenberg, who refused to plead guilty to save their lives?[20] Isn't Socrates' outright defiance of capital punishment echoed in Algerian FLN militant Djamila Bouhired's famous laughter upon hearing her condemnation to death by a French military court in 1957? And what do we make of the eerie similarity of wording between Socrates' address to his juror/judges "men of Athens, I am now far from making a defense speech on my behalf, as someone might suppose. I do it rather on your behalf,"[21] and Saddam Hussein's exclamation "I am not defending myself, I'm defending you!" as he pointed with his index finger at the judge in his 2005 Dujail trial? Importantly, the two exclamations, although very similar, do two quite different things: one is the "I" of a liminal figure of a critic, the philosopher-pariah about to be banished from the body politic, who claims to defend "you" from "yourselves" who have indicted "yourselves" by indicting "me," whereas the other is the "I" of a deposed sovereign who attempts to reclaim the prerogative to speak on behalf of "you."

Nevertheless, the contemporary frequency of such tropes in political trials—the arrogation of the defense of the body politic, counter-indictment, counter-condemnation, ridicule, defiance of punishment, and martyrdom through refusal of mitigation or mercy—may account for why so many of the available publications on political trials seem born out of a temptation to trace the political defense speech as a genre unto itself. This in turn says something about the unique effectiveness of the criminal trial as a platform for the political defendant. Where the stakes of speech are so high as to be a matter of life or death, freedom or incarceration, condemnation or exoneration, the performative potential of speech acts becomes virtually unbounded. It is perhaps not exactly a coincidence that published speeches of political defendants were all the rage in tsarist Russia in the lead-up to the Bolshevik Revolution.[22] Nor is it exactly an exaggeration to identify Nelson Mandela's famous Rivonia trial speech as articulating "a new constitutional order, one that had yet to come into being."[23] Then again, the nature of the defense is rarely identified in the literature on political trials as definitive, as that which renders a trial political—it is the prosecution itself that is understood to give the proceedings their political character, in response to which the heroic defendant puts up resistance. One key exception in this regard is the work of the late French Vietnamese lawyer Jacques Vergès, who is often credited as the originator of the theory and practice of the "strategy of rupture."[24] This is a strategy of explosive incommensurability. It is the refusal to enter into dialogue with the court about the facts of the case or the points of law. Such radical noncompliance with the terms provided by the legal system and advanced by the prosecution is meant to tend toward an outright defiance of the political order itself. Thus the strategy of rupture aims to take the trial outside the courtroom.[25] Importantly, Vergès indicates in his *De la stratégie judiciaire* that rupture strategy need not be limited to political trials. Although we cannot derive the significance of this from his practice as a lawyer,[26] in theory, what determines the politics of a trial for Vergès is the attitude of the defense toward the social order represented by the court, rather than the nature of the crime or the stature of the criminal.

In my consideration of political trials in this book, I move away from the excessive and at times fetishistic emphasis on the heroic resistance of the political defendant, although, as indicated, a performative perspective does provide a framework for making sense of this emphasis. Instead, in taking Kirchheimer's, Arendt's, and Shklar's work on political trials as my starting point, I pursue a shift of register, namely, the attempt to think the politics of political trials beyond immediate questions of expediency and resistance. I am, fortunately, not alone in this pursuit. My work in this book is indebted to and follows in the steps of two books published at the beginning of this century. These are Leora Bilsky's *Transformative Justice: Israeli Identity on Trial* and Shoshana Felman's *The Juridical Unconscious: Trials and Traumas in the Twentieth Century.*[27] In her book, Bilsky re-evaluates the politics of political trials

by placing particular emphasis on the transformative potential of trials as ve-
hicles for rearticulating national identity, through brilliant close readings of
four Israeli trials. Bilsky's choice of the term "transformative" is part of a larger
project for articulating the constitutional significance of political trials in the
ongoing life of a regime, rather than just focusing on the "transitional" moment in which a successor regime takes recourse to legal proceedings in an
act of re-founding. Inspired by her thinking on the constitutional potentials
of political trials, I likewise attend to the transformative capacities of trials. Bilsky's primary emphasis is on "transformation," which in her account is first
and foremost a transformation of public consciousness. By instead turning to
the conceptual idiom of performativity, I seek to further attend to the unconscious processes and legacies of violence that political trials mediate. In turn,
I borrow this emphasis on the role of the unconscious in trials from Shoshana
Felman's inspiring study.

In the *Juridical Unconscious*, Felman analyzes striking instances of entanglement between spectacular public trials and collective traumas. In the course
of her compelling analyses of the trials of O. J. Simpson and Adolf Eichmann
alongside literary texts, Felman makes a number of key proposals toward a reading practice that can take measure of a wide range of political, social, historical, and spectral dynamics that a trial can mediate, often unknowingly.
Importantly, Felman shows that law cannot always contain the traumas that it
is meant to address, and that trials can serve as fora where meanings that cannot be captured by legal language can nevertheless be dramatically articulated.
Although she does not take much recourse to the idiom of performativity here,
her earlier concern with infelicitous performatives and "the scandal of the
speaking body" appears in *The Juridical Unconscious* in fruitful ways. For example, Felman questions how the body "matters in the courtroom"[28] and asks:
"What is the role of human fallibility in trials? Can moments of disruption of
convention and of discourse—moments of unpredictability that take the legal
institution by surprise—nevertheless contribute to the formulation of a legal
meaning?" (131). These questions serve as important departure points for my
work in this book.

As an analysis framed within trauma studies, the *Juridical Unconscious* is
primarily preoccupied with the promises and failures of legal trials in doing
justice to traumatic histories. Felman's ensuing emphasis on the reparative potentials of legal trials often comes at the cost of inquiring after the question of
legal violence. The question occasionally comes up in the book, but it is never
allowed to set the scene of Felman's analysis. We might explain this as an
effect of the thrall of Nuremberg and its mythopoetics that casts political

violence as law's other. For example, in an opening passage, Felman writes with regard to Nuremberg:

> In setting up a precedent and a new paradigm of trial, the interna-
> tional community attempted to restore the world's balance by re-
> establishing the law's monopoly on violence, and by conceiving of
> justice not simply as punishment but as a marked symbolic exit from
> the injuries of a traumatic history: as liberation from violence itself. (1)

I part with Felman's perspective in the more central emphasis I place on legal violence itself in this book. This is to some extent an effect of shifting the frame of analysis from trauma studies to critical legal studies, with more attention placed on the language(s), methodologies, and technologies of law in evaluating its potentials, limits, and inevitable violence. A guiding light that accompanies my analysis of legal violence in this book is the important conceptualization of the entanglements and co-implications of law and violence that Walter Benjamin offers in his 1921 text "Toward the Critique of Violence."

Law and Violence: An Oblique Address

My emphasis on the co-implications of law and violence is also a consequence of the archive I focus on in Part II of this book. This is a fragmentary archive of political trials that are in one way or another concerned with the 1915 Armenian genocide. Unlike the trials concerning the Holocaust, which have determined much of our contemporary ways of understanding the potentials and limits of law in responding to past political violence, the legal aftermaths of this earlier genocide tells a different story about the relationship between law and violence.

I begin my work on this archive with a close study of the 1921 Berlin trial of Soghomon Tehlirian. Tehlirian was a survivor of the genocide. He killed Talat Pasha, who was the Ottoman Minister of Interior at the time of the genocide, and is considered one of its architects. In Tehlirian's trial, the "political" transpired as a shared state of haunting following the defendant's introduction into the courtroom of the figure of a ghost, namely, the apparition of his mother who had perished in the death marches, and who, the defendant claimed, ordered him to kill Talat. The invocation of this singular ghost brought many other ghosts into the hearings, haunting the trial in myriad ways. I trace the signs of this collective state of haunting through a careful reading of the transcript, seeking its inflections in the interventions of the presiding judge, the testimony of witnesses and experts, the arguments of the defense counsel, and finally, in the verdict of the jury. While archival research indicates that there were various political strategies and damage limitation exercises at work in how the case was prosecuted, defended, and judged, none of these consciously willed strategies had the final word on its outcome. Rather, it was the figure of the ghost itself that created a performative effect that was beyond calculation. Thus Tehlirian's trial allows us to appreciate how performatives do not require self-presence in order to be felicitous; how the inadvertent, the ghostly and the speculative come to inhabit legal forms; and how the political can assume spectral agency in law. The main effect of the ghost in Tehlirian's trial was to give form to the impossible recognition of that which would later be termed genocide. But then again, this was a spectral form.

In building my fragmentary archive, I consider the fore- and afterlives of the Tehlirian trial in a number of processes that it was haunted by, and those that it came to haunt. Importantly, the legacy of the Tehlirian affair is not limited to legal processes; it also bears on a history of sanctioned and unsanctioned acts of political violence by states, organizations, and individuals. I thus offer an account of the events of law and events of violence that bear the traces of the Tehlirian affair, and track the ways in which the history of the Armenian genocide itself acquires a ghostly status in these events: *there, but not there.* In this vein, I dedicate a more extended analysis to the killing of Armenian Turkish journalist Hrant Dink in Istanbul in 2007 and its legal aftermath. This assassination bore uncanny traces of the Tehlirian affair, while also effectively bringing back the specters of the Armenian genocide into Turkey's public sphere. At the same time, the labyrinthine process in the Dink murder case has served as a peculiar return of the law-positing violence of the genocide, including its fact-destroying oblivion. Through a close reading of the Dink murder case and its vicissitudes, I explore the continuities of law-positing violence in law-preserving violence, and the seemingly inevitable failure of law to either break free from this cycle of continuity, or to shift register altogether to serve a memorial function. This analysis paves the way for my consideration of the promises and limits of memory laws in the final chapter, which I offer through a close reading of the 2015 European Court of Human Rights (ECtHR) case *Perinçek v. Switzerland.* The case addressed whether the denial of the Armenian genocide constitutes hate speech and notably it was the first case before the ECtHR on the criminalization of the denial of a genocide other than the Holocaust. This exceptional status had the effect of reinscribing Holocaust exceptionalism in ECtHR's jurisprudence. I propose that the *Perinçek* case is important to consider in terms of understanding the deferrals, disclaimers, and ellipses that structure law's relation to history, and particularly its own historicity.

These lesser known legal encounters with genocide complicate our understanding of the relationship between law and political violence by highlighting circuits and continuities that are rendered less visible due to their eclipse by the overall meaning and reading of Nuremberg. So I offer this fragmentary archive in an attempt to challenge discourses and theoretical frameworks that take for granted law's ability to provide closure and to serve a memorial function in the face of past political violence. In effect, a performative account of trials shows that legal procedure rarely effects closure as such, instead opening new areas of strife and new legal methods of contestation, if not new wounds. Such "openings" may indeed be more characteristic of law as a body of methods than the closure it is often assumed to promise.

PART I
A Performative Theory of Political Trials

1
Theorizing Political Trials

The early 1960s was an interesting moment of theorizing on political trials. Until then, much of the literature on the subject addressed political trials as at best morally questionable instances in which law was instrumentalized for the sake of political expediency. The epithet "political trial" was used interchangeably with "show trial" and referred to, as it still often does, an unholy mixing of law and politics, two spheres that were ideally kept apart. Often, the focus would be on resistance: the dignified performance of the political defendant who called out the masquerade and defied the authorities on the stage of the trial, claiming a higher moral ground. But then we have an interesting cluster of works in the early 1960s that spoke and thought of political trials in a different register. This is when Otto Kirchheimer published *Political Justice: The Use of Legal Procedure for Political Ends* in 1961, Hannah Arendt published her "report" on the trial of Adolf Eichmann first as a series of articles in the *New Yorker*, and then in book form, *Eichmann in Jerusalem: A Report on the Banality of Evil* in 1963, and Judith N. Shklar published *Legalism: Law, Morals, and Political Trials* the following year.[1] All released in the United States but with clearly global concerns, these works appeared following a period that may ironically be deemed the "golden era" of political trials, namely, the three turbulent decades in the mid-twentieth century that witnessed the Moscow Trials of the late 1930s in the USSR, the trials of dissidents in the Third Reich, the Cold War trials of communists in the United States during the 1940s and '50s, the show trials around the same time in Hungary, Czechoslovakia, and other Eastern Bloc countries, the Nuremberg and Tokyo trials in the wake of World War II, the trial of Nazi functionary Adolf Eichmann in 1961 in Israel, and the famous South African political trials: the Treason trial and Nelson

Mandela's incitement trial, among others. But the works are significant because they go beyond the predictable and conventional legalistic outrage vis-à-vis political trials and instead offer a keen thinking of the intersections, interpenetrations, and entanglements of law and politics on the stage of trials. It is also in these works that we find a shift of focus from the political instrumentality of trials to what may be understood as their performativity. Importantly, this shift is accompanied by a sustained awareness of the operations of legal violence through procedure.

All three works are, on one level, attempts to come to terms with and reformulate the legacy of the International Military Tribunal (IMT) at Nuremberg. This is not necessarily immediately evident: Otto Kirchheimer's *Political Justice*, still the most comprehensive and systematic attempt to address, categorize, and theorize the role of political concerns in legal proceedings, covers several hundreds of pages, two centuries, and numerous jurisdictions before it gives its main "concern" away, only in the last chapters: How can we historicize our understanding of the Trial of the Major War Criminals before the IMT at Nuremberg within a generalized context of political justice? A similar movement marks Judith Shklar's work on what she refers to as the social ethos or ideology of legalism: In the last quarter of her influential *Legalism* we understand that the foregoing legal-philosophical critique serves as the groundwork for an attempt to mold a new perspective on the Nuremberg trial, one in which politics can and must be seen as a key element of certain types of legal proceedings. In turn, Hannah Arendt's report on Nazi functionary Adolf Eichmann's trial in Israel is first and foremost that, a thorough account of the proceedings. However, it also operates as Arendt's alternative indictment, defense, judgment, and sentencing of the defendant, whereby the report takes the form of a textual tribunal that accommodates and adjudicates a plurality of voices and positions. When we read it as such, one of Arendt's primary concerns in the text emerges as the attempt to lend more of a conceptual substance to the notion of crimes against humanity, which had received too narrow an interpretation in Nuremberg.[2] In evaluating the Jerusalem court's performance and pointing out its shortcomings, Arendt uses the Nuremberg trial as a critical precedent—one that also failed in certain key regards.

Thus the shift that these works effect can be understood as a consequence of their attempts to grapple with three intertwined characteristics of the Nuremberg trial:[3] its perceived necessity (i.e., as a legal response to the so-called criminal state and the atrocities it performed in the middle of Europe), its undeniably political nature (e.g., a certain selectivity and retroactivity which in turn constituted "victor's justice"), and its law-making, constitutive claims (i.e., its ostensible status as a precedent for international criminal law). Insofar as these three studies articulate the political with regard to this legacy explicitly (and as I argue, performatively in Arendt's case), they provide more nuanced articulations and explorations of what until then had mainly been addressed in terms of deviation from the true course of justice. This was in part a necessity imposed by their very milieu: World War II and the ensuing trials appear to have forced these authors to think in new ways about the uneasy relationship between politics and law in the space of the courtroom, precisely because a retreat into the ideal of the mutual autonomy of these two spheres was no longer an option. But rather than romanticizing and monumentalizing Nuremberg, these studies address the unease directly, starting with framing the hearings before the IMT as "political trials," which has since then become increasingly rare in scholarship that ascribes positive value and status as precedent to these proceedings. The works thus struggle with a key tension between the perceived necessity of a legal response to atrocity as a form of repair, on the one hand, and an awareness of the various ways in which such response can misfire, on the other. It is in attempting to address that tension and grapple with the violence of the law that these thinkers go beyond a purely instrumentalist account of political trials and begin to theorize (as well as speculatively experiment with, in Arendt's case) what I will argue are the performative operations of political trials, with a clear grasp of the functions of legal procedure and its potentials for misfire.

Kirchheimer: Setting the Parameters

Otto Kirchheimer's *Political Justice* is an impressive study of the various facets of the relationship between politics and the legal form. Mainly focusing on the nineteenth and twentieth centuries with occasional forays into the eighteenth century, Shakespeare, and antiquity, this comprehensive attempt to address, categorize, and theorize political trials provides a survey map of the field, as it were, setting out the parameters by which to understand any given political trial structurally and strategically. Kirchheimer presents the trials that he discusses in their historical and political contexts so as to emphasize their political function and public effect, and to expose the sometimes failed schemes of the authorities involved. It is a staggeringly sober account—the flair of the text is in its intellectual deeds rather than its rhetorical feats. The author's position is almost never stated, only revealed through the very quality and rigor of the critical labor constituting the work. Thus the catalytic "problem" and organizing principle of the text become recognizable only when this critical rigor becomes somewhat compromised, a thitherto absent ambivalence emerges, along with the more personalized voice of the author. This is how

I read Kirchheimer's introduction of the Nuremberg trial toward the end of his book, which in turn has an effect of resignifying the preceding investigation and analysis as an attempt to contextualize this particular political trial. In this section, I present a skeletal version of Kirchheimer's theory of political trials, to then move on in the next section to his discussion of the Nuremberg trial, which, though bracketed by his general theory, is nevertheless not properly contained by it, thereby obliging the reluctant author to the beginnings of a new formulation of the politics of trials.

Kirchheimer defines political justice as the use of the "devices of justice to bolster or create new power positions" and identifies three main categories of political trials: a politically significant trial involving a common crime; a regime's attempt to eliminate its political foe (the "classic" political trial); and defamation, perjury, and contempt trials manipulated to bring disrepute upon a political foe (the "derivative" political trial).[4] The first and the third categories are quite straightforward. In the first, the prosecution of a common crime is imbued with political significance due to its politically tinged motive, content, dramatis personae, context, or public effect—for example, a trial concerning the assassination of a political figure. The third category, the derivative political trial, is "a volatile, ambiguous, widespread device opening up opportunities for those who are excluded from the fruits of political power" (76), whereby an ordinary member of the public may manage to provoke an established political figure into initiating a defamation suit. If a trial ensues, the plaintiff's character and virtues, private life, and political decisions will come under public scrutiny, providing a forum for their lay adversaries. The example Kirchheimer offers is Friedrich Ebert's libel case against a German nationalist agitator who called him a traitor (81); another significant example is the 1954–55 Kastner trial in Israel.[5]

Most of Kirchheimer's discussion in the book revolves around the second category, the "classic" political trial, whereby a regime may attempt to incriminate its foe's public behavior, use the trial as an opportunity to elicit information that sheds unfavorable light on its foe, and/or portray its foe's opposition to official policies as treason so as to secure judicially sanctioned repression (52, 62). The classic political trial is sometimes only "a skirmish in a continuing battle," sometimes "a flourish after decisive action has been taken elsewhere," and in rarer instances a crystallization of the conflict between the established authorities and their enemies (232). Kirchheimer also provides a subcategorization for the classic political trial: An established authority's political resort to courts may be a matter of necessity, choice, or convenience. As a matter of *necessity*, it is merely a technical device such as when, to follow the example given in the book, a political dignitary is assassinated, the assassin is caught, and it is necessary that they should be tried in court for the crime (419). Even though the standard criminal procedure may be applied in such a case, Kirchheimer would deem it different from an ordinary murder trial; that is, it is political, if only by virtue of the stature of the individuals involved (48), in this case that of the victim. The recourse to court as a matter of *choice* connotes the preference of judicial action instead of (or along with) the many other methods available to repress a political adversary (i.e., extralegal or administrative repression). According to Kirchheimer, political trials motivated by choice may not always go according to plan, as the cooperation of the judiciary must be secured in order to legitimize the repression of opponents (421–22). Finally, a regime's motive for launching a political trial may have to do with *convenience*: It may have recourse to a trial in order to create effective political images as part of a propaganda campaign to manipulate public opinion (419).

For Kirchheimer, the image-creating capacity of a legal proceeding is essential: Characterized by the "dramatic configuration of a contest" and conducted under the "glaring lights of publicity," the process is most tellingly utilized in political trials, whether for "pedagogical effect," "internal mobilization," or the upper hand in a "popularity contest" of ideologies (109, 18, 233n13). Kirchheimer deems a political trial's image-creating effect vastly superior compared with other political strategies: In employing a telling image, the political trial "elevates the image from the realm of private happenings and partisan constructions to an official, authoritative, quasi-neutral sphere" (422). Furthermore, the political trial is more successful than parliamentary proceedings in providing the masses with a more intimate sense of political participation: "Its rules are intricate. Its immediate results may be quite spectacular. Its illusions are sufficiently hidden from the onlooker not to disturb his sense of drama and aesthetic enjoyment" (430). By using a complete and effective (though not necessarily meaningful) image, the political trial offers a reduced and simplified understanding of history, which further enlivens the show (423). Kirchheimer emphasizes the spectacular aspect of a political trial throughout the text, with a telling choice of words including "the show," "fireworks," "cinerama," and "cinematic episode" (53, 54, 114).

It is important to note here that Kirchheimer introduces a crucial distinction between political trials and show trials: The political trial, no matter how carefully staged, always involves an *irreducible element of risk* for the political authorities, threatening to break through the façade and invite alternative interpretations of what is actually at stake in the proceedings. This is defined in comparison with, for example, the Soviet show trials, in which the element of risk was fully eliminated, as they were "total" productions in which even the

defendants' role, participation, and "confessions" were stage-managed and orchestrated. The political trial, in contrast, has to play itself out on a public that
is host and witness to the process, is preoccupied and identified with it, and
perhaps even entertained by it. Kirchheimer's identification of this irreducible
risk as the essential condition of a "political trial" effectively crystallizes his
resignification of the notion as distinct from a "show trial." It is important to
note that this intervention comes in the midst of the Cold War, when the two
designations, political trial and show trial, were often used interchangeably and
mostly reserved for legal proceedings in undemocratic regimes. Thus Kirchheimer's understanding of the "risk" in a political trial proper: The event is
shot through with uncertainties stemming from legal procedure, political commitments of witnesses, and interpretation of defendants, who may be able to
hijack the proceedings to create very effective alternative images (118). Another
source of uncertainty is the very "judicial space" itself, namely, the freedom
of the judge or jury in deciding a case based on their own interpretation and
evaluation.[6] While noting that any jury is driven by the "urge towards spontaneous conformity" and therefore structurally conservative (223), and taking
heed of the restrictions on a judge's supposed and championed impartiality
(such as specific political inclinations and sentiments that stem from their
membership in an elite), Kirchheimer nevertheless locates a progressive possibility in the space of judgment: "the most awesome as well as the most creative part of the judicial experience: the entertaining of a small but persistent
grain of doubt in the purposes of [one's] own society" (233). So, although bound
by the parameters of established authority and the urge to guard and conserve
it, judges can still partake creatively in the political fate of the community.

   This discussion of the "judicial space" is one of the only signs of a positive
evaluation of the place of the political in legal proceedings in the entire text,
and unlike the rest of the discussion, this glimmer of possibility is formulated
not in terms of instrumentalization of the legal form, but rather in terms of an
opening for innovation within it. The discussion is also crucial insofar as it
introduces a split, or a differentiated signification, in the notion of "the political" as it is deployed in the text, whereby it begins to designate something other
than expediency. And yet this nuance is neither explored nor openly acknowledged within the text, creating a tension that undermines the strength of the
analysis. We will later see that Judith Shklar's understanding of political trials
begins with a diagnosis of precisely this problem of the split within the "political" of political trials. But in Kirchheimer, the tension created by this as yet
unacknowledged split is transferred onto, and reflected in, his discussion of
the Nuremberg trial, a discussion that incorporates the performative element
in political trials, albeit without naming it as such.

Judgment on Nuremberg

Notably, Kirchheimer locates the Nuremberg trial in the context of a wider discussion of "trials by fiat of the successor regime"—i e., cases in which a new regime uses the trial form to publicly pass judgment on the policies and deeds of the previous regime, as a way to differentiate itself from the previous regime and thereby define itself in idealized terms: "Setting the new regime from the old and sitting in judgment over the latter's policies and practices may belong to the constitutive acts of the new regime." Thus, Kirchheimer asks: "Which are the value structures that transcend the lifetime of a political regime against which acts of predecessors can be measured?" (308). A classic answer to this in national contexts is patriotism, so that, for example, toppled monarchs are tried for "treason" and former leaders are accused of acting against the best interests of the nation. But then, and this is how Kirchheimer introduces the Nuremberg trial into his discussion, such nation-bound value structures will fall short of evaluating the criminality of the deeds of a regime such as the Nazi rule in Germany. Thus, he suggests, the Nuremberg proceedings call for the necessity to define a universal yardstick, "a fundamental notion to which all groups and nations must at least submit, if not always subscribe" (319). Contextualizing it in this rather odd way, Kirchheimer goes on to discuss the Nuremberg trial before the IMT in detail as "the most important 'successor' trial in modern history" (323). His treatment of the subject is characteristically thorough, but rather than following the order of his argument and offering a detailed summary, I focus here on three aspects of his discussion that I find significant in terms of a performative theory of political trials: a reaffirmation of the possibility of innovation within the judicial space; an unequivocal affirmation of the constitutive potential of the Nuremberg trial; and an investment in the notion of "crimes against humanity" as a universal yardstick, despite and beyond all his reservations.

Kirchheimer's reaffirmation, within the Nuremberg context, of innovation in judicial space, comes curiously incorporated in his rebuttal of the defense argument regarding victor's justice, namely, the accusation that the court was prejudicial and partisan. Kirchheimer's response is that law is always already an instrument and medium of power:

> The rebuttal is simple and unavoidable. It goes straight to the very nature of political trials. In all political trials conducted by the judges of the successor regime, the judges are in a certain sense the victor's judges. . . . In a somewhat wider sense, all judges, not only those of a successor regime, are working under the conditions of the existing

legal and political system which they are duty-bound to uphold. (Kirchheimer, 332)

Enter stage left, a previously absent cynicism in argument. Kirchheimer then goes on to relate an anecdote from the London Conference where the Charter for the IMT was drawn up: USSR representative Iona Nikitschenko explained their vision for a speedy procedure that would guarantee the execution of the convictions as they had been previously announced by the heads of the Allied establishments, whereupon US representative Justice Robert H. Jackson took it upon himself to expound on the traditional liberal democratic position regarding the distinction between the executive power to set up a tribunal and organize the prosecution, and the independent role of the trial judges evaluating the evidence presented to them. "Both the cynical realism of the USSR representative and the apparent traditionalism of Justice Jackson," Kirchheimer concludes, "overstate their respective cases" (333). His no-illusions position on the matter is: The acknowledgment that it is a successor (i.e., political) trial need not rule out an expectation for some level of independence in the judicial space. The corroboration for the existence of such independence at the trial of the major war criminals came, for Kirchheimer, in the form of three acquittals, delivered despite the protests of the USSR team.

As for his further elaboration on the constitutive potential of a political trial, in what I can discern to be his only recourse to the first person in the text, Kirchheimer states that "this kind of hybrid prosecution, which mixes political accountability for planning and initiation of aggressive war with criminal responsibility for inhuman conduct, has to our eyes a politically justified element" (324). The reference to hybridity here has to do with the question of responsibility and the nature of the crimes: The "crimes against peace" formulation is meant to establish the responsibility of the governing ranks of the regime for the policy course they had taken. The other two charges are devised for establishing personal responsibility, directly concerned as they are, with the quality of human action "regardless of the hierarchical level at which it occurred" (326). The "politically justified element" of this hybrid prosecution has to do with the historical moment—Kirchheimer is convinced that warfare in contemporary society will necessarily lead to the very negation of the human condition, that is, to crimes against humanity. Thus he understands the constellation of the three charges as appropriate for the context that necessitated the elimination of aggressive war. And yet right after this statement he goes on to explain how the "crimes against peace" notion failed to set a precedent, as the coalition behind the IMT broke up "before the ink on the Nuremberg judgment had time to dry":

> Had the noble purpose of the crime against peace charge succeeded,
> had it helped to lay a foundation for a new world order, the uncertain
> juridical foundation of the charge would now be overlooked and the
> enterprise praised as the rock on which the withdrawal of the states'
> right to conduct aggressive warfare came to rest. (324)

Here we find an unequivocal affirmation of the performative promise of political justice, albeit formulated in view of its failure. Had it not failed, Kirchheimer proposes, the enterprise could not have been discredited on charges
of political justice.[7] This can be read as a succinct articulation of the performative potential of political trials to enact into being their own foundation,
through the kind of temporal operation that Jacques Derrida would later identify as a "fabulous retroactivity."[8] This insight, however, is not integrated into
Kirchheimer's wider theoretical investigation of the subject.

Finally, Kirchheimer finds in the formulation of "crimes against humanity" a universal measure, namely, the answer to his earlier question concerning the "fundamental notion to which all groups and nations must at least
submit, if not always subscribe." By way of concluding his discussion on Nuremberg, he suggests that the typical infirmities of the trial stemming from its
very conditions of existence and structure as a successor trial should not hin-
der us from acknowledging its "lasting contribution":

> that it defined where the realm of politics ends or, rather, is trans-
> formed into the concerns of the human condition, the survival of
> mankind in both its universality and diversity. . . . The feeble begin-
> ning of transnational control of the crime against the human condi-
> tion raises the Nuremberg judgment a notch above the level of
> political justice by fiat of a successor regime. (Kirchheimer, 341)

We may question the wisdom of this split between political concerns and concerns regarding the human condition, and note that it is based on a rather
limited conceptualization of the political as such. Perhaps more importantly,
the rhetorical strength of this conclusion does not quite follow from Kirchheimer's own analyses concerning the impossibility of enforcing a common
guideline for crimes against humanity in the absence of a "world authority to
establish the boundary line between atrocity beyond the pale and legitimate
policy reserved for the individual state" (326). In clarifying the difficulty produced by this absence, Kirchheimer gestures toward the various policies of systemic cruelty underway in the world at the time of writing, such as the French
in Algeria, the South African government, and the Hungarian regime—they
"might continue to have a very different viewpoint on the meaning of the

concept" (326), he asserts with typical restraint. He further suggests that this may have been a reason why the IMT had very limited recourse to the crimes against humanity charge, opting instead for the war crimes charge where possible. In that sense, and within the boundaries of Kirchheimer's critique, the precise content of Nuremberg's "lasting contribution" is not actually clear.

Indeed, in his further and final remarks on Nuremberg in the conclusion of the book, we find a slightly different articulation. The lasting contribution of the trial, we are told this time, is the image that it created. The permanence of this image will not be effaced by any criticism of the trial, nor did it owe its strength to the mastery of the tribunal: The record of the Nazi regime was "so clear-cut that the image produced in court could not but appear a reasonably truthful replica of reality." Remarkably for this otherwise decisively declarative jurist, Kirchheimer's final judgment on Nuremberg comes in the form of a rhetorical question:

> While it retained many overtones of the convenience type of trial, did the Nuremberg trial, with all the hypocrisy and grotesqueness deriving from its very subject, not belong very profoundly in the category of a morally and historically necessary operation? (423)

This is perhaps a more truthful presentation of the "problem" that Nuremberg posed for Kirchheimer, namely, the quandary of being forced to affirm political justice, not in principle, but in the face of atrocities beyond the pale. It explains something of the exceptional treatment Nuremberg receives in a book dedicated "to the past, present, and future victims of political justice," and committed to an incisive critical dismantling of such judicial productions. Nevertheless, it is also this exception that seems to have catalyzed and informed the grand project itself, while allowing or imposing on it the slow beginnings of a different way of thinking about political trials. What we are left with, however, is an emphasis on the trial's necessity as a historical and moral operation, namely, a historiographic operation: An effective and spectacular image of the Nazi regime had to be produced and condemned. As we will see, this historiographic function has since become a key rationale in the mainstreaming of the notion that political trials are not only necessary but also desirable in the aftermath of a deposed regime's atrocities and lesser legal transgressions.

Yet Kirchheimer's caution and hesitation is noteworthy. It is in searching for the "universal yardstick" that Nuremberg might have produced that he moves away from a mostly instrumentalist account of political trials to an acknowledgment of their performative potentials. Then again, framing the trial of the major war criminals in Nuremberg as a "successor trial" implies that it was an attempt to both redefine the previous "regime" and to mark the beginning of a new "regime." As an international tribunal, the previous regime that would be marked and sealed off could not be limited to the National Socialist rule in Germany, but implied an international order that allowed World War II and its atrocities. And yet the postwar trials not only excluded any consideration of war crimes committed by the Allies but also failed to effectively set a precedent for the crimes of aggression, even "before the ink on the Nuremberg judgment had time to dry." Kirchheimer can neither remain fully cynical with regard to the trial's legacy, nor uncritically embrace it. The tether he holds on to is the third element of the indictment, "crimes against humanity." But noting the wider contexts of colonialism, apartheid, and authoritarianism, Kirchheimer is cautious with regard to its status as a "universal yardstick," unwilling to fully articulate its promise. As we will see, Hannah Arendt goes further than Kirchheimer in this task of substantiation, with a kindred critical sensibility.

Arendt: A Trial of One's Own?

Much of Kirchheimer's discernment about the politics of trials in general, and of the Nuremberg trial in particular, including his suggestion that the trial could have signaled the feeble beginnings of a desirable transnational control over "crimes against humanity," is shared by Hannah Arendt in her work on the 1961 Eichmann trial, which appeared in print first as a series of articles in the *New Yorker* in early 1963, and was published as a book later that year. Unlike Kirchheimer's encyclopedic approach, Arendt's report is focused on a single trial; it offers no general theory of political trials, not even a section dedicated to the subject. It is nevertheless an important address of the question, and it has been taken up as such.[9] Now even the subject of a major motion picture,[10] the book has been widely read and commented on, and some of its analyses and claims continue to be the subject of debate and controversy. My focus here is narrow: I am interested in how Arendt's account of the Eichmann trial is anchored by an acute understanding of a range of the performative possibilities it held, namely, what it could effectively constitute by means of its very enactment. In this, the reading I most closely follow is Leora Bilsky's detailed and insightful analysis of both the Eichmann trial and Arendt's report of it, which Bilsky suggests captures the "transformative" possibilities of the trial.[11] Bilsky writes: "It was only because Arendt realized these possibilities that she became so critical of what she considered the failure of the Israeli prosecution and the limited success of the judges in the Eichmann trial in exploring these possibilities."[12] Arendt's own vision for the performative potential of the Eichmann trial was indeed at odds with both the investments of the trial's architects and the actual conclusions of the court.

Arendt's so-called report is in effect best read as a "retrial," during the course of which she reorganizes and supplements the evidence presented at the trial, provides her own responses to various legal arguments within the trial and the legal debates surrounding the trial, passes her own judgment, and formulates her own sentencing remarks. So Arendt not only describes what may retrospectively be understood as the performative operations of the Eichmann trial in this text, but she also performs an alternative version of the trial through the text. Arendt was explicit about this operation of the report in a later essay in which she referred to *Eichmann in Jerusalem* as "my 'sitting in judgment.'"[13] The most insightful commentaries work with this fascinating feature of the text. For example, Ariella Azoulay and Bonnie Honig have suggested that "we look not only at what she *says* in *Eichmann* but also what she *does* in that book, not only at what she accounts for in a report-like mode but also at what she recovers from the trial as she casts about for resources that may help renew judgment, responsibility, spontaneity, creativity, and imagination."[14] In an essay that pauses on the implications of Arendt's rather startling appropriation of a vengeful judicial voice in sentencing Eichmann to death in a direct second person address at the end of her report, Judith Butler departs from a similar insight: "Something is being written and displayed in a book. The book of justice is being written and shown in Arendt's own text."[15] As these commentaries indicate, it is necessary to be attuned to the performative modalities of *Eichmann in Jerusalem*, particularly in exploring the ways in which the text offers the incipient formulation of a performative theory of political trials.

The case itself is well known: In May 1960, Nazi functionary Adolf Eichmann, responsible for overseeing the mass deportation of Jews to extermination camps in Eastern Europe, was abducted by Israeli secret service operatives from Argentina, where he had been living under a false identity. He was secretly transferred to Jerusalem to be tried under Israeli law for crimes committed against the Jewish people during World War II. The affair sparked controversy internationally, and Israel's right to try Eichmann was challenged on several legal bases, most importantly: the illegality of Eichmann's abduction (that he was brought to Israel in violation of Argentina's sovereignty); the problem of Israel's territorial jurisdiction (Israel was to try Eichmann, who was not an Israeli citizen, for crimes committed outside Israel, against persons who were not Israeli citizens); the problem of retrospectivity (Israel was to try Eichmann under its Nazis and Nazi Collaborators [Punishment] Law of 1950 for crimes committed before the institution of the law, thereby suspending the principle of legality); and the issue of what could be referred to as "retrospective sovereignty" in that Israel was to try crimes that were committed before its own establishment (this is also a bridge between the criticism regarding territorial jurisdiction and the one regarding retrospectivity).[16] However, Israeli Prime Minister David Ben-Gurion had made up his mind; the trial did happen and was quite a happening. For the first time in Israel's then brief legal history, cameras were allowed into the courtroom which rendered the trial an early international media event.[17] The hearings lasted four months. After another four months of deliberation, the court convicted Eichmann on all charges and sentenced him to death. Both his appeal and plea for mercy were rejected, and Eichmann was hanged in May 1962.

In an interview he gave to the *New York Times*, Ben-Gurion was asked, "What do you hope to achieve by bringing Eichmann to trial?" The diplomatic answer most appropriate in the midst of much controversy would perhaps have been something along the lines of "the truth concerning Adolf Eichmann's culpability for Nazi crimes." Even a vague, unsubstantiated invocation of "justice" would perhaps suffice as a measured answer to what the trial was supposed to achieve. But instead, Ben-Gurion took this as an opportunity to explain in detail what he aimed to achieve. First, he wanted to "establish before the nations of the world" the evils of anti-Semitism: "They should know that anti-Semitism is dangerous and they should be ashamed of it"—a warning to potential foes. Second, he wanted the Israeli youth, the generation who had grown up since the Holocaust, to know the most tragic facts in their history—state-sanctioned historiography. Third, he wanted to show the Jewish Diaspora that Judaism always faced a hostile world and only the establishment of a Jewish state had enabled the Jews to hit back—Zionist propaganda.[18] And finally, the trial was to address Israel's neighbors on its unhappy borders: "It may be that Eichmann's trial will help to ferret out other Nazis, for example, the connection between Nazis and some Arab rulers"—a threat to actual enemies.[19] As such, the trial was obviously a political trial of the convenience variety in Kirchheimer's sense, meant to make images for a variety of public audiences.[20]

One of the central narrative strategies that Hannah Arendt employs in her account of the trial is an adversarial setup, not between the prosecution and the defense as one would expect, but rather between the prosecutor and the judges. She accuses Attorney General Gideon Hausner of "doing his best, his very best, to obey his master," that is, Ben-Gurion, who is described in turn as the "invisible stage manager of the proceedings." In turn, the judges are said to serve "Justice as faithfully as Mr. Hausner serves the State of Israel" (Arendt, *Eichmann*, 5). Attempts on Hausner's part to render the proceedings a show trial that would suit Ben-Gurion's vision were to some extent neutralized by the sobriety of the judges, Arendt reports. Aside from problems of performance, she finds the prosecution's case seriously flawed on a variety of bases. First, it was built "on what the Jews had suffered, not on what Eichmann had done" (6). Hausner introduced an endless procession of survivors as witnesses, though their testimony on truly atrocious facts rarely implicated Eichmann directly. In response to this problem, Arendt stresses, over and over again in her account, that the sole legitimate concern of a criminal trial is to determine individual responsibility and punishment.[21] Second, the prosecution misunderstood and misrepresented the novelty of the crime in question. Rather than recognizing in it a new type of criminality, directed at blotting out a whole ethnic group from the face of the earth, Hausner chose to contextualize it within the long history of anti-Semitism, beginning his opening address with Pharaoh in Egypt and Haman's decree. Arendt ruled: "It was bad history and cheap rhetoric; worse, it was clearly at cross-purposes with putting Eichmann on trial, suggesting that perhaps he was only an innocent executor of some mysteriously foreordained destiny" (19). Third, the prosecution's case was flawed in its representation of the criminal in question, attempting to prove him a monster, an evil mastermind, "superior of Himmler and the inspirer of Hitler" (211). Arendt's response to this is her controversial "banality of evil" formulation, which she explains as a profound inability to think for oneself, namely, from the standpoint of somebody else, living instead by borrowed clichés that only serve to shield one off from relationality, and by implication, from reality (48–49). In addition to these substantive contentions, Arendt criticizes the prosecution's case on the basis of its own raison d'être. If the aim was to expose the full picture with regard to anti-Semitism and the Holocaust, they should have ventured into the complicity of "all German offices and authorities in the Final Solution—of all civil servants in the state ministries, of the regular armed forces, with their General Staff, of the judiciary, and of the business world" (18), rather than being "so careful not to embarrass the Adenauer administration" (119). And if it was to serve as a show trial, the prosecution's case should have been properly produced for one: "A show trial needs even more urgently than an ordinary trial a limited and well-defined outline of what was done and how it was done" (9).

From the first pages onward Arendt's audacious tone is palpable. It is as if she's saying, you have made a fine mess of this trial, let me show you how it's done. Arendt's so-called report on the trial can thus be read effectively as a retrial. She presents her own prosecutorial case, in which she radically reorganizes the evidence presented at the trial to specifically pinpoint Eichmann's responsibility. She draws on evidence gathered by the authorities in the preparations for the trial but omitted by the prosecutor (such as the 3,564-page German transcript of the autobiography that Eichmann "had spontaneously given the police examiner" [235]), and she also supplements this with her own research on the legal, political, and bureaucratic developments in Nazi Germany to situate Eichmann in his immediate milieu. Then, in a move that was to spark the greatest controversy, Arendt presents a case for the defense as well, introducing[22] the matter of Eichmann's collaboration with Jewish councils and well-known Zionist leaders, devoting a substantial section to the collaboration of the Judenrate in the expulsion of the Jews from Germany before the war (56–67), and a separate discussion of their collaboration in the so-called Final Solution (117–26).

Consistent with the general form of her retrial disguised as a report, Arendt also provides her own judgment in the case. This takes the form of an analysis and supplementation of the actual judgment passed by the court. For example, she expresses her approval of the court's refusal to follow the prosecutor's "general pictures," instead strictly addressing itself to weighing the charges brought against the accused (253–54). She also acknowledges the various difficulties the judges faced in handling certain aspects of the evidence (208–9, 219). Arendt then summarizes the court's response to the various objections brought to its jurisdiction point by point, and often unsatisfied by the court's arguments, she provides, in detailed and lengthy arguments, her own justifications regarding jurisdictional concerns that have been posed (254–67). This includes, among other feats, the jurisprudential dismantling of the passive personality principle which the actual judgment relied on (260–61) and a fascinating, if odd, reformulation of the principle of territoriality to argue Israel's right to sit in judgment for crimes committed against the Jewish people (262–63). Then Arendt passes her verdict on the court's judgment: The failure of the court, she explains, consisted in its not coming to grips with three fundamental issues that have been debated widely since the establishment of the IMT at Nuremberg (274). The first of these was the problem of impaired justice in the court of the victors, which comes with the usual crisis of inequality between prosecution and defense in preparing for the trial. In Arendt's judgment, the Jerusalem court fared worse than Nuremberg in this regard. Because the attorney general did not agree to a blanket immunity for potential defense witnesses, the defense was effectively barred from calling on any. The second problem was the court's inability to provide a valid definition of the crimes against humanity. At Nuremberg, the Allies had handled this new charge timidly, subsuming it under the category of war crimes, and the judges "felt so uncomfortable" with it that they left it in a "tantalizing state of ambiguity" (257).[23] Arendt credits the Jerusalem court for doing better than its predecessor on this issue, and attributes this to its very raison d'être, that it was established to address the Holocaust and to focus on the crimes against the Jewish people. Then again, for Arendt, it was precisely the court's recourse to this particular and particularist idiom of "crimes against the Jewish people" that fell short of the task of providing a valid definition of crimes against humanity—I will return to this point in the next section in further detail. Third, the court failed to arrive at a clear recognition of the new criminal who commits this crime, who was not a monster but rather "terribly and terrifyingly normal" (276).

After providing her own prosecutorial case, her own case for the defense, and her own judgment, Arendt finally offers her own sentencing remarks for Eichmann in the final passages of her epilogue. She prefaces these passages with a note to the effect that her reformulation of the sentencing remarks is made in terms she thinks the judges would have "dared" to adopt, had they been prepared to depart from precedents to properly judge the crime and the criminal. At this point Arendt startlingly launches into a direct second person address to Eichmann, beginning with "You admitted that the crime committed against the Jewish people during the war was the greatest crime in recorded history, and you admitted your role in it" (277–78). Arrogating the voice of the bench,[24] Arendt offers rejoinders to Eichmann's attempts to deflect culpability. In this, Arendt's passages both mirror and compete with the structure of the actual judgment, in which, after analyzing the findings of fact in light of the various counts of charges in the indictment and before formulating their final verdict, the judges consider the lines of defense that Eichmann presented. Arendt's rejoinders to Eichmann's defense are very much at odds with those of the actual judgment and thus imply her critique of the court's inability to understand the new criminal.[25]

What does it mean for a sole author to reenact an entire judicial process after her own fashion in the course of a text? In arrogating multiple positions, including those of the prosecutor, the defense counsel, and the judges throughout the text, Arendt does expose herself to the charge of arrogance with which her critics attacked her in the aftermath of the publication. The "who are you to judge?" was primarily directed at her critique of the role of the Judenrate in the Holocaust, but it may well have been provoked by the cumulative effect of the text as a daring retrial of the Eichmann case, formulated by this woman, a survivor in the diaspora, who defied the injunction to uncritically celebrate the trial as the sovereign spectacle it was meant to be. But the attribution of Arendt's arrogation of numerous voices and positions to mere arrogance misses the fascinating performative experimentation that her report constitutes. The complex structure of the text and Arendt's inhabitation of a plurality of voices and positions therein is better read as an engagement with the practice of reflective judgment that she would come to theorize in later work.[26] In accommodating a multiplicity of voices and positions in the text, at times ventriloquizing and at other times contesting them, Arendt renders her report a textual tribunal, creating a forum that may afford a forensics of the crime in question—not in the sense of a strictly medical and scientific practice of forensics, but *forensis* in the sense of a critical and political practice of collectively seeking the truth of the matter.[27] Arendt's frustration with the actual legal process, palpable across the pages of her report, suggests that she would likely have been glad to abrogate her textual tribunal for sake of a more appropriate forum, such as an internationally constituted tribunal—unlike Israel, which regarded all calls for an international tribunal to try Eichmann as a slighting of its sovereignty.

The Breach That Speaks the Bind

Arendt's alternative sentencing remarks contain, in summary form, her substantiation of the notion of "crimes against humanity" for which the judgment of the Jerusalem court could not provide a valid definition in her opinion. In focusing primarily on "crimes against the Jewish people," the court failed to recognize "the possibility that extermination of whole ethnic groups—the Jews, or the Poles, or the Gypsies—might be more than a crime against the Jewish or the Polish or the Gypsy people, that the international order, and mankind in its entirety, might have been grievously hurt and endangered" (Arendt, *Eichmann*, 275–76). Arendt's understanding here is based on the modern conception of criminal law, whereby a crime is first and foremost a breach of the law of the community, of what binds the community. A criminal proceeding, therefore, is not carried out in the name of the victim, but in the name of the community whose bond has been breached. Criminal justice is aimed at restoring order to the community, rather than enacting vengeance for the victim (261). Crimes against humanity are crimes against the human condition of diversity and plurality for Arendt, precisely because the attempt to disappear a people from the face of the earth is an attack upon "human diversity as such, that is, upon a characteristic of the 'human status' without which the very words 'mankind' or 'humanity' would be devoid of meaning" (269). Therefore, the crime of murder and crimes against humanity are not of the same order, "The point of the latter is that an altogether different order is broken and an altogether different community is violated" (272).

In one sense, in Arendt's retrial of the Eichmann case, the very formulation of "crimes against humanity" becomes the performative foundation of this "altogether different community." The necessity to address the atrocity through law is meant to result in the performative production of not only the law that retrospectively censures the atrocity as a crime but also of the community which the law is understood to stem from. In other words, it is the crime in its "novelty" that produces the law and the community, but law's performative operation can allow it to cast this entire operation as its own. This is why, as part of this discussion, Arendt argues that the only proper court to try these crimes is an international criminal court, in the absence of which the Israeli authorities could have called for one upon capturing Eichmann, or they could have rendered the court in Jerusalem an international one. Another option altogether was that after the District Court of Jerusalem passed its judgment and sentenced Eichmann, Israel could have waived its right to carry out the sentence, turning instead to the United Nations to "make trouble" by "asking again and again just what it should do with this man whom it was holding prisoner; constant repetition would have impressed on worldwide public opinion the need for a permanent international criminal court" (270). The repetition of such a demand would potentially result in the performative production of such a court and with it the "altogether different order" and "altogether different community." Arendt's emphasis here is significant, given that repetition is a key element of performativity.

In what may be understood as an early post-Zionist positioning, Arendt does not contest Israel's right to try Eichmann; she recognizes and "understands" but also criticizes the sovereign investment in it; and she is convinced it was not the right option. She laments that Israel was too caught up in its own drama of sovereignty—that after almost two millennia a Jewish sovereign state could finally sit in judgment of crimes committed against the Jewish people—to recognize there was much more at stake here. Further, in casting the Holocaust as yet another grave injury suffered by the Jewish people without the protection of a national state (a historical status finally redeemed by the establishment of Israel), this theater of sovereignty failed to capture the crime in its full significance and its "unprecedentedness."[28] This is how we can read the somewhat obscure "yes, but" formulation that Arendt reaches at the conclusion of her report: "Insofar as the victims were Jews, it was right and proper that a Jewish court should sit in judgment; but insofar as the crime was a crime against humanity, it needed an international tribunal to do justice to it."[29] Importantly, Arendt appends a parenthetical note to this formulation expressing her surprise at the failure of the Jerusalem court to draw this distinction, recalling that it had been made by Pinchas Rosen, the former Israeli Minister of Justice, who in 1950 had insisted on a distinction between the "crime against the Jewish People" as defined by the bill that would later be adopted as the Nazis and Nazi Collaborators (Punishment) Law, on the one hand, and the crime of genocide as defined by the UN Convention, on the other. This is actually a crucial distinction that does goes to the heart of Arendt's critique of the Jerusalem court's focus on the crime as "against the Jewish People" as defined by the Israeli law. According to Arendt, Israel should have recognized that "The Nazis and Nazi Collaborators (Punishment) Law of 1950 is wrong, it is in contradiction to what actually happened, it does not cover the facts" (Arendt, *Eichmann*, 272).

It is worthwhile analyzing in more detail this law that does not meet the challenge of grasping the facts of the Holocaust and how the court in Jerusalem interpreted it. The judgment of the District Court of Jerusalem, in passages establishing Israel's jurisdiction over the case, explains that the "crime against the Jewish People" found in Section 1(b) of the Nazis and Nazi Collaborators (Punishment) Law of 1950 "is defined on the pattern of the genocide crime" as provided by the 1948 UN Convention for the Prevention and Punishment of Genocide.[30] Indeed, the Israeli definition of the crime against the Jewish people very much mirrors the wording of the UN definition of genocide. Where the latter states: "Genocide means any of the following acts committed with intent to destroy, in whole or in part, a national, ethnical or religious group," the former states: "'Crime against the Jewish People' means any of the following acts, committed with intent to destroy the Jewish People in whole or in part." In detailing the "acts" that constitute crimes against the Jewish people, the Israeli law borrows almost all of the wording of the Genocide Convention, only substituting "Jews" for the Genocide Convention's "members of the group." In pointing this pattern out, the judgment subsumes the "crime against the Jewish people" under the crime of genocide, which in turn it subsumes under the category of "crimes against humanity": "It is hardly necessary to add that the 'crime against the Jewish People,' which constitutes the crime of 'genocide' is nothing but the gravest type of 'crime against humanity'" (para. 26). One of the problems that this serial operation of subsumption cannot quite resolve in the judgment is the exclusion of universal jurisdiction in the UN Genocide Convention. Another, deeper, issue that the judgment cannot fully grapple with in subsuming crimes against the Jewish people under genocide and the latter under crimes against humanity, is the effect of what is lost in the Israeli law's particularization of genocide as crimes against the Jewish people. In this, both the Israeli law that defines this latter category, and the District Court of Jerusalem that works with it are greatly hampered by the different genealogies of the two separate categories of genocide and crimes against humanity.

This difference is crucially highlighted in Philippe Sands's 2016 book *East West Street: On the Origins of Genocide and Crimes against Humanity*, which

traces the life stories of Rafael Lemkin and Hersch Lauterpacht and their respective formulations of "genocide" and "crimes against humanity." A thread
that runs throughout Sands's book, which also incorporates the author's own
family history and first person perspective as a practitioner, is the way in which
these two concepts were in a fundamental way opposed to each other, despite
being coeval: Whereas the notion of "genocide" takes as its pivot the group
(atrocities against a group), the pivot for the notion of "crimes against humanity" is the individual (atrocities against individual civilians). Insofar as the mass
atrocities of the twentieth century were indeed directed at individuals not qua
individuals but because they happened to be members of a particular group,
Lemkin's formulation has merit. But it comes with its own problems: "There
were practical difficulties evoked by Lauterpacht: How did one actually prove
the intent to destroy a group? And there were objections of principle, of the
kind evoked by Leopold Kohr, that Lemkin had fallen into the trap of 'bio-
logical thinking,' focusing on groups in a manner that gave rise to anti-Semitism
and anti-Germanism."[31] As a practicing international lawyer, Philippe Sands
testifies that these issues have indeed been borne out in the recent life of international criminal law:

> Proving the crime of genocide is difficult, and in litigating cases I have
> seen for myself how the need to prove the intent to destroy a group in
> whole or in part, as the Genocide convention requires, can have
> unhappy psychological consequences. . . . The term "genocide" with
> its focus on the group, tends to heighten a sense of "them" and "us,"
> burnishes feelings of group identity and may unwittingly give rise to
> the very conditions that it seeks to address: by pitting one group against
> another, it makes reconciliation less likely. I fear that the crime of geno-
> cide has distorted the prosecution of war crimes and crimes against
> humanity, because the desire to be labelled a victim of genocide brings
> pressure on prosecutors to indict for that crime. For some, to be labelled
> a victim of genocide becomes "an essential component of national
> identity" without contributing to the resolution of historical disputes or
> making mass killings less frequent.[32]

The problematic vein in the definition of genocide, the performative effects
of its focus on the "national, ethnical, racial or religious group," that Sands
elaborates in his book became reified in the Israeli law's particularization of
the crime of genocide as "crimes against the Jewish people." Arendt does not
seem to have been aware of the subtle opposition between "genocide" and
"crimes against humanity," and she uses these categories interchangeably in
the course of her text, as do the majority of commentators on her text. Arendt

concluded that the Nazis and Nazi Collaborators (Punishment) Law of 1950 was "wrong," because she considered that particularizing crimes against humanity in terms of "crimes against the Jewish people" was inappropriate, and that it missed the whole point of the former category. However, it is noteworthy that "crimes against the Jewish people" was not actually a particularization of "crimes against humanity," but rather of "genocide," which with its focus on "the group" does carry the kernel of such a particularistic and particularizing tendency. This in turn is significant for the consideration of the performative power of legal definitions, their world-making and community-defining force—something that Arendt was keenly attuned to as evidenced by so many strands of her text.

Shklar: "There's Politics and Politics"

Published perhaps too soon after Arendt's *Eichmann in Jerusalem* to incorporate a response, and three years after Kirchheimer's somewhat tormented treatment of the Nuremberg trial, *Legalism* by Judith Shklar (1964) is rather forthright about this earlier trial, also situating a discussion of Nuremberg within a more general, if not as exhaustive, discussion about political trials. The main thrust of Shklar's book is an illuminating critique of what she refers to as legalism, "the ethical attitude that holds moral conduct to be a matter of rule following, and moral relationships to consist of duties and rights determined by rules."[33] Shklar suggests that legalism not only determines individual codes of conduct but also works as an ideology, or a widespread "social ethos" that is particularly common among the legal profession but also finds expression in numerous organizations and institutions in democracies, reaching its most perfected form "in the great legal systems of the European world" (Shklar, *Legalism*, 1). Despite this rather broad initial definition, Shklar's critique of legalism focuses mainly on one of its key characteristics, namely, the conviction that law can be understood, conceptualized, studied, and practiced in isolation from all other aspects of social and political life. In the legalistic ideology, Shklar suggests, "Law is endowed with its own discrete, integral history, its own 'science,' and its own values, which are all treated as a single 'block' sealed off from general social history, from general social theory, from politics and from morality" (2). Shklar defines the task of her "belligerent" book as "an effort to explain and judge legalism as an ideological manifestation" (4). She presents her critique in two long essays. The first essay of the book engages with both positivist and naturalist jurisprudence to challenge the legalistic distinction between law and morals. The second essay is a critique of legalism's strict separation between law and politics, executed mainly through a discussion of political trials. Her explanation for the prominence of political trials is that they "reveal the intellectual rigidities and unrealities of legalism as no other occasion can" (112). In a footnote (237n45), she indicates that her take on political trials is very much indebted to Kirchheimer's *Political Justice*, and there is indeed a clearly discernible conversation between the two books.

Shklar suggests that the traditional difficulty of thinking creatively and critically about political trials is one that is rooted in this widespread ideology of legalism, which posits law and politics as mutually exclusive: Law is seen as separate from political life, but also as superior to mere politics (8); law aims at justice whereas politics looks only to expediency; the former is neutral and objective whereas the latter is the unpredictable product of competing interests and ideologies, and so on (111). According to Shklar, the traditional adherents of legalism, "in their determination to preserve law from politics, fail to recognize that they too have made a choice among political values" (8). Legalism is itself a particular political attitude, finding expression in policies domestically and internationally, and, further, law itself should be seen as a form of political action. This is not in the sense that law is always and everywhere a political instrument for protecting the interests of the ruling classes; it can serve other political functions, such as settling group conflicts by recourse to rules in pluralistic societies. So the wider social and political context is crucial for understanding the question "What sort of politics can law maintain and reflect?" (144). Although she cannot be credited with anywhere near a satisfactory materialist analysis of politics,[34] this is one of the more interesting aspects of Shklar's approach: As a philosopher and political theorist committed to liberalism "without illusions," she values the politics of legalism but is frustrated with its disavowal of its own political functions. Shklar thus affirms the politics of legalism and particularly its ability to give rise to the sort of political climate in which judicial and other institutions flourish. But she is also highly critical of the ideology's inability to recognize its own role in these very terms, of its constant denial of its own political contribution:[35] "Legalism as an ideology is too inflexible to recognize the enormous potentialities of legalism as a creative policy, but exhausts itself in intoning traditional pieties and principles which are incapable of realization" (Shklar, *Legalism*, 112). For Shklar, political trials in general and the Nuremberg trial in particular crystallize this paradox.

Shklar notes that anyone who suggests that the judicial process is not the antithesis of politics, but just one form of political action among others will be accused of Vyshinskyism.[36] Her retort is simple and goes to the heart of the split in Kirchheimer's discussion: "There's politics and politics" (Shklar, *Legalism*, 143). In other words, the crux of the matter is not whether trials are political institutions but rather what political values they serve (220): "It is the quality of politics pursued in them that distinguishes one political trial from another" (145). However, despite this rather bold opening, on the whole, Shklar is disparaging about political trials. This is not because they represent an unholy mixing of law and politics, but because they are often used to serve the politics of persecution. She offers her own categorization for political trials on the basis of the principle of legality: There shall be no crime without law, and no punishment without a crime. She suggests that in a political trial either the law or the crime may be missing, or both may be present. Her three categories are:

1. there is law but no criminal act: legally innocent acts will be misinterpreted so as to seem criminal;
2. there is no law which designates the actual acts performed as criminal: laws may be invented on the spot or drawn by analogy, or rules (or their interpretation) may be so vague that virtually any public action can be construed to appear criminal;
3. there is both law and criminal act: trials involving espionage, treason, sedition whereby the aim is the elimination of a specific sort of political enemy. (152–53)

Even this third category, which neatly corresponds to Kirchheimer's category of classical political trials and which is sound from a legalistic perspective insofar as there is both the law and the criminal act, is not palatable for Shklar, because political crimes are difficult to square with tolerance, which she considers a primary liberal virtue. But after announcing it as "the last and third possibility," she goes on to state that "there is, however, a very rare situation in which there is no law, no government, no political order, and people have committed acts so profoundly shocking that something must be done about them" (153). This is her introduction of the Nuremberg trial into the discussion, as a political trial, but an exceptional one that defies the closure of her own categorization. Note that this initial formulation of the trial's necessity in terms of the primacy of the atrocity in question echoes the devolvement in Kirchheimer's discussion of the Nuremberg trial, where his inability to fully invest in the future of either "crimes against peace," or "crimes against humanity" had left him face to face with the atrocity, which in turn became the sole irreducible ground for the necessity of the legal proceedings: a historical record had to be kept, judgment had to be passed.

Yet Shklar has her own reason for thinking that the Nuremberg trial was a necessary operation, and she actually dismisses many of the rationales that were put forward on its behalf as fictions that the architects of the trial had to come up with in order to alleviate their own legalistic concerns. One such fiction was that an international legal system analogous to municipal law existed. Another was that the law was "there" by virtue of various previous war conventions.[37] And finally that the judgment was going to be an act within a legal system, enhancing the strength of that system, contributing to the future of international criminal law (Shklar, *Legalism*, 146–47). None of this is valid for Shklar. Her alternative verdict on the significance of the Nuremberg trial can be presented as follows: As a great legalistic act, and particularly as it concerned itself with crimes against humanity, naming them for what they were on the basis of incontrovertible evidence of the atrocities, the trial could help the immediate future of Germany in its ideological impact. Even though the court lacked a strict legal justification, and although there wasn't even a pseudo-legal basis for "crimes against humanity," the trial was effective insofar as it reminded the German political elite of the value of legalism. By basing itself on indisputable evidence and by taking the form of a fairly executed exercise in legalism, it contributed to reviving a legalistic ethos in Germany among the political elite (151), specifically reinforcing the dormant legal consciousness, the traditional legalism of Germany's professional and bureaucratic classes (156). Therefore, in Shklar's evaluation, based on not whether or not a trial is political, but what kind of politics it promotes, the Nuremberg trial as a political trial actually served liberal ends, promoting "legalistic values in such a way as to contribute to constitutional politics and to a decent legal system" (145).

Then again, Shklar is cautious not to overestimate this function of the trial to then go on to attribute to it either the power to shape the remote future or an authoritative historiographic value. What was at stake was far from a great pedagogic spectacle that would ensure the "re-education and democratization of Germany" (156). The "only value" of the trial "was an entirely unintended" and a rather limited one in Shklar's account:

> The Trial, by forcing defense lawyers to concentrate on the legality of both the entire Trial and its specific charges, induced the German legal profession to rediscover and publicly proclaim anew the value of the principle of legality in criminal law, which for so many years had been forgotten and openly disdained. (165–66)

The performative element of the Nuremberg trial is thus confined to the immediate future of its immediate context: According to Shklar, the best we could hope for the Nuremberg trial to have achieved is the reinstitution of legalism in Germany, in that it was an exercise in restoring order by means of an enactment of orderliness.[38] We may note in passing that this idea that legalistic rituals like the Nuremberg trial will reanimate Germany's legalistic culture resembles the structure of ideological conversion that Slavoj Žižek formulates with reference to Blaise Pascal: Go through the motions of faith, and the faith will come.[39] Importantly, none of the other political trials referred to in the book (the Tokyo trial, the Moscow trials, *US v. Dennis*, the trial of the Rosenbergs) are discussed in such terms, that is, as serving liberal ends in any way. Thus, what is promised as an exceptional take on political trials in general and the Nuremberg trial in particular ends up devolving into a discussion of Nuremberg as exception. Shklar's suggestion that we look at what kind of politics is advanced in a political trial does not yield much, except in its application to the Nuremberg trial. Her conclusion concerning political trials in her epilogue to the book further emphasizes Nuremberg as exception: In countries where constitutional politics prevail, the political trial "can only be a destructive device." In a totalitarian system, political trials are "no better and no worse than the politics of such an order in general." But "where there is no established law and order, in a political vacuum, political trials may be both unavoidable and constructive" (Shklar, *Legalism*, 220).

Nevertheless, there is something very sober and sobering in Shklar's approach to Nuremberg, particularly in her rejection of all the lofty rationales for it. She calls out all the legalistic and most of the political performative investments in that process as either illusionary or unsound. Consider, for example, Shklar's dismissal of the inherent value of the "crimes against peace" formulation. Although for most liberal commentators back then and today, the trial's attempt to outlaw "wars of aggression" was laudable in and of itself, for Shklar it was not only illusionary but also misconceived:

> At worst, the emphasis placed on "aggression" may have the effect of making some types of war "defensive" in purpose, respectable, and even morally desirable. However, the distance between this outworn conception of the morality of war and the present actualities of warfare seems too great to make the survival of the theory of the "just war" likely. (173)

This is prescient in retrospect, even if Shklar was wrong in her prediction that "just war" rationales for "defensive" war would become extinct on account of the tried and tested catastrophic nature of modern warfare. But her foresight of the dangerous legacy that this formulation could lead to was indeed very much on target:

> The idea of self-defense as rendering war legitimate has only the effect of making the "defensive" belligerent feel that he is morally entitled to use any military means whatever to win his just cause. The psychological

consequences of legalism may well be an intransigence fed by self-righteousness. (178)

Shklar can thus be credited with foreseeing the kind of sanctimony that would drive hawkish liberalism and humanitarian interventionism in the early twenty-first century.

Consider also her claim that the "grandiose claims to revolutionize international law" (156) through the Nuremberg trial were misguided and those who believed that this process was "a great contribution to world law . . . were deceiving themselves" (159–60). For Shklar, there was no precedent set by Nuremberg:

> If the Trial had been part of an established legal order, it might have been a legal precedent, for better or worse. Since it was nothing of the sort, both the hopes and fears for the distant future of international law were groundless. The Trial was not, and could not be, a precedent, except by way of vague analogy, for the future. (160)

Once again, given the ways in which the legacy of the IMT at Nuremberg is claimed and celebrated today across the various institutional and ideological settings for international criminal justice, transitional justice, and human rights, Shklar was wrong in what she predicted would not happen. She was, however, accurate in precisely identifying the fictions and disavowals that such legacy-making would require. In an essay that attempts to revive Shklar's work in *Legalism* for the theory of international criminal justice, Samuel Moyn flags this as a key takeaway from Shklar:

> The availability and character of postwar justice is inextricable from the nature and conclusion of the prior war that leads to it. In short, international criminal justice presupposes a political—and most often military—victory that it does not itself provide and that its theorists do not consider, but that nevertheless seems an essential part of the calculus of what its legalism could or does contribute overall.[40]

It is a rather simple point: What founds law is force/violence. As Moyn points out, "Much of *Legalism* is written in a tone, sometimes ironic and sometimes irritated, indicating Shklar could not understand why smart people avoided such an obvious fact,"[41] instead insisting on approaching law as a self-contained body of rules, as entirely isolated from its conditions of emergence.

Most notable in this regard is Shklar's impatience with the unrealistic formalism of the the conception of law as a self-generating structure, whereby rules are understood to "generate rules, nationally and internationally" (Shklar,

Legalism, 131). Using Hans Kelsen as representative, who, she suggests, "saves himself the trouble of historical reflection by retreating into formalism" (131), Shklar argues that the projection of the autogenesis of law thesis onto the international sphere exposes it as the fallacy that it is:

> Law does not by itself generate institutions, cause wars to end, or states to behave as they should. It does not create a community. Only the disingenuous misuse of the word "autogenesis," allowing as it does the confusion of the validation of rules with their historic causes, origins, and force, can permit anyone to believe that law will create world society through operative judicial tribunals. (131)

Shklar thus approaches the question of an "international community" with a very different attitude than that with which Arendt approaches the question of humanity as legal community. On the one hand, it is not possible to read Shklar's and Arendt's approaches to the status of Nuremberg as precedent as if these approaches are entirely commensurate, to then argue that they reach the opposite conclusions. They have different concerns: Whereas Shklar is responding to the legalistic investment in a notion of "world society" that she deems politically fanciful, Arendt is concerned with the political philosophical significance of the notion of "humanity" as legally defined by crimes against humanity. On the other hand, however, despite their different approaches and the seeming opposition of their conclusions, we can discern a kindred sensibility in both authors' prioritization of the political vis-à-vis the legal. Impatient with the legalistic obsession with precedents, Arendt champions self-consciously precedent-setting legal acts of judgment, just as she champions self-consciously world-making political acts of founding. Similarly, impatient with the closed-circuit self-referentiality of legalism, Shklar flags the political force that conditions and precedes any legal order. In this, and particularly in her point about the "confusion of the validation of rules with their historic causes, origins, and force," we can discern an unexpected echo of Walter Benjamin's analysis in "Toward the Critique of Violence" concerning the positivist inclination to regard law as sealed off from its own history and from the violence/force at its foundation that it inevitably repeats, reenacts, and reinstitutes. Although Benjamin, the Marxist-leaning messianic anarchist, and Shklar, a champion of bare-bones liberalism, are unlikely allies, it is significant that what drove Shklar's analysis in *Legalism* was precisely the threat and possibility of legal violence so astutely theorized by Benjamin. With regard to every other political trial she discusses, Shklar is explicit about the threat of legal violence. With regard to the Nuremberg trial, Shklar's solution is to narrowly confine this threat to a targeted and limited performative operation (reawakening the legalism of Germany's ruling elite) and to refuse to invest in any further performative functions, particularly if these are to be effected in denial of law's violence.

Between Atrocity and Legal Violence

Kirchheimer, Arendt, and Shklar grappled in different ways with political trials in the aftermath of World War II. Kirchheimer's rigor is complemented by sober caution in his writing, lending the work an authoritative and principled credibility that may camouflage the deep ambivalence of his evaluation of the Nuremberg trial. In contrast, Arendt and Shklar are staggeringly forthright in their prose. The fights they pick are very different ones, though neither less valiantly than the other: Arendt takes on a powerful political edifice and analytical consensus surrounding the trial of Adolf Eichmann, while Shklar confronts virtually all strands of legal theory that were dominant at the time. There are, however, two important and interrelated points of convergence between the three works that have served as the focus of this chapter. One has to do with a shared sense of critical urgency vis-à-vis the intersection of law and politics as this emerges in political trials; another has to do with the attempt to name, analyze, work with, respond to, or argue against the performativity of legal proceedings.

The shared sense of critical urgency can be explained as an effect of the milieu that Kirchheimer, Arendt, and Shklar cohabited: The necessity of some kind of politico-legal response to Nazi atrocities stood out against a background of various unsavory practices in political justice that had left nothing much redeemable of "the use of legal procedure for political ends." This combination of necessity and controversy can be understood to account for the tangible urgency and the keen thinking of the political that are discernible in these studies, each a rather enormous undertaking in its own right. The urgency becomes even more manifest as each writer acknowledges in his or her own way the difficulty, if not the impossibility, of properly addressing the atrocities within the legal idiom. Every legal formulation of the Nuremberg trial falls to pieces in Kirchheimer's hands, who still feels obliged to confirm the moral and historical necessity of the operation. "There are no civilized responses that are fitting," Shklar admits, "and certainly no legal norms that can cope with what the Nazis did to Europe."[42] "The Nazi crimes, it seems to me," Arendt wrote to Karl Jaspers in 1946, "explode the limits of the law."[43] Then again, it may be worth remembering that this much-cited line was privately communicated to a friend, rather than one elaborated in public writings. And when Arendt did invoke it again in a public essay she wrote in 1964, she couched it in the past tense: "At the time the horror itself, in its naked monstrosity, seemed not only to me but to many others to transcend all moral categories and to explode all standards of jurisdiction."[44] The frustration we read in Arendt's work on the Eichmann trial is thus the frustration of one who has identified a direction for legal innovation to go beyond the "speechless horror" before the atrocity, a horror "in which one learns nothing,"[45] only to find a more parochial performative operation at work in the trial, indexed to the atrocity in pursuit of what she considered misdirected political aims.

The recognition of the performative possibilities of political trials is perhaps most pronounced in Hannah Arendt's work, and this is not surprising given that an understanding of politics as inherently performative is one of the cornerstones of her political theory.[46] In addition to experimenting with a range of legal doctrines in her text, Arendt invests in the legal substantiation of the notion of "crimes against humanity" as a way to performatively produce humanity as a legal community. Kirchheimer's analysis of numerous structural dynamics of trials can also be read as an incipient grasp of the performativity of political justice, particularly his discussions of the "irreducible risk" inherent in the legal procedure, the openings for innovation in the "judicial space," and the image-making capacity of political trials for historiographic and pedagogic effect, as well as his discernment of the ability of the law to enact its own foundations into being through a process such as the Nuremberg trial. In contrast, Shklar is resolutely, and perhaps somewhat hyperbolically, skeptical and dismissive about the performative potentials of political trials. But in arguing against the rationales for Nuremberg as precedent, she astutely identifies the disavowals and self-righteous intransigences that are required for such precedenting or legacy-making. In this sense, Shklar can be understood as diagnosing the force or violence that conditions and continuously informs the law in its performative operations.

Importantly, most studies that draw on the works of these thinkers to address political trials from a liberal perspective tend to jettison the urgency and abandon the critical thinking of politics and law that permeates their writings. What is preserved from this legacy is the idea that trials can have politics and that need not be a bad thing. But what seems to have been relinquished is that keen thinking of legal violence. For example, in what has now become a classic text of transitional justice literature, Mark Osiel suggests that his book is "little more than an elaboration and defense of Shklar's argument" in *Legalism*. Shklar is represented as arguing that political trials are fine as long as they are "placed in the service of the *right kind* of politics."[47] Thus Shklar's extremely cautious and narrow endorsement of the particular political function of legalism in the Nuremberg trial is incorporated into a study that passionately advocates for the value of the "monumental didactics" of "liberal show trials" in the aftermath of administrative massacre. For Osiel the illiberal use of courts for liberal ends, particularly for historiographic and pedagogical aims, such as influencing the collective memory of historical episodes of atrocity, is fully justified. His disavowal of legal violence and the ways in which it might misfire or backfire is right on the surface of the text, as he writes, for example: "A criminal trial is one useful way to begin a discussion with an initially un-willing interlocutor"[48]—the "interlocutor" here being the defendant facing the death penalty or life imprisonment. Another American legal scholar, Eric Posner, cites the 1960s literature to coolly explain that while unavoidable, politi-cal trials in liberal democracies posit an institutional design and manage-ment challenge. What is at stake in a political trial according to Posner is a "liberty-security trade-off": It is a matter of balancing due process and the pub-lic's need for security. The best way to strike the right balance between liberty and security is to make a distinction between political opponents, on the one hand, and public threats, on the other. The latter category in this scholar's imaginary includes "anarchists, communists, Islamic terrorists."[49] When dealing with people who can be allocated to one of these categories, con-cerns over security can legitimately be prioritized over due process. The 1960s uneasy critique of the use of legal procedure for political ends is thus mobi-lized for a comfortable argument advocating the use of legal procedure for fencing out the undesirables from the political sphere.

In this chapter, I have argued that the cluster of works by Kirchheimer, Arendt, and Shklar published in the early 1960s marked a shift in the literature on po-litical trials, as each went beyond the classic approach that more or less suf-ficed with being scandalized by the combination of "political" and "trial." Instead, these thinkers crafted thoughtful accounts of the relationship between politics and law, and of the materializations of this relationship in a trial. I pro-posed that a common element of these works was the recognition of the vari-ous ways in which legal proceedings operate performatively, while always keeping in play the cognizance of the question of legal violence—something that is often dispensed with in these works' contemporary uptakes. Over the next two chapters I turn to a close engagement with performative theory to tease out its relevance for conceptualizing how law operates, without either disavowing or underestimating the vagaries of legal violence. The philosophi-cal idiom of performativity proves helpful both for rethinking the role of per-formance in trials, and for understanding the various ways in which violence is addressed, negotiated, reenacted, transformed, and perpetuated through legal proceedings. Against readings that approach the political trial as a scene of mastery, that is, as a convenient instrument of sovereign power through which political violence is wielded (for the sake of persecuting political adversaries) or contained (through pedagogic spectacle or therapeutic working-through), a performative account allows us to avoid such overdeterminations of the political. Instead, it sharpens our awareness as to the ways in which trials can fail to serve sovereign schemes, how law's structural unconscious may play out in a trial, manifesting the violence at its origin, and how embodied practices bring fears, desires, anxieties, fantasies, and hauntings into the scene of the trial to unsettle and recast its political meaning and effects.

2

The Form and Substance of Doing Justice

Law, Performativity, Performance

You are more than entitled to know what the word "performative" means. It is a new word and an ugly word, and perhaps it does not mean anything very much. But at any rate there is one thing in its favor, it is not a profound word.

—J. L. AUSTIN, *PHILOSOPHICAL PAPERS*

English ordinary language philosopher J. L. Austin's term "performative" has been revised, rethought, rearticulated, and reworked in various ways since its coinage, not only by his successors in that same tradition of philosophy such as John R. Searle and Jerrold Katz, but also, and much more influentially for critical theory, by Jacques Derrida, Shoshana Felman, Judith Butler, and Eve Sedgwick, among others. It would not be an exaggeration to say that the term has had an eventful history as the subject and scene of some polemic and controversy. I have in mind, for example, Derrida's flamboyantly scathing responses to Searle in the course of their exchange in the pages of the journal *Glyph* in the late seventies and the various inexplicably outraged responses to Butler's reworking of the term for gender theory in the early nineties. Then again, a certain amount of intimacy with theories of performativity begets the sense that there is actually something quite outrageous about the notion itself. Felman has masterfully traced this "scandal" as already part and parcel of not only Austin's coinage but also the very style of his thought.[1] In this chapter, as well as the next, I endeavor to bring something of this scandal to bear on a conceptualization of political trials.

I begin this chapter with a brief review of the promises and vagaries of the performative in Austin's conceptualization. I then move on to exploring the relevance of performativity for legal theory, first by tracing the status of law in Austin's text and then by offering a summary overview of the ways in which Austin's coinage has been taken up by legal theorists. The approach that I find particularly inspiring among the various strains of legal theoretical engagement with the theory of performativity is the deconstructive analysis of Jacques Derrida and Judith Butler. As I elaborate through a reading of Derrida's groundbreaking essay "Force of Law: 'The Mystical Foundation of Authority,'" in this approach, rather than effecting a formalistic (or, indeed, legalistic) isolation of law from its historical, political, and social context, the idiom of performativity allows the questions of law's historicity and its force/violence to remain in play in legal analyses. My discussion in the first half of this chapter attempts to demonstrate that the theory of performativity is relevant for law not because law must strictly be studied *as* language, but rather because the conceptual apparatus of performativity emerges precisely from an inquiry into the relationship of force, authority, and conventionality—elements that are essential for conceptualizing law. As Derrida states, "The juridical is at work in the performative."[2]

In the second half of this chapter, my discussion highlights something that Austin introduces in passing: the idea that performatives often masquerade as constatives. This ties in with Derrida's proposal in his reading of Thomas Jefferson's draft of the US Declaration of Independence that the masquerade of legal performatives as constatives is not accidental but rather a necessary mode for law's operation. I elaborate on this idea of masquerade and its relevance for studying trials by drawing on Butler's conceptualization of the centrality of conventionality, understood as a sedimented historicity, for performativity. I conclude this chapter by arguing that the various performative operations of legal proceedings are often disguised as constative functions partially through the hyper-conventionality of trial performance. This, then, anchors a new perspective on the coupling between performance and performativity in the trial: Conventions of embodied trial performance assist in disguising a trial's performative operations and allow law to operate as if it were fate. In other words, the overlaps between performance and performativity work to create an appearance of inevitability. In this analysis, political trials can be defined as legal proceedings the performative structures of which are publicly exposed, thereby resisting the closure of inevitability.

Not a Profound Word

Since J. L. Austin's coinage in the late 1940s, the word "performative" has been taken up and reworked as a concept in diverse ways and has found its way into various disciplines across the humanities and social sciences as a key term.

Austin's most extensive elaboration of what he meant by "performative" is found in his William James Lectures delivered at Harvard University in 1955, posthumously edited and published as *How to Do Things with Words*. That this volume has come to serve as the definitive resource for Austin's speech act theory is somewhat curious, for it is not quite conclusive and certainly not as clear-cut as other work he published during his lifetime. The lectures begin with his now well-known distinction between constative and performative utterances. Constatives correspond to the classic "statements" of analytic philosophy, describing some state of affairs or stating facts, either truly or falsely. Performatives are distinct from constatives in that they do not describe, report, or constate a reality, but rather enact what they say in their very utterance. For example, the utterance "You are sentenced to imprisonment for life" when spoken by a judge addressing the defendant in a criminal trial during sentencing remarks is a performative. The saying is the doing, the utterance is the act of sentencing itself; it doesn't describe a preexisting situation; it creates the situation that it refers to: The defendant gets life. Early on in the lectures, Austin warns that performatives can be difficult to identify because they often take on the grammatical guise of a statement, seemingly constating a reality. Indeed, if these very same words "You are sentenced to imprisonment for life" were spoken by someone else in the same scenario, say, repeated by the defense counsel to the defendant, that would be a constative utterance because it would be merely describing the situation that was brought into being by the performative speech act of the judge. So in Austin's scheme, performative utterances *do* rather than describe; they produce or transform a situation, or at least attempt to do so.

Unlike constatives for which their referent provides a truth value, performatives cannot be said to be "true" or "false" as such, but they succeed or fail in other ways. To such success or failure Austin refers in terms of the "felicity" or "infelicity" of an utterance. So instead of truth-conditions, performatives have "conditions of felicity," and Austin sets these out in six rules.[3] The first rule concerns the existence of a conventional procedure that allows the performative to do what it does. In our example the conventional procedure would be the criminal trial itself, in which a conviction is followed by sentencing, and only in that procedural context does the judge's utterance produce the situation whereby the defendant gets life. The second rule is about the appropriateness of the persons invoking the procedure and of the circumstances in which the procedure is invoked. So if the words "You are sentenced to life imprisonment" were spoken by the defendant addressing the judge; or spoken by the judge following an acquittal, these would be failed or infelicitous performatives—unless there is a revolution unfolding at the time of the utterance, or a thoroughly topsy-turvy justice system, respectively. The third and fourth rules concern the execution of the procedure: "It must be executed by all participants both correctly and completely" (15). The fifth and sixth rules have to do with thoughts, feelings, and the follow-up actions of the participants in the procedure and are less consequential in terms of the effectiveness of utterances. That is, it doesn't make a difference if the judge believes that the defendant doesn't really deserve the life sentence—if all other conditions are fulfilled, the sentence will be in effect: "Here, we say, the performance is *not* void, although it is still unhappy" (39). Austin discusses these six rules under the rubric of "the doctrine of the *Infelicities*" and provides a thorough categorization of all the ways in which a performative utterance can fail: Breaches of the first four rules constitute "misfires," and those of the last two rules constitute "abuses." A "misfire" can be a "misinvocation" (rules 1 and 2), or a "misexecution" (rules 3 and 4); and so on.

Austin lays out the hazardous path of performativity in such detail that his neat categories of failure eventually begin to overflow their boundaries. Midway into the lectures he goes on to undo the clean-cut constative/performative distinction by considering in what way some infelicities that are proper to performatives can also afflict constatives, and in turn, how performatives can be said to be "true" or "false" in certain ways. Timothy Gould incisively interprets this particular move in Austin as a strategy

> to drag the fetish of true and false into the same swamp of assessment
> and judgment in which we find the dimension of happiness and
> unhappiness that afflicts our performative utterances . . . to seduce us
> away from the reassurances of that dichotomy into a larger apprecia-
> tion of the common miseries of utterance—whether constative *or*
> performative.[4]

Indeed, toward the end of the lectures, Austin does confess a desire to "play Old Harry with two fetishes which I admit to an inclination to play Old Harry with, viz. 1) the true/false fetish, 2) the value/fact fetish" (Austin, *How to Do Things with Words*, 151). It is as part of this attempt to bedevil entrenched categories of truth/falsity and is/ought that Austin puts aside the performative/constative distinction in favor of seeking "more general *families* of related and overlapping speech acts" (150). Introducing a tripartite classification of the "locutionary" as the act *of* saying something, the "illocutionary" as the act *in* saying something, and the "perlocutionary" as the act *by* saying something, Austin attempts to formulate the beginnings of a new doctrine pertaining to all the possible forces of utterances, or as he puts it elsewhere, of *"what one is doing in saying something*, in all the sense of that ambiguous phrase."[5] But rather than entirely fulfilling this promise in *How to Do Things with Words*, he suffices with a preliminary classification of verbs regarding their potential locutionary, illocutionary, and perlocutionary force in speech acts.

Instrumentalized thus as a provisional category to "clear up some mistakes in philosophy"[6] and later suspended as an ultimately untenable designation by its coiner himself, the word "performative" nevertheless has significant currency in both theoretical and everyday usage. In ordinary language it is nowadays mostly used as the adjectival form of "performance," to refer to something akin to "theatrical," sometimes even "spectacular," and too often in the sense of "not genuine," "not true," "not really real," or "just for show." This particular usage is increasingly quite common in scholarly literature as well, particularly when "performative" is used casually rather than conceptually, so that the term is encountered surprisingly often in a forgetfulness or disavowal of its basis in ordinary language philosophy. That "performative" of all terms is afflicted with such forgetting of origins may be read as something of a philosophical in-joke.[7] Austin himself would have taken issue with the conflation of performativity with performance in the sense of "twice-behaved behavior," particularly given his methodological exclusion of language used in recitational practice in his consideration of performatives.[8]

In its conceptual deployments, however, the term "performative" and the more expansive notion of "performativity" have proved rather fecund across the humanities and social sciences, though no longer necessarily with direct reference to Austin. The main yield in philosophy of language and linguistics is speech act theory, which was developed largely by the American philosopher John R. Searle, who built on and refined Austin's conceptual scheme.[9] In literary studies, particularly in the United States in the last quarter of the twentieth century, the concept of performativity was widely used for deconstructive analysis. The main influence in this uptake was Jacques Derrida, whose engagement with Austin in his 1972 essay "Signature Event Context" led to a rather vituperative debate between Derrida and Searle in the journal *Glyph*, which published the English translation of Derrida's essay in its inaugural issue in 1977. Derrida's revision of the notion of the performative has provoked some of the more imaginative openings in critical thought, for example, in the work of Shoshana Felman, Judith Butler, and Eve Sedgwick. Meanwhile, American philosopher Stanley Cavell can be said to have forged a separate path in philosophy of language for Austin's influence, steering clear of both speech act theory and the deconstructionist take on performativity. But perhaps the most influential theorist of performativity to date is Judith Butler, who expanded the conceptual apparatus of performativity beyond the question of linguistic functions to theorize social and political processes, including the construction of gender, the legal regulation of speech, and the political significance of acting in concert. It is through these various key inflections that theories of performativity have taken root not only in the humanities but also in social and political thought, and even found their way into less likely disciplines such as economics, geography, and, of course, legal studies.

Law and Performativity

Austin himself was very much interested in the intersection of law and performativity. While it may be a stretch to claim that he attempted to read law through the notion of the performative, it would be accurate to suggest that he often understood and explained performatives through law. H. L. A. Hart, speaking of Austin as a colleague and friend in an interview he gave in 1988, said, "He was naturally interested in law. He would have made a formidable QC."[10] In reading Austin, one does get a palpable sense of how intrigued he must have been not only by legal uses of language but also by law as a discipline. He explicitly acknowledges the insights that legal language affords into ordinary language, in his essay on excuses:[11] "It is a perpetual and salutary surprise to discover how much is to be learned from the law" (188). The categories, distinctions, and precautions Austin finds in law afford him a certain analytic clarity that he draws on to explore the workings of ordinary language, including the role, function, and problems of performative utterances: "Examples are more easily seen in the law; they are naturally not so definite in ordinary life, where allowances are made."[12] Many such remarks throughout the William James lectures gesture toward law as a kind of solid ground, as opposed to the "boggy" consistency of ordinary language in which Austin finds himself "floundering."[13] Hart, who admits to being "tremendously impressed" by Austin's work on performatives and cites him among the primary sources of influence for his brand of legal positivism,[14] recognized this clearly when he stated that in Austin's idea of performative utterances, "the law came into its own."[15]

Austin recognizes that "many of the 'acts' which concern the jurist are or include the utterance of performatives."[16] He further notes that the legal profession is particularly attuned to the peculiarities of the performative (19), ready with a terminology to cope with them (24), and takes special precautions to avoid the many varieties of infelicity to which such speech acts are exposed (28). He draws heavily on legal scenarios for examples. Further, the primacy of legal language in Austin's project survives the abandonment of the performative/constative scheme. In his later tripartite classification of locutionary, illocutionary, and perlocutionary force of utterances, Austin chooses to focus mostly on the illocutionary. An illocutionary act is the force of an utterance *in* saying something, so this category can be understood as the new counterpart of the earlier definition of performative utterances. By way of an explication, Austin provides a list of verbs that, when used in the first person singular present indicative active form, have explicit illocutionary force.[17] A quick glance at this list indicates how many of the conventional utterances that are quintessential to legal procedure include verbs with explicit illocutionary force: acquit, convict, find (as a matter of fact), hold (as a matter of law), appoint, dismiss, order, command, sentence, fine, pardon, plead, press, quash, annul, repeal, and the list goes on (153–63). Austin classifies such verbs under five categories, the first three of which are primarily used in legal language: verdictives "typified by the giving of a verdict, as the name implies, by a jury, arbitrator or umpire"; exertives, "the exercising of powers, rights, or influence"; and commissives "typified by promising or otherwise undertaking" (150). Hence at first glance, legal language seems to be a fertile resource for many of Austin's examples, utilized liberally for purposes of illustration. But on more careful reading, it becomes clear that law for Austin actually serves as a privileged order vis-à-vis performativity. His evaluative scheme for determining the force of these utterances corroborates this. Recall the doctrine of infelicities: According to Austin, the effectiveness of a performative utterance depends primarily on the existence of an accepted *conventional procedure*, the appropriateness of the *circumstances* for invoking such procedure, whether the person invoking the procedure has the genuine *authority* to do so in the given circumstances, and whether the procedure is executed by all participants correctly and completely (14–15). So already in this initial evaluative configuration, it is as if we find ourselves in a scene of law.

In addition to H. L. A. Hart, a relatively early and direct uptake of Austin's work in legal thought is by the Swedish jurist Karl Olivecrona, who advocated for a critical approach to legal language that could capture the fact that it does not mirror reality but shapes it, and discussed legal performatives as part of his analysis.[18] In later work, Olivecrona coined the phrase "performatory imperatives" for conceptualizing certain performative legal formulations as imperatives without addressee.[19] Further, Olivecrona understood performative utterances as "the language of magic"[20] and thus as providing a clue for the historical link between the modern languages of law and ancient law's magical formulae.[21] Danish legal philosopher Alf Ross also engaged with Austin's work on speech acts, proposing to replace the term "performative" by "normative," and to bring a definition of "legal acts" and "conventional acts" under this new concept of "normative acts."[22] Later utilizations of Austin's conceptual scheme in its relevance to law are mostly found across the wide terrain of law and language scholarship, but here John R. Searle's reading of Austin tends to dominate. Work by linguists provides technical analyses of legal speech acts[23] and offers specific taxonomies of the legal use of performatives.[24] However, some legal scholars who engage with speech acts downplay their jurisprudential significance.[25] Some go so far as to caution that "it is a dangerous mistake" to think that the theory of performatives is important to legal theory, though without explaining what exactly the danger may be [26] Such hasty dismissal proves injudicious when we consider, for example, the work of legal philosopher Marianne Constable, whose imaginative uses of speech act theory may have something to do with the fact that she chooses to bypass the Searlian inflection of Austin.[27]

For my own purposes in this book, namely, for a performative theory of political trials that can account for the ways in which they go awry, both falling short of and exceeding the intentions invested in them, it is the deconstructive analyses of the relationship between law and performativity that are most illuminating. In this approach, the analysis is not limited to the question of how language functions in law or how legal utterances work performatively. The conceptual apparatus of performativity is further made to serve as a wider analytic frame for legal theory. Austin's work does lend itself to this particular uptake more readily than may be conceded by his "legitimate" heirs in speech act theory. For example, in detailing conventionality, circumstances, and authority as conditions of felicity, Austin not only draws his examples from law but also chooses curious ones that begin to broach legal theory. When he discusses the question of convention, he invokes the practice of *talaq* in Islamic law—namely, a husband's ability to effect a divorce by repeatedly pronouncing "I divorce you"—to suggest that the conventional procedure must not only exist but also be accepted, that is, it must be valid in the jurisdiction in which it is invoked.[28] In detailing the ways in which a conventional procedure may fail to be executed completely, Austin makes an interesting allusion to social contract theory, recasting it in the form of a prior performative ("I promise to do what you order me to do") that potentially conditions the validity of the authority that does the ordering (29). And when he explains the possible mismatch between convention and circumstance, he does so with reference to how lawyers work with the notion of precedent, proposing that the limits of applicability of any conventional procedure is inherently and necessarily vague: "Can I baptize a dog?" Austin asks, and leaves the question unanswered (31). Already in these remarks, which may be read as minor forays into jurisprudence, we find the seeds of a deconstructive analysis of legal performativity. For example, in Austin's allusion to the social contract, what is at stake is the traditional jurisprudential question of the ground of law; to reformulate this as a matter of a previous performative can be understood to foreshadow Jacques Derrida's proposal that law is grounded performatively. Or Austin's quip about baptizing a dog and his preceding discussion of the inherent ambivalence of the applicability of a convention can be said to anticipate Judith Butler's understanding of norms as performatively constituted and therefore open to subversion and resignification.

One of the important aspects of the deconstructive uptake of theories of performativity for purposes of legal theory is its inscription of the question of force / violence into any analysis of law, rather than withdrawing into a formalism that evaluates law as an entirely self-contained structure. The text that can be credited with facilitating the transfer of the language of performativity from ordinary language philosophy to deconstructive jurisprudence is Jacques Derrida's "Force of Law: 'The Mystical Foundation of Authority,'" which was the keynote address to the 1989 colloquium "Deconstruction and the Possibility of Justice." In this text, Derrida approaches his task of inquiring into the relationship between deconstruction and justice by introducing law as a third term. He locates "the possibility of the exercise of deconstruction" in the interval between the undeconstructability of justice and the deconstructability of law. Law, he proposes, is deconstructable owing to its performativity. His interpretation of law as performative pertains first and foremost to the question of its foundation but also includes an understanding of law's subsequent operation as likewise performative. Departing from a comparative reading of Pascal and Montaigne on the "mystical foundation of the authority of laws," Derrida suggests that what founds law and preserves its authority is not any intrinsic link to justice, but rather the performative force at its foundation: "The very emergence of justice and law, the instituting, founding, and justifying moment of law implies a performative force, that is to say always an interpretative force and a call to faith."[29] But this link between law and force, he cautions, should not be reduced to an instrumentalist account that sees law as merely "*in the service* of force, its docile instrument, servile and thus exterior to the dominant power . . . for example an economic, political, ideological power that would exist outside or before it and that it would have to accommodate or bend to when useful" (241). There is a "more intrinsic structure" linking law and force that any critical approach to law must take heed of, which is a structure of co-implication between law and force / violence. Derrida dedicates the second part of his essay to a close reading of Walter Benjamin's 1921 essay "Toward the Critique of Violence," in which he takes recourse to the language of performativity to elaborate this "more intrinsic structure" whereby law and force / violence are always co-implicated.

As an idiom for theorizing force, authority/authorization, and convention-ality, the language of performativity does indeed easily accommodate Ben-jamin's important understanding of the relationship between law and force/violence. For example, in paraphrasing Benjamin's note on the opera-tion of the monopoly of violence (his proposal that law punishes unsanctioned use of force/violence by individuals, not because such use breaches this or that law, but because it threatens the very legal order itself), Derrida writes:

> This monopoly does not strive to protect any given just and legal ends but law itself. This seems like a tautological triviality. . . . Performative tautology or a priori synthesis, which structures any founding [*fonda-tion*] of the law [*loi*] upon which one performatively produces the conventions (or the "credit" of which we spoke earlier) that guarantee the validity of the performative, thanks to which one gives oneself the means to decide between legal and illegal violence. The expressions tautology, *a priori synthesis*, and especially the word *performative* are not Benjaminian, but I dare believe that they do not betray his purposes. (267)

Here the proposal is that any given modern legal order can be described as a structure of serial performativity whereby the order of conventionality that is instituted by a performative founding becomes the context and measure of each further performative operation of law. But unlike the language of "nor-mativity" or "autogenesis" that serves to bracket law off from the historical con-ditions of its emergence, the idiom of performativity keeps in play the question of the force/violence of the founding.

Since Derrida's "Force of Law" continues to resonate as a keynote in con-temporary critical legal thought, there is often an echo of Benjamin's essay in discussions of legal performativity that are informed by this deconstructive analysis. A brief consideration of Benjamin's classic text will therefore assist in elaborating the openings that the idiom of performativity allows for legal the-ory. Benjamin begins his famous essay with an evaluation of the seeming op-position between theories of natural and positive law in terms of their evaluation of violence. He exposes the point of convergence of both of these approaches as the legitimization of violence in terms of a means-ends relationship, and provisionally sides with the approach of positive law, which, in maintaining that means justify ends, allows for "a differentiation in the sphere of means itself, without regard for the ends they serve."[30] Benjamin's temporary prefer-ence for positive law must be understood in relation to his wider project in this text, which is to provide "an outline for a politics of pure mediacy,"[31] or to attempt to conceive of justice in the sphere of human action and freedom without falling back on criteria that are driven by logics of instrumentality. Then again, this is just a provisional alliance, as Benjamin points out the ways in which this approach closes in on itself: its failure to take account of the historicity of posited law, its inability to question how law became law in the first place, and its consequent inadequacy for a critique of the wider framework of instrumentality in which posited law serves as a means to the ends of the modern state. Accordingly, Benjamin presents his own undertaking in the essay as "a historical-philosophical reflection on law."[32]

Benjamin parts with the isolation of law from its historicity through his discussion of the relationship between what he terms law-positing force/violence and law-preserving force/violence. Benjamin introduces the former as the force or violence that makes law (e.g., war, revolution, colonization) and the latter as the force or violence that preserves the law that has been posited (e.g., the police, the criminal trial, the penal system). He then proposes that law-preserving violence always implicates and repeats law-positing violence, as readily seen in examples such as the death penalty (where the origins of the legal order "are represented as they burst into the status quo, manifesting themselves in a fearsome manner") and the institution of the police (where "the separation of law-positing and law-preserving violence is annulled"). Derrida inscribes the analysis of performativity into Benjamin's distinction between law-positing violence and law-preserving violence by recasting the former in terms of the "performatives that institute" and the latter in terms of "derived performatives that suppose anterior conventions."[33] As in Benjamin's approach, these two types of performatives ought not be conceived of in a relationship of hierarchy that prioritizes the "original" over and above the "copy." This is because the performative force at the origin of law contains within itself a certain iterability, whereby "the possibility of repetition" is inscribed "at the heart of the originary":

> Consequently, there is no more pure foundation or pure position of law, and so a pure founding violence, than there is a purely preserving violence. Positing is already iterability, a call for self-preserving repetition. Preservation in its turn refounds, so that it can preserve what it claims to found. Thus there can be no rigorous opposition between positing and preserving, only what I will call (and Benjamin does not name it) a *differential contamination* between the two, with all the paradoxes that this may lead to. (272)

In other words, each performative operation of posited law both reenacts (repeats, represents, re-performs) and reinstitutes (founds, instates, inaugurates again) the performative violence of the founding of the legal order. Derrida writes that since a performative has to ground "itself in on conventions and so on other performatives, buried or not, it always maintains within itself some irruptive violence" (256).

In Derrida's scheme this irruptive violence is also what enables critical thinking on law or law's deconstructability. As I discuss in detail in the next chapter, it can also serve as a methodological departure point for interpreting the politics of political trials as both exceeding and undoing the sovereign investments that ostensibly drive such proceedings. Judith Butler's work on performativity is particularly significant in this regard, because it offers a keen thinking of performative agency in relation to the operation and temporality of conventions. In *Excitable Speech*, Butler trains their gaze on the force of convention and the logic of iterability which is inherent in convention and yet "governs the possibility of social transformation."[34] Since their main interest lies in sketching the potentials as well as the limits of performative agency, they provide an insightful reading of the vagaries of the relation between the performative and its context of convention. This relation is almost always one of institution (each performative utterance reinstitutes the convention), but it is *not necessarily* so, also offering a possibility of rupture and insurrection. Herein lies another key appeal of the theories of performativity: The analysis of how performatives operate includes the recognition of not only performative failure (infelicities) but also performative contradiction and subversion. The theory holds out the possibility of rupture in the horizon of conventionality whereby a reiteration need not necessarily function as a reinstitution. Thus the context of convention need not be figured as an immovable mover, but rather understood in its contingency, as a process of "historical sedimentation."[35]

For Butler, each performative utterance that draws on "the force of reiterated convention" is a "condensed historicity." This points to the particular temporality of performatives that Butler explains with reference to their "ritual or ceremonial" form identified by Austin:

> They work to the extent that they are given in the form of a ritual, that is, repeated in time, and, hence, maintain a sphere of operation that is not restricted to the moment of the utterance itself. The illocutionary speech act performs its deed *at the moment* of the utterance, and yet to the extent that the moment is ritualized, it is never merely a single moment. The "moment" in ritual is a condensed historicity: it exceeds itself in past and future directions, an effect of prior and future invocations that constitute and escape the instance of the utterance.[36]

In this account, the performative is always more than its presence and present tense, as it is extended both into the past and the future. It stretches into the past insofar as it owes its conditions of being and felicity to a historical sedimentation of conventionality, and into the future insofar as it constitutes a reinscription (or potentially, transformation) of that conventionality. Butler's temporalization of the role of convention in the theory of performativity renders the latter a powerful analytical instrument for law, as Ritu Birla points out, posing "context as more than just the historical and empirical framework *for* law, contemplating it instead as the historicity of law itself, of law understood as ever-shifting convention, or the always already situated norms that become sites for citation."[37]

One of the general criticisms directed at deconstructive analysis is that it treats all of its objects as if they are textual, thereby reducing diverse phenomena to language and its forms. But to inquire into the performative foundation and operation of law is not necessarily to study law strictly *as* language. As I have tried to highlight in this section, the relevance of the idiom of performativity for law is owed not so much to law's linguisticity as to its conventionality. In other words, it is the conventionality of law, or law as convention, that renders a performative perspective key for theorizing law and the force of law, capturing aspects of law that are not in the final instance reducible to language and its forms. The deconstructive uptake of performative theory for legal analysis allows law's historicity to remain in focus, and maintains an attunement to the operations of force and violence in law, thereby parting with both a solely instrumental (i.e., political) and a solely formal (i.e., legalistic) account of the intersection of law and the political.

Masquerade and Fate

The question of how conventionality works—what it effects and what it obscures—is therefore rather crucial for understanding legal performativity. There is an important clue to the effects of conventionality in law in Austin's work, one that requires a detour in returning to the question that I began this chapter with, namely that of the significance of the obfuscation of performance and performativity in law. Early on during the very first of his lectures, in a section aptly titled "Preliminary Isolation of the Performative," Austin warns against the capacity of performatives to disguise themselves as constatives:

> The type of utterance we are to consider here is . . . one of our second class—the masqueraders. But it does not by any means necessarily masquerade as a statement of fact, descriptive or constative. Yet it does

quite commonly do so, and that, oddly enough, when it assumes its
most explicit form. Grammarians have not, I believe, seen through
this "disguise," and philosophers only at best "incidentally."[38]

Thus the performative is said to often *masquerade* as a descriptive or constative
statement, seeming to display a relation of externality to its reference, and
thereby deceiving us into ascribing it a "truth value" in such disguise. Even
though Austin holds the legal use and scrutiny of language in high esteem, a
curious footnote that he appends to this passage tells us that he thinks jurists
do not necessarily fully grasp the philosophical implications of their pragmatic
distinctions:

> Of all people, jurists should be best aware of the true state of affairs
> [i.e., the disguise whereby performatives masquerade as constatives].
> Perhaps some now are. Yet they will succumb to their own timorous
> fiction that a statement of "the law" is a statement of fact. (4n2)

The implicit suggestion here is that statements of law are often performatives.
So just as performatives can be distinguished from constatives, statements of
law must be distinguished from statements of fact. As experts dealing in performatives, jurists are in a privileged position to see what all grammarians and
most analytic philosophers have failed to see: They should be able to understand that what seems to pass as a statement of fact is sometimes the very production of that fact, the enactment, as it were, of the factual order in question.
Jurists must understand this, Austin seems to suggest, because this is the ordinary mode in which law operates.

Austin's idea that performatives disguise themselves as constatives is quite
significant, and his use of the metaphor of "masquerader" to describe this operation is noteworthy. The metaphor brings the excluded theatrical through
the back door into Austin's theory, as part and parcel of his initial definition of
the performative. The performative, we are told, is that which often disguises
or passes itself off as constative. So there is always already a staging involved
in the performative, whereby it disguises the fact of its enactment. The performative both stages its referent, and stages itself so as to look as if it is merely
stating rather than staging its referent. The staging is thus doubled so as to
conceal the fact that there is any staging involved. Further, the word "masquerade" happens to be charged with theoretical associations in work on the
performativity of norms. For example, in Judith Butler's *Gender Trouble*, an
extended discussion of the way masquerade figures in the works of Joan
Riviere and Jacques Lacan provides part of the groundwork for Butler's notion of the performativity of gender.[39] It is here that they offer an initial, albeit

seemingly provisional, version of what they later in the book elaborate in terms of gender performativity: "Masquerade may be understood as the performative production of a sexual ontology, an appearing that makes itself convincing as a 'being'" (60).

Admittedly, Austin is not entirely accurate in his assessment of the failure of jurists to appreciate that the statements of law are not statements of fact. As far back as 1605, Flemish jurist Leonardus Lessius wrote about promise (*promissio*) and donation (*donatio*) as being "practical signs, actuating what they mean."[40] Further, the positivist tradition from Jeremy Bentham and J.L.'s namesake John Austin onward can be read as recognizing at some level the performative quality of law. Nevertheless, suppose that one of the imaginary jurists conjured by Austin in his brief footnote were to respond, offering the rejoinder that statements of law do not resemble performative utterances as much as they resemble constative statements, in the sense that there is a law out there—whether in the form of statute or precedent, whether based on a conception of sovereign command or normative system—that exists prior to individual legal statements, and to which such statements correspond, very much in the same way that constatives correspond to facts that are outside and prior to themselves. Thus, the jurist would say, a statement of the law constates existing law, which is its "factual" referent. If such a conversation were to take place, would Austin still accuse his imaginary jurist of succumbing to a "timorous fiction that statements of 'the law' are statements of fact"? Would he say that it is misguided to speak of a law "out there," existing prior to its utterances? Would he instead suggest that it is each and every individual statement of the law that reinstates and reifies the law? Would he thus claim that what purportedly derives from law in fact performatively brings it into being?

Perhaps not. The response would more likely be a corrective, a fine-tuning of terminology, something along the lines of: To say that existing law constitutes the "fact" to which individual legal utterances pertain truthfully or falsely would be to say that a judge's "I sentence you to imprisonment for life" describes something already extant in the law, as if you were always already to be sentenced to imprisonment for life, and the judge was merely stating this fact. Applied to utterances of the law, the constative fallacy produces this kind of absurd fatalism, whereas thinking through the same scene in performative terms would help us better understand the dynamics involved.[41] Thus Austin would presumably counter-propose that existing law should not be understood as the *fact* out there that then determines the truth or falsity of statements of law, but rather as a context of *convention* that determines their felicity. Here is, Austin would say, not only an established code of procedure and set of conventions, but also often the appropriate authority with which to invoke them,

crucial elements determining the force of a performative. Thus legal conventions and legal authority would render the judge's sentence a felicitous performative, enabling him to indeed send you to prison for life with his very
utterance in the right circumstances.

The idea that performatives often masquerade as constatives is important
for critical legal thought in a number of ways, for example, in understanding
the mechanism of self-evidence by which law is founded. An illuminating
demonstration of this mechanism is offered by Derrida in his reading of the
US Declaration of Independence. Here Derrida inquires into the structure of
the language of the declaration and points out that it is not possible to decide
whether the declaration is stating the independence (i.e., as a constative) or
performatively bringing it into effect. He concludes that "this undecidability
between, let us say, a performative structure and a constative structure, is *required* to produce the sought-after effect. It is essential to the very positing or
position of a right as such."[42] Thus the masquerade of legal performatives as
constatives, or in Derrida's words "the whole game that tends to present performative utterances, as constative utterances" (11), is not accidental, but rather
necessary to certain legal operations. In this text, Derrida further highlights
that it is not only the law that is brought into being by this confounding of the
constative and the performative but also the body politic as well: The representatives sign the declaration on behalf of "the people," but the latter do not
exist as such prior to the signing. The people come into being only in the act
of the signature: "The signature invents the signer" (10). Derrida identifies this
in terms of a "fabulous retroactivity" effective in the instituting performative.[43]
A similar analysis of the confounding of the performative and the constative
in the act of legal founding as exemplified by the US Declaration of Independence is offered by Hannah Arendt. As Bonnie Honig has pointed out, although Arendt does not work with the language of performativity, her reading
of the political significance of the phrase "We hold these truths to be self-
evident," in *On Revolution*, demonstrates a keen grasp of the amalgamation
of the operations of the performative (what she refers to as the appearance of
action in words—"We hold") and the constative (the unfortunate recourse to
"an absolute" in Arendt's account, namely, self-evidence).[44]

Another way in which the performative-constative masquerade, or to put it
more precisely, the undecidability of these two modes, is relevant for critical
legal thought is in understanding the naturalization of norms, and the sedimentation of conventions so as to create truth-effects. Judith Butler's oeuvre
has been groundbreaking in conceptualizing how ritualistic repetition has the
effect of entrenching and sedimenting conventions across various scenes of
embodied social and political life so as to create truth-effects pertaining to

certain categories, such as gender. In carrying Butler's grammar of analysis over to legal-institutional settings, we may inquire into the function of established legal procedure as well as of conventions of embodied performance in law in creating the said masquerade. Costas Douzinas provides a broad account of this in his essay "The Metaphysics of Jurisdiction," in which he writes of the "common metaphysical structure that regulates jurisdiction," the latter (*juris-diction*) understood as both the speech that institutes law, that is, the saying of law or the diction that speaks the law, and what the instituted law speaks. These two aspects of law's speech "are inescapably intertwined."[45] The metaphysical structure of jurisdiction involves, according to Douzinas, two different axes that are rendered indistinguishable: "the universal and the particular as well as the performative and the constative. Their cohabitation helps confuse the four poles of the two dyads" (24). It is this confusion or the indistinguishability that upholds the metaphysics of jurisdiction. Therefore, the glimpse of "the gap between particular and universal or between performance and statement" is also a glimpse of the potential failure of law's claim (27). A grasp of these gaps allows "violence and critique [to] launch themselves in law" (27). More importantly, in Douzinas's account, the legal version of the masquerade or the performative-constative undecidability is a product of *judicial organization*, which is particularly effective in relatively stable liberal democracies where "judicial interpretation and judgment are organized in a way that conceals the original performance of the law in favor of its reasoned and coherent statement" (27). This emphasis on organization, reasoning, and coherence is particularly important in that it highlights the role of conventionality (i.e., conventions of legal procedure and of legal performance) in rendering performatives indistinguishable from constatives. In other words, the masquerade is at its most convincing when the system appears as efficacious and thus as felicitous as possible.

An effect of the masquerade is therefore the operation of law as if it were fate: You were always already to be sentenced to imprisonment for life. There is an important resonance here with Walter Benjamin's evocation of the notion fate in his essay "Toward the Critique of Violence," in which fate is figured as precisely how law presents itself. Law's power, Benjamin suggests, "resides in the notion that there is only one fate";[46] fate is understood as "underlying legal violence in all cases" (55); indeed, "the origin of law" is "violence crowned by fate" (47). It is, because it could not have been otherwise. In a more prosaic sense, this fateful effect of law's constative masquerade is perhaps something that teachers of law will be familiar with: Especially in contexts where law is experienced as entirely or mostly shielded off from the vicissitudes of the political, social, and cultural spheres, an early challenge in teaching law is that of communicating that it could have been otherwise. Let alone the difficulty of imagining a world without law or with less law—but even that this same case, with the same facts and this same body of law, could have had an entirely different outcome. As I outline in the next section, particularly in criminal trials, the main effect of established legal conventions, including those of performance, is to conceal the performative operations of trials through a series of seemingly constative functions that create this fateful effect.

The Trial: Performativity and Performance

The conceptual apparatus of performativity can be drawn on to account for what transpires in a criminal trial on a number of levels. The most obvious is a direct Austinian reading concerning the language used in a trial: Many of the key utterances in the course of a trial are performative utterances. Objecting, finding (as a matter of fact), holding (as a matter of law), convicting, acquitting, sentencing are often effected through explicit or implicit performative utterances in the trial. In effect, trials not only contain but are sustained by performatives; they provide the skeletal structure through which a trial plays itself out, the mainstays on which the linguistic rituals of trials are built.[47] But the foregoing exploration on the performative operations of law can be brought to bear on an analysis of trials beyond this immediate observation about legal language.

The criminal trial is a key instance of law-preserving violence in the modern state. While it is not the only medium for the exercise of the monopoly of violence, it remains, along with various choreographies of policing, one of the most visible features of law-preserving violence. Thus the trial can be understood as a performative instantiation of the law and a crucial medium through which the legal system continues to stage itself as if it were fate. Further, a criminal trial is the amalgamation of a number of essential performative operations, such as the establishing of facts, the interpretation of the law, and the application of substantive law to the facts of the case. On the basis of the foregoing discussion, I propose that the criminal trial is felicitous to the extent that it effectively disguises these performative operations as constative. The catch is that although these operations are best disguised in the trial as a series of constative functions, or perhaps in order that they are successfully disguised as such, the trial has to be performed. It has to take its course, play itself out, preferably without any seeming prejudice on the part of those who are to arrive at a verdict at the end of the process, so that the outcome is not fully foreseeable in advance. This quality of live performance, the process of making a case—representing, defending, arguing, challenging, evaluating narratives of fact and matters of law—in the setting of a forum is part of what lends the trial its eventual authority to pass as inevitable, as fate. Hence the necessity to submerge the trial in an avalanche of conventionality, including conventions of embodied performance.

I further propose that *the political trial can be defined as a legal proceeding whose performative structures are publicly exposed.* In other words, trials that are identified by their public audience as political tend to afford critical insight into the performative structure of proceedings, otherwise disguised in the daily grind of the courtrooms. As I discuss in more detail below, the exposure of the performativity of a trial is usually due to a crisis of masquerade, that is, a failure in one of the several ways in which performatives ordinarily disguise themselves as constatives in the course of a trial. That the question of trial performance often comes under scrutiny in political trials and accusations of theatricality ("show trial," "circus," "kangaroo court," etc.) begin to fly around can be understood as closely connected to this exposure of performativity. When the conventions of trial performance cannot bolster the sense of inevitability, they begin to stand out in their theatricality.

It is here that we may begin to address in the context of legal proceedings what Eve Sedgwick and Andrew Parker have identified as "one of the most fecund, as well as the most under-articulated" areas in theoretical writings around performativity: "the oblique intersection between performativity and the loose cluster of theatrical practices, relations and traditions known as performance."[48] In other words, we may ask: How and to what extent does the hyper-conventionality of trial performance assist the masquerade whereby the performative functions of a trial parade as constative? The rigidity of performance practices extends over every corner of the stage of the trial: the organization of space, the distribution of bodies in space, the regulation of their movement, the required bodily gestures, the ordered proceedings, the prescriptions and restrictions of attire, the authorization of speech, the formalized language, and so on. Could it be that the rather anachronistic conventions governing a trial's performance work to reinforce a perception of its absolute inevitability? Everything was performed as it ought to have been, thus the outcome is what it ought to be. Could this appearance of necessity, in turn, bolster the masquerade whereby the key performative functions of the trial pass as constative? In other words, can the overlap between performance and performativity in a trial be identified in terms of the production of an appearance of inevitability? This would mean that the conventions of embodied performance in a trial assist in disguising its performative operations.

One key performative operation of a trial has to do with its truth-seeking function, which notably involves a performance of constating. The trial au-

thorizes a fact-finding mission that is both institutional and collective in character, the latter more pronouncedly in jurisdictions that employ juries. In the
adversarial jury trial, there is further a special emphasis on live oral testimony
which is understood to enhance the truth-seeking function of the trial.[49] Witness testimony occurs live in the trial as a performance of recollection.[50] Its
authenticity is then subject to scrutiny on two main accounts: demeanor and
confrontation.[51] The attention to demeanor calls for a performance of credibility: It calls on the body of the witness to verify truthfulness, much like in
trials by ordeal where it was believed that the accused's body under ordeal
would "speak" the truth. In turn, the principle of confrontation provides the
discursive complement to the embodied truth of demeanor and renders the
adversarial trial an agonistic space of conflict over narrative and meaning. In
inquisitorial or hybrid systems where there is less of an emphasis on live testimony and more so on the documentation of the case, the case file acquires a
similar function of enacting the truth of the trial.[52]

The forensic narrative produced as to what has happened beyond reasonable doubt is then taken as authoritative: It shapes the very language of the
public discourse around the event, so that, for example, the "alleged/ly" in
public reports is dropped after factual details are decided on in a criminal trial.
The trial thus produces a privileged account for historiography. This explains,
to some extent, recourses to the criminal trial in collective attempts to negoti-
ate the past, for example, in transitional justice scenarios or post-conflict
societies. As Cornelia Vismann explains:

> The appeal of the courtroom lies . . . in the stability of its order, in
> discourse that is limited both temporally and lexically according to the
> rhetorically imposed turns for speaking and the fixed validity of words,
> coded according to the place from which they are uttered, as com-
> pared to the amorphous talk, or rather noise, by which we are normally
> surrounded.[53]

The usual cacophony of the public sphere is filtered through a highly formalized and stylized orchestration in the trial, which lends a particular weight to
its findings. This historiographical privilege is also why political powers have
been known to opt for criminal trials in attempts to authorize their version of
events as official history.[54]

Notably, the constative function of the criminal trial is often referred to as
"establishing" the facts, a verb that not only conveys the constative sense of
"confirming" and "validating" but also the more performative function of "instituting." The potential gap between the truth and its representation in the
trial has been captured by a distinction between "substantive," that is, actual

truth, and "formal legal truth," namely, "whatever is found as fact by the legal fact finder."[55] That the story could have been told otherwise always remains a possibility, but a felicitous trial is partly so because it has successfully banished this possibility from public perception, to the extent that the performativity of the retelling, of the establishing of facts is shrouded in the constative function of describing the facts.

In political trials, often the potential gap becomes visible. The trial may fail to fully convince the public that the facts that it has established—its performance of the constative—are congruent with reality, or to put it more simply, if it has failed to assure that its representation of what happened is truthful. The trial may occasion suspicions that facts have been manipulated through forged or fabricated evidence, false testimony, and the like, so as to "frame" the defendants. It may be that the evidence is suspected to be fabricated not during but before the trial by the police, the intelligence service, or a third party. Even then, how this evidence is handled in the trial, how it is substantiated or invalidated, becomes a focus of attention, revealing something about the performative operation involved in the finding of facts. A famous example is the 1951 trial and conviction of Ethel and Julius Rosenberg in the United States, on charges of conspiracy to commit espionage during wartime. An effective public campaign was launched only after their conviction, dividing international and domestic public opinion regarding their culpability at the time of their execution in 1953, and for many decades after. Although subsequent evidence has suggested that Julius Rosenberg was indeed involved in espionage for the USSR, it is still contested whether this involved the transmission of any useful information on nuclear weaponry, which was the actual reason for the capital sentence, and whether Ethel Rosenberg was involved in espionage at all.[56] Further, it remains the case that their conviction at the time was secured on the basis of false evidence.[57] The history of political trials provides many other examples in this vein. The publicity of suspicion pertaining to the truthfulness of fact-finding in a political trial occasions an exposure of the fact-finding mechanism's contingency, which in liberal democratic orders is often shrouded in performances of orderliness and solemnity.

Another key performative operation of the criminal trial can be identified as the application of laws to the case at hand, which raises the classic jurisprudential question of the fit between the facts of a case and existing law. Political trials problematize this in particularly pronounced ways. In many political trials, neither the facts, nor the law itself is in question, but the legal interpretation of the facts is. That is, the trial may not necessarily be beset by suspicions or claims that facts are being fabricated; the point of contestation and controversy is rather the legal spin that the prosecution puts on them. So, for example, various coincidences are prosecuted as a "conspiracy" (Chicago Conspiracy Trial, USA, 1969–70); the public criticism of ceaseless war is cast as "discouraging the people from military service" (the trial of superstar Bülent Ersoy, Turkey, 2008); or political performance art is legally interpreted as "hooliganism motivated by religious hatred" (the trial of Pussy Riot, Russia, 2012). In such cases, there is again the suspicion that the defendants are "framed," but this time the frame itself becomes visible and is exposed as problematic.

The starkest exposure of the frame occurs in trials concerning acts of civil disobedience: The facts of the defendants' acts are not in dispute, nor is their illegality—the defendants attempt to call the laws themselves into question as either irrelevant or illegitimate. Existing laws are contested with an appeal to justice, in the name of higher laws or principles—constitutional or moral.[58] On the flip side of civil disobedience cases, we have the kind of political trials that Kirchheimer, Shklar, and Arendt were primarily concerned with. In successor regime trials, the commonsensical temporal relation that is expected from an ordinary legal proceeding is overturned. Rather than the anticipated canny order of a narrative arc proceeding linearly from law to breach to trial to judgment, the prosecution may be understood to retrospectively institute the law where there was none. As Kirchheimer and Arendt fully grasped, when felicitous, this type of political trial institutes law, it is a constitutive moment that seemingly draws on legal conventions, but in fact founds a new order of conventionality. Thus, how faithfully procedural conventions are performed, how closely courtroom etiquette is followed and what kind of a theatrics of justice is displayed tend to be absolutely crucial in these kinds of cases for their felicity. This is because loyalty to procedure and conventions of performance can effectively stand in for the necessity for preceding legal authority.

This is how I read Arendt's critique of the prosecutor's performance in the Eichmann trial, that I have discussed in some detail in the Introduction and Chapter 1. It has been argued that Arendt's approach to this trial is beset by legalism in Shklar's sense, that her insistence on the strict separation of the legal and the extralegal within the space of the trial, her obstinate definition of the scope of the trial in terms of doing justice to the accused and nothing else, was a sign of her inability to grasp the other significant functions the trial served.[59] I believe this approach misses the point. Arendt is in fact fully aware of the limitations of a legalistic approach to the problem at hand,[60] as well as the various dimensions of the political at stake. Her argument in favor of strict adherence to procedural concerns in the proceedings is not an argument for closing the legal form onto itself. On the contrary, it is for grounding what is novel on as solid a platform as possible under the circumstances, in other words, for allowing innovation where no precedent exists, precisely on the basis of

adherence to certain other formal procedures, including conventions of embodied performance. Arendt's discomfort with how the prosecutor attempted
to stage the Eichmann trial can further be interpreted as closely related to her
understanding of the necessity for spontaneity in the task of judgment. In a
lecture Arendt prepared following the controversy unleashed by her work on
the Eichmann trial, she wrote of the faculty of judgment in the following terms:

> Only if we assume that there exists a human faculty which enables us
> to judge rationally without being carried away by either emotion or
> self-interest, and which at the same time functions spontaneously, that
> is to say, is not bound by standards and rules under which particular
> cases are simply subsumed, but on the contrary, produces its own princi-
> ples by virtue of the judging activity itself; only under this assumption
> can we risk ourselves on this very slippery moral ground with some hope
> of finding a firm footing.[61]

Here we see a formulation of judgment that particularly emphasizes its performative quality: A judgment is to bring into being the principles on which it
is based (in what Derrida would refer to as a "fabulous retroactivity"). Hence,
the responsibility to judge is linked to a responsiveness to the matter to be
judged, rather than loyalty to existing standards and rules. Although Arendt's
understanding of the task of judgment is largely incompatible with how legal
judgment must work, her emphasis on the value of the spontaneity of judgment further explains her approval of the "natural" spontaneity of the judges
in the Eichmann trial, as well as her objection to the sense of scriptedness and
the feigning of spontaneity in the prosecutor's trial performance.

What is exposed in a stark light in civil disobedience and successor regime
trials is at work in every criminal trial whereby the very event of the trial can
be said to relate to its larger context, the particular legal system of which it is
an instance, performatively. As Martha Merill Umphrey suggests:

> Trials are law-making (not just law-applying or law-interpreting) events
> *because of their performativity*. . . . They not only enact law, both
> theatrically and linguistically, in their very doing, but also performa-
> tively constitute the law they enact.[62]

Thus a trial can be understood as a reinscription of law that not only draws on
precedent and legislation but also effects their further sedimentation. However, operative in the representational strategies involved in both the retelling
of the facts in a manner that can be legally assimilated and the further performative function of applying legal rules and standards to this retelling is what
Shoshana Felman has referred to as a "cognitive view," which disguises these

processes as a series of transparent congruities. In Felman's characterization of the cognitive view, "The question of knowing is confused with the question of judging; the illocutionary act of judgment is experienced as a pure constative or cognitive."[63] The strict procedural restrictions and the stringent conventions governing the performance of the trial allow law to stage its illocutionary operations as pure constatives whereby law seemingly exercises a masterly cognition of itself, the crime, and the criminal. Notable in this regard is Ross Charnock's linguistic analysis of judgments that overrule precedents:

> Common law judges are not simply reluctant to overrule explicitly;
> they often go to the extent of denying, contrary to the evidence, that
> their overruling decisions imply a change in the law at all. They claim
> instead that these decisions are mere declarations of the true state of
> the law, in the face of misapprehensions derived from mistaken
> decisions in earlier cases.[64]

Charnock's analysis thus shows that even in the most obviously performative operation of overruling a precedent, which amounts to law-making, recourse is often sought in a constative masquerade, so that the effective institution of a new precedent is disguised as the representation of what is in fact the very truth of the law.

I have offered the analysis in this section in an attempt to explain how and why questions of performance and performativity are often intertwined in a political trial, presenting themselves as coupled and at times indistinguishable. Here the importance of conventionality for the theory of performativity and the inclination of performatives to masquerade as constatives serve as a key. Reading Butler's conceptualization of conventionality as a sedimented historicity alongside Derrida's and Douzinas's formulations regarding legal performativity, I proposed that the embodied conventions of the trial bolster the masquerade whereby its performative operations pass as constatives, allowing law to operate as if it were fate. Political trials, I suggested, lay bare the performative operations that are more difficult to discern in ordinary trials. In the next chapter, I further engage with performative theory to conceptualize the vagaries of what may be referred to as "sovereign performatives," and explore the significance of this conceptualization toward a performative theory of political trials, as distinct from approaches that suffice with instrumental analyses of the politics of trials.

3

Sovereign Infelicities

But as a performative cannot be just, in the sense of justice, except by
grounding itself in on conventions and so on other performatives,
buried or not, it always maintains within itself some irruptive violence.
— JACQUES DERRIDA, "FORCE OF LAW"

In the preceding chapter, I offered a general account of the relevance of theories of performativity for critical legal thought, and I began to formulate one
way to bring this understanding to bear on a conceptualization of the dynamics of criminal trials in general and political trials in particular. This analysis
also offered one way to make sense of the oblique intersections of performance
and performativity within the space of the trial. In this chapter, I continue to
engage with performative theory toward a proposal of how to read the politics
of trials. More specifically, I tease out the implications of performative theory's critique of sovereignty, for approaching the so-called sovereign spectacle
of political trials. The idiom of performativity complicates the scene of sovereign agency through its emphasis on iterability (or, for my purposes, conventionality) and performance (or embodied practice). These are two necessary
conditions of performativity that undermine the idealized attributes of sovereign agency such as absolute presence, unfettered intentionality, felicitous willing, and transitivity. I rework this particular orientation for a practice of
reading the politics of trials. My proposal is that a performative perspective
allows the conceptualization of the "political" in political trials beyond its overdetermination in terms of expedient instrumentality or sovereign agency, that
is, beyond its intentional and willed status, instead attuning us to what comes
to haunt the scene of the sovereign spectacle. To indicate the various dynam-

ics that can be captured by such a perspective, I begin this chapter with descriptions of three scenes from three different political trials, and I return to these scenes at the end of the chapter for brief analyses. These are intended as a cursory demonstration of the relevance of performative theories of agency for capturing what transpires on the stage of a political trial. I offer more detailed readings of other cases in the second part of this book, also based on the particular orientation elaborated over this first part.

Three Scenes

The first scene is from a trial that is relatively well known: The 1969–70 Chicago Conspiracy Trial[1] was the trial of eight activists charged with the conspiracy to cross state lines to incite a riot.[2] In effect, it was an extension of the government's "law and order" response to the massive protests in Chicago in August 1968, organized to coincide with the Democratic National Convention, and brutally repressed by the Chicago police. The defendants included local organizers, student activists, a Christian pacifist, "Yippies" Abbie Hoffman and Jerry Rubin, and most famously, the co-founder and chairman of the Black Panther Party (BPP), Bobby Seale. Represented by radical lawyers such as William Kunstler and Leonard Weinglass, the defendants opted for a spectacularly disruptive approach to the proceedings. The anti-authoritarian Yippies were already well known for guerrilla theater, and Hoffman and Rubin took the trial as an occasion to improvise. In addition to staging several acts during the trial, they generally played havoc with courtroom conventions, and their co-defendants played along: They refused to rise with the comings and goings of the judge, shouted insults at him, refused to address him with the usual "Your Honor," cracked jokes, laughed out loud, and so on.

Bobby Seale had his own reasons to be disruptive. From the beginning of the trial he insisted that none of the defense attorneys present represented him. He would either be represented by the BPP lawyer Charles R. Garry, or represent himself. Garry was initially the chief attorney on the defense team but had to undergo a surgery that coincided with the beginning of the trial. Judge Julius J. Hoffman refused to allow a six-week delay to accommodate this, and Garry had to leave the team, passing the lead to Kunstler. Seale refused to acknowledge Kunstler as his attorney and demanded his constitutional right to represent himself. Judge Hoffman denied him the right on the basis of a technicality. Kunstler respected Seale's decision and did not attempt to represent him. This left Seale in direct confrontation with the judge. During the first few weeks of the trial, Seale continuously disrupted the proceedings with the demand to represent himself and attempts to cross-examine the witnesses. By the fifth week of the trial, with the antics of the other defendants in the background, the confrontation between Judge Hoffman and Seale escalated to the point where the judge ordered Seale to be bound and gagged. This was initially on a simple folding chair with handcuffs and a towel gag, and when that proved ineffective, he was bound on a wooden throne chair with heavier straps, a massive gag, and adhesive tape. For two whole days, on 30 and 31 October 1969, the hearings proceeded with the only Black defendant on trial bound and gagged in the courtroom, struggling with the straps and his speech muffled by the gag.[3]

The second scene is a brief moment from the early days of Saddam Hussein's 2005 Dujail trial at the Iraqi Special Tribunal. Presiding over the proceedings was Rizgar Mohammed Amin, who would later be replaced due to his perceived lack of authority. The following exchange took place between Hussein and Amin, and it was recorded on video:[4]

> HUSSEIN: I only say this so that the defendant—
> JUDGE: [quietly] He's the prosecutor, not the defendant.
> HUSSEIN: Excuse me?
> VOICES IN COURT: The prosecutor.
> HUSSEIN: The prosecutor, eh [makes head gesture]. . . . The prosecutor
> and the witness should listen . . .

Saddam Hussein makes a slip of the tongue and refers to the "defendant" during a hearing where he is the chief defendant. But he means neither himself nor a co-defendant; he's referring to someone else. The judge interrupts to correct him and says somewhat sheepishly, "He's the prosecutor, not the defendant." For a split second Hussein does not understand why he has been interrupted; then he does, and the shadow of a smile crosses his face; he makes a gesture with his head as if to say "whatever, same difference." The footage cuts to the judge who inexplicably returns the smile before Hussein continues to speak.

The third scene is also a brief moment, from a trial that concluded in March 2013 at Woolwich Crown Court in the United Kingdom. This was the third trial of two students, Alfie Meadows and Zak King, who had been involved in the 2010 protests against the austerity measures and extortionate university tuition fee hikes introduced by the government. Meadows had made the news at the time, as he had to undergo emergency brain surgery after being hit on the head with a police baton while kettled during the 9 December 2010 protest in London's Parliament Square. His injury was critical, but he miraculously survived without brain damage, only to be subsequently charged with violent disorder. There seemed to be a cynical calculation at work: A conviction would secure the police against misconduct charges, and in any case, a prosecution would delay any civil action against the police force. Meadows and King were in the criminal justice system for a while, because their first trial ended with a hung jury in April 2012, with three other co-defendants acquitted. Their retrial in November 2012 was aborted due to insufficient time scheduled for the hearings.

As in the previous two trials, in the third and final trial, the prosecution brought to the witness stand several police officers on duty that day at the demonstration. In his cross-examination of the first two police witnesses, one of the defense attorneys established that yes, the batons must be used only as a last resort; no, they should not be used to hit people on the head; yes, the police receive extensive training to this effect, because hitting someone on the head with a police baton can cause death. The third police witness was Superintendent Woods, who had served as Bronze Commander on the day of the protest.[5] He was cross-examined in a similar vein, which seemed to increasingly agitate him. When asked whether he considered baton strikes an absolute last resort, he answered, "The absolute last resort is getting a machine gun out." As he said this, he was pointing an imaginary machine gun directly at the jury members and pretending to shoot.

Sovereign Spectacles

In his vivid discussion in the opening chapters of *Discipline and Punish*, Michel Foucault inquires into the gradual disappearance of punishment from public view. For Foucault, this disappearance signifies a historical shift in the modality of power, namely, a passage from predominantly sovereign to predominantly disciplinary power. He comments in passing, however, that the judicial spectacle, once so powerfully staged by the sensational public torture and execution of the condemned, is now transferred onto the post-Revolutionary public trial.[6] Although this is a specifically French genealogy (in common law, criminal trials were always public), the insight is valid across modern law: Sovereign power, associated with pomp and circumstance, is still operative in the courtroom, in the very spectacle of the trial, albeit bound up with a more recent mode, disciplinary power, which corresponds to an all-surveying gaze that aims at the knowledge of the criminal through expert testimony and the like.

The courtroom remains a privileged stage for the spectacle of sovereignty, and this is particularly conspicuous in political trials. The dynamics of national sovereignty that were played out in Adolf Eichmann's trial, discussed in some detail in the first chapter of this book, serve as a lucid example. The idea of the trial as sovereign spectacle is indeed commonly encountered in writings on political trials. Otto Kirchheimer's discussion of a regime's recourse to the image-making capacity of a trial captures the importance of legal spectacle for claims to sovereignty. Writing on "terror" trials that involve political perspectives of radical difference, Leora Bilsky suggests that it is unlikely that national courts will relinquish such cases to be tried by international courts, as these trials "are often viewed as the very symbol of their sovereignty (the right to adjudicate those who claim unrestricted 'war' against the state and its citizens)."[7] While similar observations are found across the various genres of writing on political trials, the same dynamic can be discerned in "ordinary" criminal trials as well, at least in principle. Here it is pertinent to note that the modern, liberal democratic rationale for the publicity of trials draws not only on the defendant's right to a fair trial, but also on the public's right to know. In other words, the principle of publicity is formulated partly in terms of popular sovereignty and the public's interest in seeing justice done in its name. Trials are thus conventionally figured as spectacular spaces where sovereign power plays itself out to itself.

This, in turn, corresponds to an aspect of the shift of sovereign spectacle from public punishment to the public trial that Foucault writes about. In Foucault's account, the juridico-political function of the spectacle of public execution was to reconstitute a momentarily injured sovereignty.[8] Since the law emanates directly from the sovereign, a crime, besides its immediate victim, is an attack on the will and the body of the sovereign himself. The public spectacle of punishment was meant to redress that injury. In the passage from absolute monarchy to popular sovereignty, the form of this operation is preserved via the general theory of the contract: Law is the bond, the contract of society; a crime is a breach of this pact; hence besides its immediate victim, the crime is understood as an injury to the body politic, whose law is breached. Trials and punishments are meant to redress this injury to the community at large, rather than avenge the victim. We have seen the effects of this modern conceptualization of criminal justice in Arendt's interpretation of crimes against humanity as the breach of the community that is global humanity.

Yet a further aspect of interest in Foucault's discussion of the spectacle of sovereignty is its very ambiguity:

> The terror of the public execution created centers of illegality: on execution days, work stopped, the taverns were full, the authorities were abused, insults or stones were thrown at the executioner, the guards and the soldiers; attempts were made to seize the condemned man, either to save him or to kill him more surely; fights broke out, and there was no better prey for thieves than the curious throng around the scaffold. (63)

Foucault further discusses the political risk that this ambiguity created through its consolidation in social solidarity among the spectators, against the sovereign. He writes, "Out of that uncertain festival in which violence was instantaneously reversible, it was this solidarity much more than the sovereign power that was likely to emerge with redoubled strength" (63). In noting that the spectacle of power is transferred onto the public trial, Foucault does not go into much detail, but we know from political trials that this ambiguity too is partly transferred onto the public trial. Kirchheimer captures this well in his discussion of the "irreducible risk" whereby the image-creating capacity of the legal procedure can be usurped to create effective "counter-images." In other words, the sovereign spectacle can turn on itself.

Then again, Kirchheimer's account of this ambiguity in trials is mostly premised on a particular conceptualization of agency. We see this in the various reasons that he gives for the irreducible risk: political commitments of witnesses who may not play along with the prosecution's vision for the trial; the interpretation of defendants who may successfully hijack the proceedings to make counter-images, and "the judicial space," that is, the freedom of the judge or jury in deciding a case based on their own interpretation and evaluation, with relative independence from the sovereign agency of the state.[9] Thus potentially pitted against the sovereign who wills the spectacle of the trial are various participants of the trial also figured as sovereign agents who are fully present to themselves, and whose actions perfectly coincide with their wills and intentions. While the analysis has some merit for trials involving particularly self-conscious political conflicts between prosecution and defense, it is important to be attuned to the subtler, unintentional, accidental, spectral, unconscious ways in which the sovereign spectacle can unravel in a trial. This would then call for an alternative formulation of the political in political trials beyond its overdetermination in terms of the intentions and designs of the parties. Since the idealized coincidence of spectator and sovereign in the modern criminal trial does not allow as clear a crystallization of parties to the conflict as Foucault describes with regard to public punishment, such an attunement may be helpful in discerning the politics of seemingly ordinary trials as well. Here the problematization of sovereignty by theories of performativity will be of assistance in conceptualizing the potential ambiguity of legal proceedings.

Sovereign Performatives?

Judith Butler coins the phrase "sovereign performatives" in one of their essays in *Excitable Speech*, as part of their critique of certain jurisprudential writings on hate speech, which turn to theories of performativity to argue how some

forms of speech must be seen as injurious conduct. They identify in these theories the attribution of a certain efficacy to individual acts of speech, an efficacy that is "modeled on the speech of a sovereign state, understood as a
sovereign speech act, a speech act with the power to do what it says."[10] Inter-
estingly, this kind of sovereign speech is fantasized by those writing on hate
speech precisely when contemporary power is no longer primarily sovereign in
character. Thus, Butler pits the Foucauldian analysis of waning sovereignty up
against the recourse to theories of performativity in conjuring this figure of the
sovereign utterer of hate speech, who is understood to be invested with the
"power of absolute and efficacious agency, performativity and transitivity at
once (it does what it says and it does what it says it will do to the one addressed
by the speech)" (77). Butler then questions whether we have in these theories
something like a nostalgia for sovereign power, a fantasy of its return:

> The emphasis on the performative phantasmatically resurrects the
> performative in language, establishing language as a displaced site of
> politics and specifying that displacement as driven by a wish to return
> to a simpler and more reassuring map of power, one in which the
> assumption of sovereignty remains secure. (78)

Butler proposes instead a departure from the conceptual model of sovereignty
in reformulating performativity, and rethinking agency and resistance from a
non-state-centered perspective. However, in doing so, they preserve a version of
the notion of "sovereign performatives" to describe "the performative power of
state-sanctioned legal language" (81). They retain this notion in order to distinguish from it the (hate) speech of ordinary citizens. Efficacious legal language,
therefore, is retained as a field where "one has the power to make happen what
one says," and the example they append to this is predictable: "as a judge backed
by law in a relatively stable political order has the power to do" (82).[11]

     In their introduction to the same book, Butler provides a critical account
of Louis Althusser's theory of interpellation, especially taking issue with the
examples he uses to elaborate his theory. According to Butler, the analogy that
Althusser formulates between his example of the policeman who hails "Hey,
you there!" and his other example of God naming Peter and thereby transform-
ing him into a subject models his theory of interpellation on the figure of the
divine voice: "In claiming that social ideology operates in an analogous way
to the divine voice, Althusser inadvertently assimilates social interpellation to
the divine performative" (Butler, 31). Butler argues for an account of ideology
that does away with this figure of the divine voice. The divine power of naming must be dissociated from the otherwise useful notion of interpellation,
because

the voice is implicated in a notion of *sovereign* power, power figured as
emanating from a subject, activated in a voice, whose effects appear to
be the magical effects of that voice. In other words, power is understood on the model of the divine power of naming, where to utter is to
create the effect uttered. Human speech rarely mimes that divine
effect except in the cases where the speech is backed by state power,
that of a judge, the immigration authority, or the police, and even then
there does sometimes exist recourse to refute that power. (32)

Here Butler does not go on to theoretically address the "recourse to refute that
power" or offer a deconstruction of this notion of the "sovereign performative."
Instead, they counter it again with its historicized outside, that is, with the Foucauldian critique, and thus pursue the question of conceptualizing interpellation "after the diffusion of sovereign power" (34). In *Excitable Speech* "sovereign
performatives" thus remain instrumental as a term, to signify speech backed
by state power, typically the speech of a judge.

Butler does, however, gesture toward a challenge to this notion in a brief
aside that follows their discussion of Althusser, by suggesting that even the
speech of the policeman who hails the person on the street is governed by conventionality. That is, his ostensibly sovereign speech is effective only due to its
citational dimension, a "historicity of [linguistic] convention that exceeds and
enables the moment of its enunciation" (33). Similarly, in a later text on performative agency, Butler writes:

With respect to illocutionary utterances, those realities brought into
being depend upon a speech act, but the speech act is a reiterated
form of discourse, so we would be mistaken to overvalue the subject
who speaks. The judge learns what to say, and must speak in codified
ways, which means that the codification and ritualization of that
discourse precedes and makes possible the subject who speaks.[12]

These notes about the speech of the policeman and the judge allude to Jacques
Derrida's discussion in "Signature Event Context"[13] on how the condition of
iterability undermines sovereign acts of speech—an important discussion that
I will turn to shortly. Still, the notion of a sovereign performative works as an
idealized reference point, and the closest approximation to it is said to be
achieved by the speech of, say, "a judge backed by law in a relatively stable political order." There is something reminiscent in this setup of Austin's fetishiza-
tion of legal language in highlighting that which is not ideally efficacious in
ordinary language, the so many ways in which the latter can fail, implying that
the former won't ever do so as scandalously. Admittedly, the figure of the judge

does provide a gauge: His or her speech can indeed be said to amount to conduct leading to injury (as hate speech is fantasized to be), unleashing the force
of law on the body of the addressee of his or her speech act. Still, we may want
to further explore the structural potential of fissure even within such ostensibly
sovereign performatives. Thus, in addition to wanting to sully Austin's fetish, I
want to extend the implications of Butler's work on the performative to question
the very possibility of a "sovereign performative" other than as fantasy—even in
that most efficacious site of performativity, the trial.

The intrinsic challenge that the idea of performativity poses to the notion
of sovereignty is closely linked to two issues: the question of conventionality
(or what Derrida refers to in terms of "iterability") and the simple fact that performatives are performed. With regard to the latter, it seems wise to take Austin at his word when he writes "a word never—well, hardly ever—shakes off its
etymology and its formation,"[14] or, indeed, when he states specifically with reference to his coinage of "performative" that "its etymology is not irrelevant."[15]
The etymological relevance he had in mind was perhaps simply a wish to emphasize that performatives "perform," but it seems crucial to be attuned to
the fact that they are also performed. Thus, an understanding of performativity that takes into account the question of performance is key here, and it is
not unrelated to the question of iterability. Ironically, precisely such an attempt
to think the performance of performativity and the performativity of performance, namely Judith Butler's work, seems to have incited in its uptakes an
uncritical conflation of the two notions, that is, the use of the term "performativity" to refer primarily to forms of theatricality. In the following sections,
I first explore the theoretical implications of this conflation in terms of an inability to grasp the critique of sovereign agency that the conceptualization of
performativity involves. Then I trace this critique back to Austin by both working with and challenging Derrida's reading of Austin with assistance from
Stanley Cavell and Shoshana Felman. I explore the further elaborations of this
critique in Derrida's, Felman's, and Butler's works, before moving on to consider the implications of this conceptual assemblage for how to read the politics of political trials.

(Mis)reading the Performative as Performance

The use of "performative" to refer to forms of theatricality is understandably
quite widespread in performance studies publications from the 1980s onward.
Yet the conflation encountered in critical thought should perhaps be traced
back to Judith Butler's reconfiguration of the term in Gender Trouble, its reception and, to some extent, misinterpretation. Notably, in this work, Butler

formulates gender performativity without any reference to J. L. Austin or his speech act theory.[16] And yet framed in terms of signs, discourse, and even "inscriptions" on the surface of the body, the idea of gender performativity is clearly not divorced from the order of language and signification. In other words, gendered corporeality is partially rendered linguistic in this work, in the sense that it is thought through in terms of discursive functions maintaining the truth-effects of the categories of gender and sex.[17] So although there are no references to speech act theory in *Gender Trouble*, certain affinities and common concerns are not difficult to discern. Further, it is possible to read Austin into Butler's book at the very least in terms of a common spirit of playful inquiry, given the two authors' recourse to performativity in a shared inclination to bedevil the fetishes of truth/falsity and fact/value. *Gender Trouble's* version of gender performativity is hardly bereft of linguistic significations of the term, but even more importantly, by paying close attention to gendered acts and gestures, and suggesting that such corporeal performance has the effect of reifying an ontology of gender, the work initiates a unique way to link the linguistic and embodied connotations of "performative." For Butler, gender performance is performative not only in that it is embodied, but also in the sense that it operates in the same mode as a performative utterance: masquerading as constative, purporting to represent a truth to gender that is external or prior to it, while in effect enacting and fabricating that truth through its very performance.

While Butler thus offered us, in their early work on gender, one significant way in which the performativity of corporeal performance can be thought as separate but related terms, a common misreading of their proposal turns precisely on a conflation of the two terms. This confusion could perhaps be attributed to Butler's discussion of drag, clearly introduced as a marginal example of gender performativity, but often misread as paradigmatic. In Butler's discussion, through its amplifications and exaggerations, that is, by the very means of its avowed artifice, drag can shed light on quotidian, normalized versions of gendered enactments that disavow their artifice. It is as a limit case of sorts that drag helps us understand the performativity of gender, the function by which certain ordinary and obvious bodily performances reify an ontology of gender. Instead, *Gender Trouble* has been widely interpreted to offer drag as the very measure and standard of gender performativity, leading many early commentators to hastily dismiss Butler's reconfiguration of performativity as a manifesto on the subversive power of cross-dressing. And because a certain degree of theatrical excess is integral to drag, Butler's notion of "gender performativity" has often been reduced in its reception to "gender performance," thus deprived of its philosophical connotations.

It is interesting to watch what happens to the question of the subject in this reduction of performativity to performance. Some readers have envisioned Butler's scene as a puppet show of sorts, a complete debunking of agency, with "discourse" as a mystified matrix of power pulling the strings. For instance, in an early response to Butler's work, Seyla Benhabib wrote: "If we are no more than the sum total of the gendered expressions we perform, is there ever any chance to stop the performance for a while, to pull the curtain down, and let it rise only if one can have a say in the production of the play itself?"[18] Then again, others who read gender performativity solely in terms of theatrical performance understand it to involve an absolutely voluntaristic notion of agency. This was a common reading in the early 1990s, but it has oddly persisted in the new century, particularly in more mainstream reception. For example, in a general readership book on the late capitalistic exploitation of body anxiety, British feminist psychoanalyst Susie Orbach writes, with specific reference to *Gender Trouble*, that "it has become a feature of postmodernist thought to . . . see embodiment, like femininity and masculinity, as something we achieve through performing or enacting the body we want to have. . . . It is believed that the body can be anything we want it to be."[19] The celebrated American literary critic J. Hillis Miller takes it to a new level, magically combining these two types of theatrical misreadings into a caricature of sorts:

> "Performativity," it now appears, means, among other things, the assumption that human beings have no innate selfhood or subjectivity but become what they are through more or less forced repetition of a certain role. . . . It is an exhilarating theory because, apparently, it blows the gaff on the familial, social, ideological, and political forces that have made me what I now think I am by forcing me to repetitive performances of that role. Once I understand that, the way is open to change society so I can be different, or even, so it appears, to take my identity into my own hands and "perform" myself into becoming some other person, some other gender, or some mixture of genders, or one person or gender today and another person or gender tomorrow.[20]

Miller is well aware of speech act theory in this article, dedicating a significant portion of it to Austin. But he not only claims that Butler's notion of performativity has nothing to do with Austin's (227), but attributes it to "performance theory," possibly because, as he explicitly admits, he depends on the Wikipedia entry for this "reading" of *Gender Trouble*.

Needless to say that neither of these forms of theatrical reductionism, that is, neither the puppet show nor the scene of spontaneously willed and absolutely intentional playacting, nor even a fanciful combination of the two, can properly stage Butler's crucial reconfiguration of performativity. In the former misreading, some phantasmic notion of "discourse" is afforded sovereign status, as the inexorable and invincible puller of strings (as fate, perhaps); in the latter, sovereignty is bestowed upon the subject as the power to turn every whimsical desire into reality. When the two are combined, as in Miller's version, the scene becomes one of a tug-of-war between discrete sovereign forces. The theatrical misreadings notably correspond to either the eradication of the political or its overdetermination.

Derrida's Austin: Sovereign Pretensions

At this point, it will be worthwhile to return to Derrida's first extensive engagement with Austin's theory of performativity in his essay "Signature Event Context," as it contains an elaboration against voluntaristic (mis)readings that bestow the agent of performativity with sovereign status. In this essay Derrida carries the predicates that constitute the classical concept of writing over to speech. In other words, certain characteristics of writing that are deemed distinctive, such as the potential non-presence of the subject who has produced the writing, or the force of rupture that severs the writing from its context (from its milieu of production and from the intentional investments of its author) while allowing it to continue functioning, are made to bear on speech itself. Thus Derrida turns to Austin's performative theory to trace in what ways presence and intention are always already compromised in speech, and how the parasitism classically attributed to writing is the very condition of language, even in its spoken form. Central to the essay is the notion that iterability introduces into language, as its very condition of possibility, a "logic that ties repetition to alterity."[21] Derrida presents this reading in a deconstructive mode, as if he is reading Austin's text over and against the inclinations and intentions of its author, and therefore not quite recognizing how much of a co-conspirator he had in Austin. Derrida's (mis)reading of Austin is nevertheless important to parse, if only because it dramatizes the implications of reading an unfettered sovereign agency into any performative scheme.

Characteristically, Derrida homes in on two exclusions that Austin explicitly acknowledges: the exclusion of the general infelicities that afflict all actions and the exclusion of citational uses of language. Both of these appear as provisional exclusions in Austin, who says, "Some very general high-level doctrine might embrace" the first subject of exclusion, and that the second "might be brought into a more general account."[22] Derrida finds Austin's deferral of such a general theory "highly significant."[23] He proposes that the infelicity of a performative is a structural possibility, interpreting Austin's first exclusion as a failure to appreciate this. For Derrida, it will not suffice to grant an accidental status to the infelicities that Austin discusses under the two main headings of "Misfires" (utterance of a performative without the requisite conventional procedure, or by a person without the requisite authority, or in circumstances inappropriate to the conventional procedure, or without executing the procedure correctly, or without executing it completely) and "Abuses" (insincere performative utterances). Instead, Derrida proposes, "The value of risk or exposure to infelicity" should be "interrogated as an essential predicate or as a *law*" (15) of performative utterances.

While Derrida's suggestion that failure is integral to the structure of the performative and thus the theory should take it into account as such is important, it is actually not so clear that Austin refuses to do so. Derrida's mistake is to quote Austin's first exclusion as evidence of his refusal to think infelicity as a structural possibility. This then allows him to claim that by virtue of the former exclusion, Austin retains the speaking subject's intention as the organizing center in his scheme of the performative utterance: "a free consciousness present to the totality of the operation" of the felicitous performative utterance, and "an absolutely meaningful speech [*vouloir-dire*] master of itself" (15). This reading of Austin as centralizing intention in his account of performative utterances has been contested by Stanley Cavell,[24] who points out that Austin's first exclusion is not an exclusion of infelicity as a necessary condition of performatives, but the exclusion of a different, a more general kind of unhappiness that afflicts all actions, perhaps what Arendt would refer to as the contingency of all human action, including but not limited to speech acts. Austin makes a distinction between the various ways in which human action can fail, on the one hand, and the specific infelicities that afflict performatives (i.e., Misfires and Abuses), on the other—he says his theory embraces the latter, though not the former. Derrida's account, however, collapses this distinction, to suggest that Austin's procedure

> consists in recognizing that the possibility of the negative (in this case, of infelicities) is in fact a structural possibility, that failure is an essential risk of the operations under consideration; then in a move which is almost *immediately simultaneous*, in the name of a kind of ideal regulation, it excludes that risk as accidental, exterior, one which teaches us nothing about the linguistic phenomenon being considered.[25]

And yet the performative attains its very definition through its countless failures in Austin, whose humorous rhetoric only reinforces this sense of the performative as a perpetual comedy of errors. A reading in this vein is offered by

Shoshana Felman who draws attention to the performativity of Austin's theorizing itself, his humorous exposure of his own failure to provide a solid ground
for the notion of the "performative." This "self-subversion, this self-transgressive
character of the Austinian performance,"[26] according to Felman, only goes to
show that "for Austin, the capacity for failure is situated not outside but *inside*
the performative, both as speech act and as theoretical instrument. Infelicity,
or failure, is not for Austin an *accident* of the performative, it is inherent in it,
essential to it" (45). Felman suggests that Austin's critics fail to take his constant jesting seriously (94–96).

Concerning the exclusion of the more general unhappinesses that afflict
all human actions (the exclusion that Austin *does* admit to in this passage)
Cavell has suggested that this is not an exclusion in Derrida's sense, that is, a
constitutive outside to his theory of performativity, but rather a reference to
elsewhere where he does discuss it in detail. In other words, it is not that Austin "rejects and defers"[27] the question by saying "I am not going into the general doctrine here," but rather means "I have discussed it elsewhere and it must
be borne in mind." Indeed, the reference is clear for those familiar with Austin's "A Plea for Excuses." In this essay, Austin proposes to imagine the variety
of situations in which we make excuses, that is, the myriad ways in which intentionality falters, fails, or is altogether absent: "If we have a lively imagination, together perhaps with an ample experience of dereliction, we shall go
far, only we need system: I do not know how many of you keep a list of the
kinds of fool you make of yourselves."[28]

Derrida's charge that Austin's ordinary language philosophy involves
"pass[ing] off as ordinary an ethical and teleological determination" of which
"the transparency of intentions" of the speaking subject is a key element,[29] and
his diagnosis to the effect that Austin's discussion of infelicities delineates the
"teleological jurisdiction of an entire field whose organizing centre remains
intention" (15) seem to be undermined also by the very status of intention in
How to Do Things with Words. One significant moment is Austin's discussion
of the type of infelicities that he refers to as Abuses, the subcategories of which
are insincerities and infractions or breaches. These infelicities arise when the
procedure is "designed for use by persons having certain thoughts, feelings,
or intentions, or for the inauguration of certain consequential conduct on the
part of any participant"[30] and the persons invoking the procedure in fact do
not have such thoughts, feelings, or intentions (e.g., I say, "I congratulate you
on your performance," while thinking it was a flop), or they do not intend to
carry on with the necessary consequential conduct (e.g., I say, "I promise I'll
be there," while having no intention to go), or even if they had the necessary
thoughts, feelings, intentions at the time and for consequential conduct, they

fail to conduct themselves subsequently (I say, "I bet you sixpence it'll rain tomorrow"; I sincerely believe it will, and I fully intend to claim my sixpence from you if it does or pay you if it doesn't, but it doesn't rain tomorrow, and I fail to give you the sixpence). Even with this category of Abuses, the crux of which seems to be the intention of the speaker, it would be a mistake to conclude that intentionality is centralized in Austin's account. Significantly, when discussing Abuses, Austin repeatedly emphasizes that such infelicities do not render the act void, so that I have still congratulated you, promised you, and entered a bet with you, regardless of my thoughts, feelings, intentions, or future conduct. This is precisely why the constative model falls short of capturing performative utterances—"I congratulate you on your performance" is *not* the description of an inward spiritual act of me congratulating you; it may indeed be anything but. Austin's classical example for this key failure of the constative model is derived from Hippolytus's utterance in Euripides' play, "My tongue swore to, but my heart did not." Austin writes:

> It is gratifying to observe in this very example how excess of profundity, or rather solemnity, at once paves the way for immodality. For one who says "promising is not merely a matter of uttering words! It is an inward and spiritual act!" is apt to appear as a solid moralist standing out against a generation of superficial theorizers: we see him as he sees himself, surveying the invisible depths of ethical space, with all the distinction of a specialist in the *sui generis*. Yet he provides Hippolytus with a let-out, the bigamist with an excuse for his "I do" and the welsher with a defense for his "I bet." Accuracy and morality alike are on the side of the plain saying that *our word is our bond.*[31]

Thus, rather than centralizing intentionality, Austin's theory of the performative must be understood as emphasizing its irrelevance in key scenarios, particularly where ritualized conventions reign.

To Cavell's suggestion that Derrida did not read Austin's work on excuses, I would add my own suspicion that Derrida's reading of *How to Do Things with Words* was distorted by French linguist Émile Benveniste's rigidifying revision of Austin's notion of the performative in a 1963 paper, in which Benveniste disapproves of Austin for "[setting] up a distinction and then immediately [going] about watering down and weakening it to the point of making one doubt its existence."[32] Benveniste thus took it upon himself to resuscitate the performative, in the meantime rendering it somewhat unrecognizable.[33] Notably, it was Benveniste who adopted and popularized Austin's notion of the performative in French thought,[34] soon after Austin introduced his coinage into French (as *"performatif"*) at a colloquium held at Royaumont.[35] Although there is no explicit reference to Benveniste's paper in "Signature Event Context," the influence of his rendition can be traced in Derrida's employment of certain phrases, as well as the key focus of his inquiry around "citationality." The challenge that Derrida poses to conceiving of the performative in terms of the "pure singularity of the event" and to its description as a "singular and original event utterance" or as "the most 'event-ridden' utterance there is" is less an argument against Austin than against Benveniste's version of Austin.[36] In fact, the word "event" is never once used in Austin's lectures as part of a description of the performative. Whereas Austin continuously emphasizes the conventionality, the ritual, or ceremonial character of performative utterances, it is Benveniste who reduces the performative to its presumed singularity, uniqueness, eventness, and unrepeatability, when he writes, for example,

> The performative utterance, being an act, has the property of being *unique.* . . . In short it is an event because it creates the event. Being an individual and historical act, a performative utterance cannot be repeated.[37]

Benveniste further proposes that utterances that have become cliché cannot be considered performative, thus potentially excluding many of Austin's paradigmatic examples. Significantly, Benveniste also refuses to take into account the theory of infelicities, which forms the very crux of Austin's discussion: "We shall neither examine the considerations of the logical 'unhappinesses' which can overtake and render inoperative either type of utterance, nor the conclusions Austin was led to by them" (234). Thus the exclusion that Derrida attributes to Austin, the allegation that Austin excludes the risk of infelicity "as accidental, exterior, one which teaches us nothing about the linguistic phenomenon being considered,"[38] much more appropriately describes Benveniste's move here. In fact, Benveniste even ends up arguing that failed performatives are not performatives at all—that, for example, a performative uttered by a person without the requisite authority is in fact not a performative:

> Anybody can shout in the public square, "I decree a general mobilization," and as it cannot be an *act* because the requisite authority is lacking, such an utterance is no more than *words*; it reduces itself to futile clamor, childishness or lunacy. A performative utterance that is not an act does not exist.[39]

If failed performatives are not performatives, what could they be? Futile clamor, childishness, or lunacy—all of which in turn can apparently be said not to exist. By rending the performative from its context of conventionality and excluding the theory of infelicities in this curious manual for how to do all or nothing with words, Benveniste effectively attributes an absolute presence, absolute intentionality, and absolute sovereignty to the one who utters performatives. Indeed, without these absolutes, the performative is not one according to Benveniste. My sense is that Austin would have argued against this rendition, and not only because it is absolutely devoid of humor. In this sense the presuppositions that Derrida criticizes in Austin (absolute intentionality, absolute presence, and uniqueness) would be more appropriately directed to Benveniste's explicitly "corrective" reading of Austin.

Performing the (Structural) Unconscious

Even if Derrida's charge against Austin concerning the centrality of intentionality to his scheme is something of a misfire itself, his proposal for "decentering intentionality" in Austin's theory is significant nevertheless, as it involves the reintegration of the excluded "citational" into the conceptual framework of the performative. Focusing on Austin's second exclusion, namely, his passage on the "not serious," "parasitic" uses and thus "etiolations" of language (i.e., utterances by an actor onstage, introduced in a poem, or spoken in soliloquy), Derrida suggests that this quality of being a quotation, this citationality, is not only a possibility available to every act of utterance, but in fact the necessary condition of all language. Language is conditioned by a structural iterability. Allowing a general theory of what Derrida calls "this structural parasitism" of all language will help construct a differential typology of forms of iterability whereby "we will be dealing with different kinds of marks or chains of iterable marks and not with an opposition between citational utterances, on the one hand, and singular and original event-utterances, on the other."[40] Thus, Austin's excluded parasite (practices that involve recitation) is to be brought in as part and parcel of a general scheme.

The interesting move here is that such an inclusion comes to have bearing on Austin's first exclusion as well, at least in the way Derrida reads the first exclusion as centralizing intentionality. In such a differential typology that embraces the fully citational utterance, the category of intention, according to Derrida, "will not disappear; it will have its place, but from that place it will no longer be able to govern the entire scene and system of utterance" (18). Notably, an absolute intentionality, one which is thoroughly present to itself and to the utterance it animates, cannot be part of this typology. The very iterability necessarily conditioning language disallows, or rather, renders impossible this kind of full saturation. Indeed, the iterability of language serves as a structural unconscious that is present to each and every utterance, placing it beyond the utterer's intention, full consciousness, or ultimate control. So Derrida is flagging the impossibility of such "singular and original event-utterances" while proposing to include Austin's excluded citational as part of the differential typology. This typology that would range between the two also exposes their impossibility and the impossibility of their ultimate opposition: There are neither fully citational utterances nor singular and original event-utterances—neither the puppet show nor sovereign volitional acting, as it were—but only gradations therein.

Judith Butler's notion of performativity shares with Derrida this differential understanding of intentionality, as an element that neither fully disappears from the scene nor fully governs it.[41] Derrida's theory of the general iterability of all language displaces intentionality as the sovereign organizer of speech (something he mistakenly attributes to Austin), by introducing a "structural unconscious" that governs every utterance. Butler, in turn, follows Derrida quite closely on this, as they explicitly acknowledge their debt to Derrida's reformulation of intentionality vis-à-vis performativity in their essay "For a Careful Reading," quoting and then closely echoing Derrida: "The category of 'intention,' indeed, the notion of 'the doer' will have its place, but this place will no longer be 'behind' the deed as its enabling source."[42] The most significant difference between Butler and Derrida in their respective appropriations of the notion of the performative has to do with the body. Although Derrida in his account of the performative argues against Austin's exclusion of the theatrical, it is not bodily performance that he wishes to bring into the scene, but rather the general condition of citationality. This is actually very faithful to the structure of Austin's exclusion, since the latter excludes the theatrical on the basis of its citationality rather than its materiality or status as bodily performance, while not giving much thought to the latter dimension. Thus in Derrida's appropriation, the performative remains linguistic, and in self-conscious irony, the closest he comes to the question of materiality is through the figure of the signature. In contrast, Butler addresses performativity in relation to bodily gestures, signs, and signification practices. This is of course an essential movement for their account of the performativity of gender; but it is crucial to note that Butler retains the significance of the bodily even when they directly address and problematize speech acts as such. Hence much of *Excitable Speech* is dedicated to thinking through "the speech act itself as a nexus of bodily and psychic forces"[43] in various aspects and several different contemporary contexts.

Derrida's exclusion of the bodily is especially striking when we note that the emphasis on citationality is an occasion for him to introduce a concept of the unconscious. Significantly, in "Signature Event Context" this is not an embodied unconscious of fears, desires, and instincts, but rather a "structural unconscious" that derives from the necessary citationality of all language. Thus the historical sedimentations that language carries by virtue of its citationality do not ever allow the subject of speech to fully consciously instrumentalize language. Rather, in each utterance, something of the structural unconscious of language speaks beyond the conscious intentions of the speaker. An implied conclusion would be that perhaps in each utterance, language speaks something of the subject's unconscious. But this latter conclusion is not quite tangible in "Signature Event Context," and even if it is implied, it is not explored. Granted, in his polemical rejoinder to John R. Searle's somewhat unfortunate response to "Signature Event Context," Derrida personalizes this "structural unconscious" as part of his rhetoric of ridicule.[44] But compared to the status of the unconscious in Shoshana Felman's contribution to the theory of performativity, Derrida's gesture here seems to be toward a more disembodied ("structural") sense of the unconscious.

Felman, in contrast, directly addresses the question of the role of the body in performative theory in her book *The Scandal of the Speaking Body*, in which she stages a dazzling encounter between Molière's *Don Juan*, J. L. Austin's work, and psychoanalytic theory. For Felman, it is crucial to be attuned to the fact that the speech act is both linguistic and bodily at once, thus obliterating the distinction between the two:

> The act, an enigmatic and problematic production of the *speaking body*, destroys from its inception the metaphysical dichotomy between the domain of the "mental" and the domain of the "physical," breaks down the opposition between body and spirit, between matter and language. "A body," Lacan says, "is speech arising as such."[45]

It is by its very virtue of being a bodily act that speech always brings the unconscious into play, which in turn poses an irreducible risk to the felicity of any and every speech act.[46] This is what Felman refers to as the "scandal" of the speaking body, which "consists in the fact that the act cannot *know what it is doing*."[47] Thus, compared to Derrida's more circuitous route to the role of the unconscious in the theory of the performative utterance, Felman identifies it as already evident in the very phraseology of speech act theory itself.

The notion of a "sovereign performative" is untenable in both Judith Butler's and Shoshana Felman's schemes, precisely because a performative speech act is performed. As bodily performance, something of the sovereign status of speech is always already undone. This undoing of sovereign speech is also found in Jacques Derrida's treatment of the performative, although it is not occasioned by the body as such. Instead the impossibility, strictly speaking, of a "sovereign performative" in Derrida's treatment is an effect of iterability as the necessary condition of any and all language—so it is not this or that particular body's desires, fears, or anxieties as such that undermine sovereign speech, but rather how language works as language, how it structurally lends itself to not only the unconscious of the speaker but also the unconscious of the language. The distinction may seem slight, but it is crucial. Butler's work on performativity is further intriguing because it not only addresses the speech act as bodily (Felman) and the necessary citationality of linguisticity (Derrida), but it also bridges these two insights to explore the citationality of bodily practices.

Undoing Sovereignty

The conceptualization of performativity thus implicates a particular model for (political) agency and involves an important challenge to forms of agency that are figured and understood as sovereign. Derrida, Felman, and Butler, following Austin, formulate this challenge as arising out of two necessary conditions of performatives: conventionality (iterability) and performance (the performative as speech *act*). In an incipient attempt to explore the significance of this vein of analysis for reading the politics of trials, I return to the three scenes that I described at the beginning of this chapter.

   The episode I described from the Chicago Conspiracy Trial serves as a particularly lucid example of the challenge posed to sovereign performativity by conventionality. Recall that in Chapter 2, I discussed the significance of conventions for legal proceedings. Admittedly, the conventionality of a trial is in one sense what promises its justice: Along with strict rules of procedure, courtroom etiquette has evolved partly with a view to the doing of justice. In a criminal trial, justice is owed to the accused as much as to the victim, thus conventions are ideally meant to protect subjects from the arbitrary imposition of punishment as a form of sovereign violence. In a political trial, although these same conventions may be followed, they may well serve to undo the sovereign will at work in the proceedings. This applies first and foremost to the classic political trial in which authorities take recourse to legal proceedings to eliminate their foes—ostensibly a sovereign performative par excellence. As I discussed earlier in this chapter, Otto Kirchheimer identifies a number of ways in which sovereign schemes are subject to risk in the political trial, due to the potentially uncontrollable effects of the political commitments, intentions, and wills of participants other than the prosecutor. I suggested that this particular formulation of risk remains within a paradigm of sovereign agency by attributing such felicity not only to the will behind the proceedings but also to the intentions of other participants who are understood to bring their own agendas to the trial. Indeed, most readings of political trials tend to focus solely on the conscious strategizing on the part of the participants or stakeholders, the various ways in which they attempt to instrumentalize the proceedings for their own discrete purposes, thus conceiving of the process as a contest of sorts. Notably, however, there is another reason Kirchheimer identifies for the "irreducible risk" and this is not premised on a notion of sovereign agency: The risk can also inhere in uncertainties stemming from legal procedure itself. In Kirchheimer's account, if allowed to follow its own course, a trial's outcome, how it eventually plays out, may be determined by the strict conventionality required procedurally. Thus conventionality, a defining feature of any legal proceeding, lodges an unpredictability at the heart of the trial. Just as it may serve to unravel sovereign claims in the trial, this unpredictability is also the trial's structural promise of justice, no matter what the political will behind the effort is.

A common dynamic linked to this uncertainty in political trials is the mobilization of the legal conventions by persons, often defendants, who are unauthorized to do so. Thus the "irreducible risk" of the political trial becomes the risk of untethering the court's conventions from the sovereign schemes of the state, allocating the force of the performative outside its control. The fact that conventions can be wielded by various participants in the trial beyond the intentions of the political will subtending the proceedings is nothing exceptional if the counter-mobilization remains within the boundaries of what would be considered an "effective defense." But another dynamic is at work in a process like the Chicago Conspiracy Trial where conventions were taken up beyond the limits of authorized conduct to the point of effective subversion of the entire proceedings. The resultant image could not be reduced to any participant's intentions or strategy, but instead can be interpreted as a revelation of law's structural unconscious, that which was "violently resolved, that is to say buried, dissimulated, repressed" in the "founding of law or in its institution."[48]

In his repeated attempts to exercise his right to represent himself, Bobby Seale ventured, for example, to cross-examine all witnesses for the prosecution. He would thus strategically disrupt the proceedings, but crucially, he would speak *only* when he would have been allowed to speak had he been granted the right to defend himself. This careful deployment of convention lent his unauthorized speech a veritable authority. As Judith Butler suggests, "being authorized to speak" and "speaking with authority" are not necessarily equivalent, and further "it is precisely the *expropriability* of the dominant, 'authorized' discourse that constitutes one potential site of its subversive resignification."[49] That Seale spoke with authority in the courtroom was indeed corroborated by another scene: As the conflict between Seale and Judge Hoffman mounted, the spectator seats were filled with increasing numbers of young Black Panthers. When Judge Hoffman cautioned the audience, Seale told him that "they would not take orders from 'racist judges' but he could convey the orders."[50] Surprisingly, Seale was taken up on his offer on the following day, when the marshals asked him, in the name of the judge and themselves, to caution the Panthers in the audience, and Seale agreed to do so (61).

Increasingly frustrated with the progress of the trial, Seale also began directly usurping the judge's speech:

> THE COURT: Let the record show that the defendant Seale has refused to be quiet in the face of the admonition and direction of the court.
> MR. SEALE: Let the record show that Bobby Seale speaks out in behalf of his constitutional rights, his right to defend himself, his right to speak on behalf of himself in this courtroom.
> THE COURT: Again let the record show that he has disobeyed the order of the court. Bring in the jury, Mr. Marshal.
> MR. SEALE: Please do.
> . . .
> THE COURT: Ladies and gentlemen of the jury, good morning.
> MR. SEALE: Good morning, ladies and gentlemen of the jury.[51]

Then, later:

> THE COURT: Let the record show that the defendant—
> MR. SEALE: Let the record show you violated that and a black man cannot be discriminated against in relation to his legal defense and that is exactly what you have done. You know you have. Let the record show that.
> THE COURT: The record shows exactly to the contrary.
> MR. SEALE: The record shows that you are violating, that you violated my constitutional rights. I want to cross examine the witness. I want to cross examine the witness.
> THE COURT: . . . I admonish you, sir, that you have a lot of contemptuous conduct against you.
> MR. SEALE: Admonish you. You are in contempt of people's constitutional rights. You are in contempt of the constitutional rights of the mass of the people of the United States. You are the one in contempt of people's constitutional rights. I am not in contempt of nothing. You are the one who is in contempt. The people of America need to admonish you and the whole Nixon administration.[52]

These instances, later cited at length by the trial judge as part of specifications for contempt charges, were allowed precisely by the citationality of legal procedure as its inherent possibility. By mimicking, and indeed parasitizing conventional judicial speech, Seale revealed and deployed its potential of structural infelicity. The unauthorized usurpation of the speech of authority worked to destabilize authority. Responding to Pierre Bourdieu's emphasis on the decisive factor of social power in determining the efficacy of a speech act, Butler questions whether the context of legitimacy must be figured as necessarily immovable:

> Is there a sure way of distinguishing between the imposter and the real authority? And are there moments in which the utterance forces a blurring between the two, where the utterance calls into question the established grounds of legitimacy, where the utterance, in fact, performatively produces a shift in the terms of legitimacy as an *effect* of the utterance itself?[53]

The performativity of Seale's speech in the trial can be understood to precisely reconfigure the terms of legitimacy.

In this respect, the culmination of this entire affair in the binding and gagging of Seale is revealing: Judge Hoffman had already intimated during the previous day that he might take recourse to such a measure on the basis of a recent precedent.[54] On the day, Seale continued insisting on his right to cross-examine the witnesses, and when denied, he pointed to the portraits hanging on the courtroom wall behind the judge and said, "You have George Washington and Benjamin Franklin sitting in a picture behind you, and they was slave owners. That's what they were. They owned slaves. You are acting in the same manner, denying me my constitutional rights being able to cross examine this witness."[55] When the judge reminded Seale of what "might happen to you," Seale responded: "Happen to me? What can happen to me more than what Benjamin Franklin and George Washington did to black people in slavery? What can happen to me more than that?" (383). The binding and gagging took place very soon after this exchange, revealing and reenacting some aspect of the foundational violence of slavery in the trial. The locus of this reenactment was the very body of the defendant who spoke of the continuity between law-positing and law-preserving violence, and the reenactment was triggered by his speech. In this sense, although he was the victim of what William Kunstler called out as "this medieval torture" (385) somewhat missing the mark in his identification of what historical period the whole episode actually summoned, Seale's intervention was felicitous insofar as it unraveled the sovereign spectacle. Moments after Seale spoke of the legacies of the constitutive violence of slavery, a scene highly evocative of that constitutive violence materialized before everyone's eyes. This is of course not to say that he brought it on himself, but precisely the unauthorized mobilization of conventionality destabilized the spectacle of sovereignty to reveal the performative violence instituting and perpetuating that conventionality. In other words, what surfaced in the spectacle of a Black man bound and gagged in a US district court in the second half of the twentieth century can indeed be interpreted as the very structural unconscious of law.

If the Chicago Conspiracy Trial thus visibly stages the structural infelicity that stems from the conventionality of trial performance, the other two scenes I introduced at the beginning of this chapter illustrate the exposure of sovereign performatives to infelicity due to the vagaries of embodied performance. Saddam Hussein's Dujail trial was, by all means, a classic political trial: a former head of state tried by fiat of the successor regime. It was meant to institute law retrospectively, to recast as crime what had passed as legitimate under dictatorial prerogative. Hussein, like most defendants in classic political trials, chose to play havoc with the very conventions of the trial, and the fact that this was a "special" tribunal facilitated his performance. His aim, a classic political defense strategy, was to advance his own counter-images so as to challenge the legitimacy of the trial and its performative outcomes. But perhaps we find the most succinct exposure or unraveling of the trial's sovereign performativity in that scene of the slip of the tongue as a result of which the distinctions between the positions of witness, prosecutor, and defendant became muddled in a particularly telling way. This happens beyond the intentions of Hussein himself, through an unconscious lapsus, which is then addressed by the judge first in a significantly tentative way: In offering a corrective, Amin speaks quietly, hesitantly, as if not entirely certain himself, or as if he doesn't want to overemphasize the point. The judge signals that when Hussein spoke of the "defendant," he was referring to the prosecutor—but we don't know, Hussein may have been referring to the witness. This would render the judge's corrective even more interesting, making him the unwitting author of the complete reversal of positions. Simultaneously, as Hussein masters his slip, he also discerns the humor in it; he is amused by his own mistake. Then he moves on to capitalize on the amusing moment to suggest with his head gesture, "whatever." Whatever indeed, the prosecutor and/or the witness who testified against him would have been "defendants" under his authority—the judge smiles back, sharing in the humor of the situation. Saddam Hussein's slip of the tongue cuts through the spectacular conflict of sovereign claims in the courtroom to reveal just how thin a façade the trial constitutes.

Finally, the trial of the UK student protesters was an attempt by the Metropolitan Police to legitimize having caused near-fatal injury to a protester. Unlike the other two trials I have discussed here, the trial of Meadows and King did not have much of a public life as a political trial, except in certain limited circles. The hung jury in the first trial meant that the police were close to securing a retroactive authorization of their violence. But when Superintendent Woods shot at the jury with an imaginary machine gun as a "last resort," he reenacted something of the sovereign violence to which the police seemed to feel entitled in the 2010 student demonstrations. The performance disrupted and unraveled the performativity at work in the trial. The playacted shooting of the jury was further the enactment of a threat on the members of the jury— an unconscious threat that must have been registered by the jury at some level, at least unconsciously. This inadvertent performance entirely reconfigured the scene so that the respective positions in the trial were redistributed to effect a sea change in the performative dynamics of the proceedings: The witness became perpetrator, defendant became victim, and jury members became potential victims as well as fresh witnesses. The sovereign performative initially at work was thereby undermined, to give way to an entirely different truth-effect. In this third run, the trial resulted in a unanimous acquittal.

The double-edged nature of trial performance whereby it can make or break the sovereign spectacle cannot ultimately be fully attributed to the political designs, intentions, and strategies of the participants or architects of the trial. The disturbance of sovereign spectacle should be identified as transpiring also in subtler ways, beyond the intentions and designs of the parties, though nevertheless revealing much about the political dynamics at stake, including the violence that posits and preserves the legal order. In the brief examples above, I have tried to tease out the undecidability lodged in legal proceedings not only by their very conventionality, but also by the involvement of bodies that "arise as such" in speech, with their desires, fears, fantasies, anxieties. In the next chapter, I offer a more detailed case study, analyzed in this particular vein, paying close attention not only to the political calculations invested in the trial, but also to the unintended effects of legal procedure, courtroom conventions, and embodiment, to further explore the vagaries of the political in political trials. My close reading in Chapter 4 of a literally "haunted" trial, held in Berlin in 1921 in the aftermath of the Armenian genocide, also serves as the opening of Part II of this book, which looks past the Holocaust and its trials to the Armenian genocide and its fragmentary and oblique legal aftermaths. This oblique vantage point allows a reopening of the questions of law's relation to memory and history, and of law's presumed ability to master past political violence.

PART II
Tracing the Specters in the Spectacles

4

Ghosts in the Courtroom

The Trial of Soghomon Tehlirian

HAMLET: Speak, I am bound to hear.
GHOST: So art thou to revenge when thou shalt hear.
—SHAKESPEARE, *HAMLET*, 1.5.7–8

On 15 March 1921, a young Armenian man named Soghomon Tehlirian assassinated Talat Pasha, the Ottoman statesman who devised and ordered the
mass deportations that led to the annihilation of a great majority of the empire's Armenian citizens. Tehlirian killed Talat on the sidewalk of a busy street
in Berlin's Charlottenburg district, in broad daylight, with a single bullet to
the back of his head. When the assassin was captured on the spot by a somewhat violent citizens' arrest, he said to his captors in broken German, "I am
an Armenian. He is a Turk. It is no loss to Germany."[1] He received an injury
to his head during the commotion,[2] and was eventually delivered to the police. Although he suffered from loss of blood and a high fever during the night,
he was interrogated by the police the next morning and testified. In this preliminary investigation, Tehlirian stated that his only reason for coming to Germany was to assassinate Talat in an act of vengeance, and that his conscience
was clear.[3] In his trial, Tehlirian stated that he had come to Germany to study,
and that he ran into Talat on the street by chance, he was then haunted by his
mother's ghost, compelling him to kill Talat. His trial lasted two days, over
2–3 June 1921, in a Berlin District Court, and resulted in acquittal.

Technically, the acquittal was secured by this figure of a ghost—the apparition of Tehlirian's mother, who had perished in the death marches, understood in the trial as having haunted his capacity for voluntary action. In turn,
the invocation of this singular ghost brought thousands of others into the

courtroom, haunting the trial in myriad ways. Tehlirian's is a curious one among political trials: It remained politicized despite the efforts of the prosecutor, the presiding judge, and the defendant himself to play down the political significance of the crime and the proceedings. Ironically, this inadvertent politicization was effected by the ghost that was initially introduced by the defendant as a way to depoliticize the crime. The figure of the ghost derailed the various wills invested in this particular process and brought about its own performative effects. The trial can thus be read as a case study in the logic and temporalities of haunting as a political category, revealing the workings of the political beyond considerations of expediency, interest, calculation, and other such states of sovereign willing. Instead, the political in this trial partially takes shape as a shared sense of haunting—a state of having, or a process of coming to have, ghosts in common.

In Tehlirian's trial we can also discern a very early emergence of a trauma framing in the legal attempt to assimilate thought-defying atrocity. However, this framing effects a crucial trade-off insofar as the factuality of the genocide is legally recast in terms of personal trauma. In what follows in this chapter, I trace the workings of the ghost in the Tehlirian trial: what it reveals, what it conceals, and how it recasts history itself as ghostly. In the next chapter, I move on to a consideration of the fore- and afterlives of the Tehlirian trial, not only in terms of the legal processes that it was haunted by, and those that it came to haunt, but also in terms of its disparate legacies of political violence.

Talat

The victim of the assassination, Ottoman politician Mehmet Talat, had come to prominence with the 1908 Young Turk Revolution, which reinstituted constitutional rule in the Ottoman Empire[4] and installed in government the organization known as the Committee of Union and Progress (*İttihat ve Terakki Cemiyeti*). Although initially only a Unionist deputy, Talat was among the professional committee organizers who from early on "held the real power and indeed became more influential than cabinet ministers or even grand viziers."[5] He became minister of the interior in 1912. Following a brief interlude of several months out of government, he achieved full power in the bloody coup d'état of 26 January 1913, as one of the triumvirate along with Enver and Cemal Pashas, both of whom were military officers, unlike Talat, a civilian. Still, Talat is considered to have been the "most important single member of the Committee, giving it much of its character";[6] or in a more orientalist figuration, he was "the Big Boss of Turkey," as Henry Morgenthau, American Ambassador to the Ottoman Empire from 1913 to 1916, referred to him in his memoirs.[7] During World War I, the Ottomans sided with Germany, and Talat's role in this alliance was acknowledged by the kaiser with the highest honor, the Order of the Black Eagle, in March 1917.[8] It was also in 1917 that he became Grand Vizier, leading the cabinet until its resignation in October 1918. On 30 October 1918, the Ottoman Empire's defeat was confirmed by an armistice agreement signed with the Allies. Two days later, on 1 November 1918, Talat and six others of the Unionist inner circle fled the country with the help of the German military. Talat then settled in Berlin under the pseudonym Ali Salih Bey.

It has been suggested that Talat's own reasons for his escape included his culpability for wartime atrocities against Armenians.[9] Historian Vahakn N. Dadrian derives this from the first person accounts of Midhat Şükrü, the secretary-general of the Committee of Union and Progress, who relayed an intimate conversation between himself and Talat only hours before his flight in which the latter spoke of "the burden of responsibility" regarding the Armenian massacres. Talat's public statements do not corroborate it, but if there is any truth to the suggestion that he was indeed haunted by the massacres in this way, his assassination by a man who lost family members in the massacres acquires a particularly striking figurative force. It is not a matter of historical contestation that Talat and Enver Pashas conceived of, engineered, and ordered the mass deportations of the Armenian civilian population. Rather, the contention turns on whether the deportations were ordered with the "intent to destroy" this population "in whole or in part," as provided ex post facto by Article II of the United Nations Convention on the Prevention and Punishment of the Crime of Genocide 1948. As the Ottoman Empire's successor state, the Republic of Turkey's official position is that the deportations were a matter of military necessity—they were wartime measures taken against a rebellious population and thus justified. Relying on exaggerated accounts of atrocities perpetrated by Armenian militia groups prior to the deportations, this "provocation thesis" forms the basis of Turkey's official denial of genocide and significantly downplays the extent and magnitude of the deportations, the resultant atrocities (the brutal assaults on and the mass murder of the deportees by the gendarmes, soldiers, and gangs), as well as the ensuing appropriation of the deportees' wealth by local governments and families. More crucially, it denies any link of intentionality between the deportation orders and these consequences.

However, this was not always the official Turkish stance on the issue. Following the dismantling of the Committee of Union and Progress and the flight of its leaders at the end of World War I, the Ottoman parliament was dominated by an assortment of anti-Unionist politicians. This allowed the unleashing of widespread and unequivocal condemnations of Unionist leaders for their responsibility and role in the genocide, across print media and in parliament.[10] Indeed, the postwar Ottoman government initiated a series of prosecutions concerning crimes committed during the war, and Unionist party leaders and functionaries were tried in the Special Military Tribunal (*Divan-ı Harbi Örfi*). Mostly held in Istanbul, these trials were conducted from 1919 until 1922, when they were truncated due to the Turkish war of independence and the ensuing regime change, the establishment of today's republic. At least sixty-three of these trials directly involved crimes committed against the Armenians.[11] Talat was tried in absentia as a "perpetrator of the crimes of massacres," along with other leading Unionist members and wartime cabinet ministers, Drawing on witness testimonies, memoranda, coded telegrams, letters, and other written documents, the indictment claimed that the massacres of Armenians subjected to deportation were "carried out under the [express] orders and with the knowledge of Talat, Enver and Cemal Beys." On 5 July 1919, Talat was sentenced to death in absentia, for crimes that would later be formulated as genocide.

Would the sentence be carried out had the postwar Ottoman authorities gotten hold of Talat, we will never know. An extradition request made by the Turkish Ambassador to Germany on 11 November 1918, only ten days after Talat's flight, was refused by the Berlin government on 16 November 1918.[12] Germany's then Foreign Minister Wilhelm Solf stated, "Talat stuck with us faithfully, and our country remains open to him."[13] Later, Article 228 of the Treaty of Versailles, signed in June 1919 between Germany and the Allies, required Germany to hand over "all persons accused of having committed an act in violation of the laws and customs of war," and even though Talat was one such accused, he was never extradited. When the assassinated "Ali Salih Bey" was identified as Talat, Germany's official position was that the authorities had no idea that he was resident in their territory.[14] This is, of course, highly unlikely.[15] In Berlin, Talat seems to have had an active social life and lived with his wife in relative luxury. On the morning of 15 March 1921, Talat was taking his usual morning stroll in his well-to-do neighborhood in West Berlin, walking on Hardenbergstrasse toward the zoo.

Tehlirian

We glean one version of the biography of the twenty-four-year-old assassin Soghomon Tehlirian from his own statements at the beginning of his trial. We owe this detailed autobiographical account both to a structural element of German criminal trials in which key emphasis is placed on the defendant's account of events, and to a particular decision made by the panel of judges in Tehlirian's case. Section 243 of the 1877 German Code of Criminal Procedure requires[16] that after the case is called up and the judge has ascertained that participants are present, the witnesses leave the courtroom and the proceedings begin with an initial examination of the defendant by the presiding judge as to his or her personal circumstances. Then the indictment is read, and the defendant is informed that they may, but are not required to, respond to the charges. This option is constructed in section 136(2) of the Code of Criminal Procedure in terms of presenting the accused an opportunity to remove the grounds for suspicion existing against them and to present the facts that are favorable to them. If the defendant chooses to make use of this opportunity, they are further examined by the judge on the charges.[17] Although the examination of the defendant as to their personal circumstances at the very beginning is often limited and the main part of the initial interview is this latter examination on the specific charges after the indictment is read, in Tehlirian's case, the panel of judges decided on hearing Tehlirian's account of the massacres before the charges were put to him, despite the prosecutor's objection.

During his interview in court, Tehlirian related the following: He was born in a village near Erzincan, an eastern Anatolian province of the Ottoman Empire. In June 1915, when Tehlirian was eighteen years old, an order was issued for Armenian inhabitants of Erzincan to leave the city. Three days later, people were taken out of the city, divided into groups and marched off in caravans (ST 6). Tehlirian was in a group with his family, traveling on foot. Gendarmes, cavalry, and other soldiers guarded the convoy on the sides so that no one would escape. Once they were at a distance from the city, they were attacked by the gendarmes (ST 7) and mobs. He witnessed his sister being taken away, raped, and killed, his younger brother's skull being cracked open with an axe, and his mother shot down with a bullet (ST 8). Then he was struck on the head, went unconscious, and was probably taken for dead. He regained consciousness a few days later and had to climb out from under his older brother's corpse. He then found his way to a mountain village in the Kurdish town of Dersim, where he was taken care of by an old woman and her family for about two months (ST 9). When his injuries were sufficiently healed, he set out for Iran, and eventually found his way to Berlin after a circuitous route covering Tbilisi, Erzincan, then back to Tbilisi, Istanbul, Thessaloniki, Serbia, then back to Thessaloniki, Paris, and Geneva (ST 10–16). He did not find a trace of any family members (ST 9).

The indictment was read to Tehlirian following this account. Unlike his statement during the preliminary police interrogation to the effect that he only came to Berlin to assassinate Talat, in his trial testimony Tehlirian stated that he moved to Berlin to study engineering (ST 15). In this version

of his story, it wasn't that he hunted Talat down, but rather a chance encounter with Talat on the streets of Berlin provided the twist of fate that led
to the assassination. As he was going on with his life in Berlin as a student
of mechanical engineering and trying to improve his German through private tuition, one day he chanced upon a group of three or four men speaking Turkish among themselves, on a street near the zoo. One was addressed
by the others as "Pasha," and when Tehlirian looked carefully, he recognized Talat from the pictures he had seen in newspapers (*ST* 17, 25). Tehlirian claimed in the trial that his mother's ghost appeared to him following
this chance encounter with Talat.

Enter Ghost

In the trial, the ghost is invoked soon after the indictment is read to Tehlirian:
He is accused of killing with intention and premeditation under Article 211 of
the 1871 German Penal Code. Tehlirian pleads not guilty. His counsel requests
that the judge ask the defendant why he does not consider himself guilty, the
judge relays the question. Tehlirian answers:

> DEFENDANT: I do not consider myself guilty because my conscience is
>   clear.
> PRESIDING JUSTICE: Why is your conscience clear?
> DEFENDANT: I have killed a man. But I am not a murderer. (*ST* 14)

The judge then tries to ascertain whether Tehlirian is objecting to a key element of the charge, and begins to inquire whether the killing was "premeditated."[18] This must have been because intentional killing without premeditation
was a different charge under Article 212, and incurred a considerably lighter
sentence (a minimum of five years imprisonment) than an Article 211 conviction which called for death by decapitation. The judge asks:

> PRESIDING JUSTICE: When did the idea first occur to you to kill Talat?
> DEFENDANT: Approximately two weeks before the incident. I was feel-
>   ing very bad. I kept seeing over and over again the scenes of the
>   massacres. I saw my mother's corpse. The corpse just stood up be-
>   fore me and told me, "You know Talat is here and yet you do not
>   seem to be concerned. You are no longer my son."
> PRESIDING JUSTICE: (*repeats those words to the jury*) (*ST* 15)

Here, between the parentheses, we see the ghost making an immediate impression upon its first mention: Tehlirian recounts his encounter with his
mother's ghost in Armenian, his interpreter repeats the account of the encoun-

ter in German, then the judge repeats these German words to the jury once again. The ghost story echoes in the courtroom. After Tehlirian's harrowing account of the massacres, it probably resonates, too. Newspaper reports of the trial mention attendance in great numbers by the Armenian community of Berlin.[19] Given that the trial took place soon after the war, we can surmise that many others present either as participants or spectators were living with ghosts of their own. Since the record is restricted to the legally authorized speech that takes place in the hearings, we can only conjecture the full range of resonances, but the transcript itself does allow some insight into the various levels of haunting, especially in retrospect.

A little while after the entry of the ghost into the courtroom, the judge's seeming absorption by this figure is evidenced once more as he continues his examination of the defendant:

> PRESIDING JUSTICE: How did it come about that you committed this homicide?
> DEFENDANT: It was because of what my mother told me. I was thinking about that and on March 15th I saw Talat.
> PRESIDING JUSTICE: Where did you see him?
> DEFENDANT: While I was walking around in my room, I was reading and I saw Talat leave his house. . . . When he stepped out of the house, my mother came to my mind. I again saw her before me. Then, I also saw Talat, the man who was responsible for the deaths of my parents, my brothers, and my sisters.
> PRESIDING JUSTICE: You also saw your relatives before your eyes and thought that Talat Pasha was responsible not only for their deaths but also for the deaths of your fellow nationals. (ST 21)

Here the judge feels the need to intervene to supplement the defendant's story, seemingly so captivated by it that he cannot stop himself from participating in its telling. It is pertinent that whereas in Tehlirian's account the business of the ghost is strictly a family affair, in the supplement that the judge offers, its significance is generalized to include vengeance for sake of "fellow nationals"— this is a generalization that is at once a politicization, as a narrative of kinship is reconfigured into one about ethnic belonging.[20] So already at this early stage of the trial, the ghost is politicized by the judge's interpretation. This is but one instance of the gradual politicization of the trial by the ghost. The process mainly unfolds through the testimonies of witnesses introduced by the defense. As a significant part of the two-day trial is flooded by the horrific stories of the genocide, the singular ghost of Tehlirian's mother is recast as one of the many ghosts of the Armenian genocide.

A key figure effecting this ghostly pluralization was Christine Terzibashian, who, along with her husband and brother, seems to have been a close friend to Tehlirian in Berlin. Herself a survivor of the genocide, Terzibashian testified through an interpreter about her own experience of the death marches. She spoke of being forced to march over the bodies of deportees who had recently been killed, of her legs being covered with the blood of the corpses she stepped on, of some five hundred youths being tied together in groups and pushed into the wild currents of a river, of gendarmes crushing the pelvic bones of pregnant women to tear out the fetuses (ST 73–74). Her account caused several commotions of outrage and incredulity in the courtroom, prompting the judge to ask:

> PRESIDING JUSTICE: Is all this really true? You are not imagining it?
> WITNESS: What I have said is the truth. In reality, it was much more horrible than it is possible for me to relate. (ST 75)

At the end of her testimony the judge broached the question of responsibility, signaling a key shift in the focus of the hearings:

> PRESIDING JUSTICE: At the time, who was thought to be the person responsible for this terror?
> WITNESS: Enver Pasha[21] was the one who gave the orders and the soldiers forced us to kneel and cry out "Long live the Pasha," because the Pasha had permitted us to live. (*Commotion*) (ibid.)

From this point in the trial, the question of responsibility for Talat's death became temporarily engulfed by the question of responsibility for the plight of the Ottoman Armenians, further discussed by the following witnesses, including very prominent ones.

One such prominent figure was Dr. Johannes Lepsius, a German missionary who had written books and articles on the Armenian massacres and was considered to be the foremost expert on the subject in Germany at the time.[22] In affect, Lepsius's testimony was contrapuntal to Terzibashian's, and in content, it lent the latter some leverage by providing a more general, historico-political perspective. He suggested that there are over a hundred eyewitness accounts published in German and English, and that these accounts are similar in content to Tehlirian's and Terzibashian's (ST 77). He stated that Talat, among other Young Turk leaders, was directly responsible for the annihilation of Ottoman Armenians, and that he could verify this by official written proof based on German and Turkish documents (ST 81). Lepsius also broached the question of how these events came to take place, a question that many scholars have shied away from until recently, due to the fear that the attempt to explain the causes of the genocide would amount to an attempt to justify it, in a landscape of historical research polarized and distorted by Turkey's official denial.[23]

The second celebrity witness was Otto Liman von Sanders, a German general who was sent to Istanbul in 1913 for modernizing and reorganizing the Ottoman Army and had remained there through the war, heading various campaigns. Liman von Sanders's position on the question of high-level responsibility for the massacres was characteristic of the German military stance. He suggested that while the deportation orders were indeed given by the government, the responsibility for the ensuing atrocities should be attributed to the lower echelons and mobs. He vaguely indicated that he saw some incriminating official orders issued by Enver, but then dismissed these as "incomprehensible," "impractical," and "nonsensical," without going into any substantial detail (ST 84). Further, he emphatically denied having witnessed anything that incriminated Talat (ST 85). However, his testimony was followed and countered by another key witness, Bishop Grigoris Balakian, one of the very few survivors of the initial wave of deportations and massacres that targeted Istanbul's Armenian intellectual elite on 24 April 1915. Balakian knew Talat personally, and testified to having seen what Liman von Sanders claimed he had not, an incriminating telegram signed by Talat.

The Telegrams

These testimonies, not of Talat's assassination, but of the massacres of Ottoman Armenians, allowed the defense to successfully reverse the positions of victim and defendant, which is a common strategy in political trials. The question of the Unionist leadership's direct responsibility for the massacres, or what can in retrospect be formulated as a question of "specific intent" as per the legal definition of genocide, had been floating in the air from the very beginning of the trial. It first found a dramatic if somewhat unthinkable shape in Terzibashian's testimony, then was recast by Lepsius into a more assimilable form. Liman von Sanders raised doubts by offering the interpretation that remains a bulwark for denialism to this day: There was no policy of extermination, the massacres were unplanned and contingent. When the following witness also submitted that extermination was state policy, the defense attorney, with Balakian still on the stand, turned to Liman von Sanders to ask:

> Von Gordon (to His Excellency Liman von Sanders): Your Excellency, you implied in your remarks that the responsibility for the massacres should be with the lower echelon officials.

WITNESS: I said the lower echelon officials were responsible for
the extreme horrors of the massacres, not for the deportation
orders. (*ST* 92)

What Liman von Sanders reiterates here by implication is that the state leaders were responsible for the deportation orders and not for the "extreme horrors of the massacres." This is when the defense attorney moves to submit documentary evidence of specific intent:

VON GORDON: In refutation of this point, I would like to present five
telegrams from the Vice-governor of Aleppo, Syria.
(*von Gordon wishes to put said telegrams on the court table*) (*ST* 92)

The record does not directly indicate whether the telegrams were indeed placed in front of the judge. Likely not, because at this point the judge intervened to say that this is not a procedurally correct moment to introduce this evidence. The attorney responded that he would at least like to describe the contents of these telegrams, and went on to describe the documents as evidencing that Talat personally gave killing orders. He added, "The witness Andonian can testify to the authenticity of these telegrams" (*ST* 92).

This is a crucial moment in the trial, the significance of which only becomes apparent if we understand what these telegrams were. They were items from the famous collection of documents widely known as the "Naim-Andonian documents," which has since become a key battlefield for denialism. Writer and journalist Aram Andonian, a survivor of the genocide, procured this collection in November 1918 from a low-level Ottoman official called Naim, who had served in Aleppo as the office secretary in the Deportation Office under the Interior Ministry led by Talat. The collection included numerous telegrams attributed to Talat, some containing his orders regarding the annihilation of the Armenian population. Andonian published a selection of the documents in his possession alongside Naim's explanatory notes in books in three languages over 1920–21. The English-language version of this book is still in print with the rather misleading title *The Memoirs of Naim Bey* and the more appropriate subtitle, *Turkish Official Documents Relating to the Deportations and Massacres of Armenians*. However, in the meantime, the actual collection has disappeared. Notably, some of this disappearance was effected during Andonian's lifetime by official legal processes, including the trial under discussion. First, the various documents that Andonian was asked to submit to the Ottoman Special Military Tribunal (which was held in postwar Istanbul and which had sentenced Talat to death in absentia) disappeared along with the entire case file of these proceedings. Those that Andonian handed to Tehlirian's defense lawyers were also never returned, and now there is no trace of them. In 1983, denialist Turkish historians Şinasi Orel and Süreyya Yuca published a seemingly authoritative book claiming that an official named Naim did not exist and that all of the documents published by Andonian were forgeries. In the absence of counter-evidence, this view was widely accepted across the different camps of historical scholarship, with even non-denialist historians staying well clear of the contents of Andonian's book as potential fabrications.

However, the recent cataloguing and systematization of the private archive of Reverend Krikor Guerguerian, a survivor who amassed over five decades an extensive collection of documents concerning the genocide, has yielded a set of documents substantiating the authenticity of those published by Andonian. Historian Taner Akçam, who has led the digitization and classification of these archives in an open-access online platform, published a first book on the basis of these documents in which he highlights that:

> The failure of the documents to be utilized in Tehlirian's trial was used by Orel and Yuca as evidence of having been fabricated. This argument is incorrect. . . . If such a discussion had indeed been held, the court would have confirmed by its own hand that the documents were real.[24]

Akçam is right: Had the telegrams been introduced into the case file, they would have been confirmed as authentic. According to a 1937 letter by Aram Andonian that surfaced in the Guerguerian archives, he had been contacted by Tehlirian's lawyers in advance of the trial, and was asked to bring the originals of some of the telegrams that he had published in the book. The lawyers knew that they would need to confirm the authenticity of the documents in Andonian's possession, so they submitted a copy of Andonian's book to Walter Rössler, who had served as Germany's consul in Aleppo during the genocide. In response, Rössler wrote a report, which has also surfaced in the Guerguerian archives, in which he was extremely critical of Andonian's framing of the documents, and particularly his accusations concerning the complicity of German officials in the massacres. However, in this same report Rössler nevertheless vouched for the authenticity of these documents in strong terms:

> Aside from these issues, I must say that the content of the book, in its details, makes a credible impression, and that the published documents, compared with the course of events, certainly have an internal probability. Many particular events with which I am familiar are portrayed with absolute accuracy; others with which I was not yet

familiar provide an explanation for phenomena that I observed but
could not explain at the time.

   . . . So the documents described as original could very well be
genuine. As far as those reconstructed from memory, one would need
to know Naim Bey's character in order to judge their degree of reliability. But I did not encounter anything internally improbable among
these. Rather, the facts that I know are well explained by the documents. Their wording, too, speaks for their authenticity rather than the
opposite.[25]

Following this exchange, Tehlirian's lawyers requested that Rössler appear as
an expert witness in the proceedings. We see the trace of this request and its
outcome in the trial transcript at the very outset of the hearing. The defense
attorney von Gordon says, addressing the bench:

We had planned to call, as an expert witness, the former German
Consul to Aleppo, Syria, Mr. Rössler, who presently is in Eger. He sent
me a telegram from there, stating that he could come as an expert
witness if the Foreign Office gave permission. The Foreign Office had
initially given permission; however, as of last night, they would not
allow the Consul to come and be heard as a witness. As to the questions that we could have asked the Consul, we are in the process of
corresponding with him and we hope to have this matter resolved
today. (ST 3)

The Foreign Office's withdrawal of permission was likely due to the potential
damages that this testimony could inflict on Germany's national interests
at the time. Rössler himself had detailed these in a statement to the Foreign
Office, effectively requesting that he not be given permission to testify:

If the German Foreign Office should give its permission that I be
examined as a witness in the proceedings against the murderer of
Talaat Pasha, I would have to be released from official secrecy and
would be obliged to answer all of the presiding judge's questions under
the oath I would swear as a witness. I would not be able to avoid
expressing my conviction that Talaat Pasha is, in fact, one of those
Turkish statesmen who wanted the Armenians to be annihilated and
carried this out according to plan. All of the softening effects that
might arise, for example from my depiction of the exceptional danger
that the Armenian question was, in fact, for Turkey as it was to be used
by Russia as a means of dividing up Turkey, would recede to the
background compared with the main impression that my testimony

would make. I suppose that the court will present me with documents that were published by the Armenian, Aram Andonian, and which contain accounts of Talaat Pasha's orders in the matter concerning the deportation and annihilation. I would have to give testimony to the effect that these documents are, in all probability, genuine. I would also have to testify that a remark made to me by the Commissioner of Deportations, who was sent from Constantinople to Aleppo, was actually made, "You do not understand what we want: we want an Armenia without Armenians."[26]

As with the withdrawal of permission for Rössler to testify, the judge's "procedural" intervention to prevent the defense lawyer from introducing the telegrams into the case file must be understood as part of the damage limitation exercise, a well-orchestrated effort on the part of German authorities in the Tehlirian trial. The telegrams could have been introduced into the case file a little later, if Aram Andonian had been heard as a witness as initially planned. It is interesting to note that it was the defense counsel who gave the court an out on this point. After being provisionally and procedurally prevented from reading out the telegrams, and after describing the contents of the telegram, Tehlirian's lawyer said: "I personally feel it is important, essential in fact, that the Jurors accept the defendant's belief that Talat was the responsible party and the author of these terrible atrocities against the Armenians. If the Jurors are willing to accept this, then I am willing to waive the reading of these telegrams." The prosecutor seized this moment as an opportunity to object to the introduction of the telegrams into the case file, but also to prevent any further testimonies on the atrocities against Ottoman Armenians:

> DISTRICT ATTORNEY: I feel that the motion [concerning the reading of the telegrams into the trial record] should be denied. Even though great latitude was granted to discuss this subject, nevertheless, it is not the purpose of this body, nor is it within its competence, to come to a historic decision pertaining to the guilt or innocence of Talat and the extent of his involvement in the massacre of the Armenians. The essential point is that the defendant believed that Talat was the responsible party and thus the motive becomes fully clear.
>
> . . .
>
> VON GORDON: In view of the position taken by the District Attorney and the effect it has had on the jurors, I would like to cancel my motion to have these telegrams read into the record.
>
> PRESIDING JUSTICE: I believe that takes care of this point. (ST 92–93)

The prosecutor's caveat with regards to the limitations of a trial as a site for exercises in historiography is not out of the ordinary, but his objection to the defense motion is at once a concession, as he acknowledges the genuineness of Tehlirian's belief in Talat's responsibility for the massacres and suggests that this suffices for the truth-seeking function of the trial, insofar as it establishes the defendant's motive. The judge seeks the defendant's consent to move on, upon which Andonian's name is heard one last time in the courtroom:

> PRESIDING JUSTICE: I would like to ask the defendant if he wishes us to examine any other witnesses.
> DEFENDANT: I would like author Aram Andonian to testify.
> PRESIDING JUSTICE: The jurors believe that at the time of the incident you were convinced that Talat Pasha was the author of the massacres.
> (*Hereupon, the defendant announces that he agrees that the interrogation of other witnesses can be dispensed with.*) (ST 93)

Thus what counted in the end was not an absolute certainty vis-à-vis Talat's responsibility, but rather the defendant's belief in Talat's responsibility. While this would not be news for criminal lawyers who will often find themselves trading in fine but crucial distinctions between "genuine" and "reasonable" even if "mistaken" beliefs, it is nevertheless important to note that history itself acquires a ghostly status here: The law withholds judgment on historical fact; it refuses to authorize the factuality of the fact, but nevertheless allows it a hold over the proceedings as subjective vision. On the verge of achieving a legal inscription, the key question of specific intent is dissipated; it turns into a question of the defendant's own beliefs and opinions.

This movement from historical fact to psychological effect will be seen to be repeated in the 2015 European Court of Human Rights case *Perinçek v. Switzerland*, which I discuss in detail in Chapter 6 of this book. In the Tehlirian trial, the move emerged as part of a damage limitation exercise. It brought the "digression," the reversal of the positions of defendant and victim, to an end, at least in the actual proceedings. It ensured that the question of Germany's responsibility in the atrocities would not be prodded further, at least in the actual proceedings. But it also had various other effects. For one, the law was made to effectively devour the evidence of specific intent: First, the five telegrams are not allowed to appear in the case file; then the telegrams are disappeared into the case file to never resurface ever again. I will discuss the implications of this in more detail in the following chapters, as part of a critique of the memorial function that law is invested with and much celebrated for, say, in most transitional justice literature. I will propose that law is as, if not more, capable of producing oblivion as it is of producing memory. Another effect of the shift from historical fact to psychological effect was the trial's resultant failure to contain the ghosts that had been unleashed into the courtroom through the accounts of the genocide. In receiving no conclusive judgment that the trial participants could accept or reject, or at least have as a tangible point of reference, history itself became "there but not there," like a ghost. The restless spirits invoked by the witness testimonies enthralled their audience to a history that remained unthinkable as fact, only assimilable through what Avery Gordon refers to as a "haunting recognition."[27] Another effect of the shift from history to psychology was, of course, to bring Tehlirian back in focus, as it was his state of mind that was said to matter in the end— how convincing he seemed in his convictions was critical.

The Haunted Hunter

In the trial, Tehlirian did indeed come across as a genuinely haunted man. A definitive moment occurred at the very beginning of the trial, during his initial interview by the judge. When he was prompted to recount his experience of the massacres, Tehlirian dramatically broke down in the telling:

> DEFENDANT: While we were being plundered, they started firing on us from the front of the caravan. At that time, one of the gendarmes pulled my sister out and took her with him. My mother cried out, "May I go blind!" . . . I cannot remember that day any longer. I do not want to be reminded of that day. It is better for me to die than describe the events of that black day.
>
> PRESIDING JUSTICE: . . . it is very important that we hear of these events from you. You are the only one that can give us information about those events. Try to pull yourself together and not lose control.
>
> DEFENDANT: I cannot say everything. Every time I relive those events. . . . They took everyone away . . . and they struck me. (ST 7)

A rather ornate account in a German newspaper relates this moment in the following words: "Tehlirian lifts his small hand on his white forehead—he does not want to be reminded of those days of horror. It takes some time to convince him of the need for accurate depiction."[28] The *New York Times* correspondent is less forgiving: "As Teilirian [sic] was narrating, through an Armenian interpreter, the Turkish atrocities in Armenia, his Oriental temperament got the better of him and he shrieked, 'Rather will I die than again live through the black days.'"[29] Notably, Tehlirian's breakdown occurs as soon as he embodies his mother's voice ("My mother cried 'May I go blind!'"), as an initial hint of the haunting that later comes to dominate the proceedings.

The character portrait drawn by witnesses corroborates something of Tehlirian's hauntedness. His first landlady who has "only good things to say about him," confesses that she could hear everything that went on in his room: "At night he seemed to have nightmares. . . . He always played his mandolin. . . . He used to sing very melancholy tunes. . . . Many times he would talk out loud to himself, making me think that there was someone with him" (ST 39–41). His second landlady testifies: "On the morning of March 15th, the day the incident occurred, the maid came in to tell me that the defendant was in his room crying" (ST 43). His German teacher: "It was easy to see that he had an emotional trauma. He always looked sad" (ST 47); then, an acquaintance: "He was always dejected and had a vacant stare" (ST 64). Reporting on his examination of Tehlirian, the court physician Dr. Robert Störmer says, "Whenever the defendant spoke of the massacres, I had the impression that what he said came straight from the heart" (ST 95).

This sad, visibly haunted figure also appears as a ghostly, haunting figure himself. He is described by the doctors at the trial as a very sick young man, weak, trembling, thin, fragile. An earlier report by a medical officer filed during Tehlirian's preliminary investigation described him as "malnourished" and "inconspicuous."[30] In the trial, it gradually emerged that Tehlirian developed epilepsy following the traumatic events. As the inquiry turned from the historical record to the subjective, Tehlirian's epilepsy became a focal point for the proceedings, especially in the testimonies of five expert witnesses—two neuropsychiatrists, two neurologists, and a physician. The psych-experts, testifying one after the other, were particularly invested in understanding the link between Tehlirian's epileptic seizures and his memories of the massacres.

People with epilepsy are known to experience the hallucination of a pungent odor just before a seizure. In Tehlirian's case the hallucinated odor was interpreted to be related to the stench of the corpses. The physician Dr. Störmer explained: "He remained for three days under corpses; he lost consciousness, coming to only because of the horrible stench arising from the corpses—a stench which has remained ingrained in his mind forever. He tells me that any time he reads anything horrifying or whenever he recalls the massacres, the stench from the corpses penetrates his olfactories and he cannot seem to overcome it" (ST 94). Except for Dr. Störmer who diagnosed Tehlirian with epilepsy, all other experts concluded that Tehlirian was suffering from "affective epilepsy" rather than "real" epilepsy. Though coined in the early twentieth century by German neurologists Bratz and Falkenberg to designate a slightly different phenomenon,[31] the term *Affekt-Epilepsie* seems to have been used in the trial to denote seizures that were psychological in origin rather than organic.[32]

The extended discussion of Tehlirian's epilepsy and detailed descriptions of his seizures must have imparted to him further mystique. In his famous essay "The 'Uncanny,'" published only two years before Tehlirian's trial, Sigmund Freud discusses the work of Ernst Jentsch, who writes about instances in which there are "doubts whether an apparently animate being is really alive; or conversely, whether a lifeless object might not be in fact animate" as having an uncanny effect.[33] For Jentsch epileptic seizures have this effect because they "excite in the spectator the impression of automatic, mechanical processes at work behind the ordinary appearance of mental activity" (226). Freud adds to this that the ordinary person sees in epileptic seizures the "workings of forces hitherto unsuspected in his fellow-men, but at the same time he is dimly aware of them in remote corners of his own being. The Middle Ages quite consistently ascribed all such maladies to the influence of demons, and in this their psychology was almost correct" (243). Elsewhere Freud calls this "uncanny disease with its incalculable, apparently unprovoked convulsive attacks" by its old name: "*morbus sacer*," the sacred disease.[34]

Such associations around epilepsy have particularly strong resonance in the figure of Soghomon Tehlirian. According to what emerges of / as his past in the trial, Tehlirian has quite literally arisen from the dead, from beneath the corpses. He is sickly and weak, and yet he demonstrates a steely, almost mechanical, automated determination to avenge the dead. The stories of his epileptic seizures bestow on him an almost netherworldly quality—at the onset of each seizure, his sense of smell returns him to the scene of carnage, the scene of his own death from which he was miraculously revived. If the classic ghost story plot dictates that the ghost must return to seek vengeance for past injustice, the telos for Tehlirian's return from the dead is only too obvious. As he is animated by forces beyond his limited physical strength to avenge the dead, his epileptic seizures serve in the narrative universe of the trial as the all too tangible sign of Tehlirian's rapport with the world of the dead. Tehlirian himself acquires an uncanny, ghostly presence as the revenant: haunted and haunting, possessed and possessing at once.

The question of whether the defense outlined in Article 51 of the German Penal Code applied to the defendant becomes particularly interesting when read in this light. Article 51 states: "If the offender at the time of the committal of an offense was in a state of unconsciousness or derangement of the intellect due to illness by which the free exercise of his will was prevented, the act is not punishable." In Tehlirian's trial, all expert witnesses were asked to consider whether Article 51 applied to the defendant, in other words, whether his free will was totally absent or not at the time of the act of killing. The experts' answers arrived in a gradual scale from no to yes. The first expert, Dr. Störmer, the court's examining physician, said no, his free will was not totally absent. The second expert, neuropsychiatrist Dr. Liepmann, also said no, but added that Tehlirian's condition was very close to falling within the purview of Article 51, as at the time of the act, he was under the influence of an "over-valued idea."[35] Liepmann also expressed regret that a doctrine of diminished responsibility had not yet been introduced into German criminal law, suggesting that such mitigation rather than a full defense would be more appropriate in this case. Expert witness number three, Dr. Richard Cassirer, also suggested that Article 51 did not apply, that Tehlirian's free will was not totally absent at the time of the incident, but similarly added that the provision came very close to applying. The fourth expert, Dr. Edmund Forster,[36] was also on the fence, but leaning toward yes. He expressed uncertainty as to how his medical judgments translate into a legal opinion, but said that Tehlirian's status comes very close to Article 51, and added, "I am even inclined to say that free will was totally absent" (ST 108). The final expert, Dr. Bruno Haake, in his very brief testimony, univocally stated yes, Article 51 did apply to Tehlirian.

In effect, this collection of testimonies functioned as so many attempts to translate the haunting into a medico-scientific language. And yet, the translation, rather than explaining the ghost away or secularizing it, instead seems to have reified the haunting to a significant extent. This was especially the case with the "over-valued idea" formulation, advanced by Dr. Liepmann and backed by the other neuropsychiatrist, Dr. Forster. In Liepmann's explanation, the recollection of a profound psychological shock "dominates the personality; it is always present; it always comes out, forcing the person to submit to its authority. . . . Tehlirian was under the influence of such a compulsive precept and he was unable to free himself from the memory of the severe shock he had endured" (ST 99). Considering that the German psychiatric profession maintained a generally hostile attitude toward psychoanalysis at the time,[37] it is not entirely surprising that we have here what reads as a clumsy theory of trauma. The concept of "over-valued idea" comes across at best as a gross misnomer for recurrent and haunting memories of a massacre. It presumes the existence of a standard gauge, a measure for how much such past experiences should normally be valued; and it bestows the neuropsychiatrist with a claim to authority over that measure. The language of psychoanalysis may have allowed a better grasp of the workings of trauma, even back in 1921,[38] as well as possibly a more self-reflexive approach on the part of the doctors, some of whom were clearly haunted by Tehlirian and his ghost.[39] By utilizing the "over-valued idea" doctrine, Liepmann seems to have in fact lent further purchase to the figure of the ghost: "The entire recollection of the calamity . . . appeared in physical form—seeing his mother" (*ST* 100–101). Thus the ghost becomes in this account the very physical manifestation of every recollection Tehlirian has of the traumatic events, the memory of which has imprisoned him. And this, the good doctor says, gives us "the singular creation of 'over-valued idea.' . . . His vision of his mother was an all-powerful force, thus making any further argument pointless" (101, translation modified).

The inevitable force of the demands of the ghost was thus melded with accounts of Tehlirian's "affective epilepsy" to yield a pseudoscientific account of his intentionality, but it was pseudo, precisely because everything that was uncanny about the haunting and the seizures was retained in an odd form of scientific reification. Although the majority of the experts actually claimed the non-applicability of Article 51, their testimonies in effect reinforced the sense that Tehlirian's volition was haunted at the time of his act. Their attempts to secularize the ghost and exorcise it failed, as evidenced in the closing statements that followed the expert testimonies. The ghostly retained its hold on the proceedings as one of the defense attorneys in his summation drew on its force. After recounting Tehlirian's entire story and his encounter with his mother's ghost in properly dramatized form, the defense counsel said:

> It is quite evident that such visions play an altogether different role in the lives of spirited Easterners than they do in the lives of us Westerners, who look upon such things from a philosophical and medical point of view. I remind you of the passage from the Holy Bible which reads: "And the angel appeared to him in his dream." A similar apparition or corporeal vision is what had the decisive effect on Tehlirian. (*ST* 124)

The double move here is noteworthy: disowning the ghost as "us Westerners," but then drawing on its persuasive force nevertheless; allocating "such things" to their proper Western site of philosophy and medicine, but then invoking the Holy Bible and its angels. The jury, in returning a verdict of not guilty, seems to have agreed with this analysis of Tehlirian's volition being haunted by the ghost, whatever its proper place in the "Western" imagination.[40]

The Many Lives of Tehlirian

As I have suggested, the positions of the victim and the defendant were temporarily reversed in Tehlirian's trial, as the ghosts of history congregated in the courtroom to reconstruct history as ghostly. The trial was first transformed from a truth-seeking effort regarding responsibility for Talat's murder to an inconclusive truth-seeking effort regarding responsibility for the catastrophic events of 1915. Then it began revolving around the inner world of the haunted, haunting defendant. This trajectory had the key effect of disappearing from the scene of the trial the various doubts and unresolved questions concerning the facts of Talat's assassination.

For example, even though early on in the investigation the police had expressed that they strongly suspected Tehlirian had accomplices,[41] in the trial that question entirely vanished, not even surfacing during Tehlirian's examination. More significantly, questions raised by the contradictions between Tehlirian's initial confessions to the police and his trial testimony, especially regarding premeditation, were dematerialized with a fascinating sleight of hand. This one was a translator's coup: Kevork Kaloustian was Tehlirian's interpreter during the police interrogation, and also later at the trial, as well as taking the stand as a witness. In both instances, Kaloustian openly admitted his admiration of Tehlirian for the deed he committed. It emerged during his trial testimony that he purposely did not sign the transcript of the police interrogation "for the simple reason that the defendant was in no condition to be interrogated" (ST 66). The absence of his signature on the transcript absolved Tehlirian of his self-incrimination, prompting the presiding judge to conclude: "There is grave doubt as to the validity of the contents of this transcript in terms of its acceptability as evidence" (ST 67).

The questions as to accomplices and premeditation thus vanished from the scene of the trial. In retrospect, especially in light of various later retellings of Soghomon Tehlirian's story, these prove to be highly significant disappearance acts. The versions of the retellings vary, but the assassination provides the organizing center to all. There is a volume of Tehlirian's memoirs as recorded and published by his friend Vahan Minakhorian in Cairo, which incorporates the original trial transcript.[42] This volume is in Western Armenian and has never been fully translated into English, though there is a very loose adaptation.[43] Then there are Tehlirian's "memoirs" as told by Lindy V. Avakian, published in English almost three decades after Tehlirian's death.[44] The structure of the narrative is strange: Avakian inhabits Tehlirian's voice and appropriates his "I" in the retelling, while intervening in the narrative with what seem like editorial, disinterested, and ostensibly objective "(COMMENT)"'s that are highlighted as such in capital letters and parentheses, usually including dry "historical facts." The effect thereby created is a split in the authorial voice, which is probably meant to authenticate the "I" as that of Tehlirian, and Avakian as the historian that the jacket proclaims him to be. Although the book contains some privileged information with regard to Tehlirian's life,[45] its historical accuracy is highly suspect, as can be discerned from the complete rewriting of the trial that has precious little to do with its offical transcript.[46]

Another account is by Edward Alexander, a retired American diplomat of Armenian descent, who, in a much more conscientious attempt to reconstruct the story, draws on the trial transcript and newspaper reports, as well as Tehlirian's 1956 memoirs, though glossing over some key conflicts between the latter and the former.[47] Additionally, there's a volume by French political thriller writer Jacques Derogy, who was commissioned to write the story of Operation Nemesis, Armenian Revolutionary Federation's (ARF's) covert vengeance campaign, which aimed to "bring justice" to those deemed responsible for the massacres.[48] In addition to various secondary sources, Derogy draws on memoirs, archival documents, and oral history for the arduous task of reconstructing the story of a series of assassinations. Notably, Tehlirian is featured in the narrative as a Nemesis agent. In a recent nonfiction book aimed at a general readership, Eric Bogosian further builds on Derogy's research, centering his account on the figure of Tehlirian and drawing on additional resources and archival material to offer a fuller narrative that is nonetheless historically accurate.[49]

Indeed, according to all these retellings, including Tehlirian's own, Tehlirian was assigned the task of assassinating Talat by Armen Garo[50] during a visit to the ARF headquarters in Boston in late 1920. Nor was Talat the first man he assassinated: In his memoirs Tehlirian admits to having killed Harootiun Mugerditchian in 1919 in Istanbul, a detail that is featured in the other retellings as well.[51] Mugerditchian's assassin remained officially unknown, and it is no surprise that Tehlirian did not volunteer this information during his 1921 police interrogation or trial testimony in Berlin, as that would have depicted him as a professional hit-man. It is also understandable why Tehlirian did not admit to having accomplices in Talat's assassination, namely other Berlin-based ARF operatives that all other accounts refer to. In these retellings, an entirely different story of the assassination emerges: Tehlirian did have accomplices, and the murder was premeditated. All of this has only recently been extensively documented with the publication of the letters and telegrams of the leaders of Operation Nemesis, by one granddaughter who inherited the archive.[52]

More crucially, according to various accounts, including Tehlirian's own memoirs and recent interviews with Tehlirian's son,[53] he was never in the death marches himself. Nor did he have any sisters. He and two of his three brothers had left Erzincan in 1914, on the eve of the war, to join their father in Serbia, while their mother and brother stayed behind. When the war broke out and he found out that there were Armenian volunteer forces fighting on Russia's side, he traveled to Tbilisi to join them. He was not allowed to go in the field due to his young age and was tasked with organizing the reception of orphans. The first time he heard of the massacres was from these orphans who had survived them. When the region was occupied by the Russians in 1916, he went to his village seeking his mother and relatives, but found no trace of them. He found his family home in ruins and had his first ever epileptic fit there, in the garden of his abandoned home.[54]

Ellis Island records corroborate Tehlirian's fateful trip to the United States, though this is one trip that is not mentioned in the seemingly endless list of travels recounted during the trial. It is difficult to know whether the ARF connection would have been discovered if the German authorities had knowledge of Tehlirian's recent trip to the United States. A remarkable detail, however, is that there are two Tehlirians even in the Ellis Island records, according to which on 22 August 1920 a "Salonon Telarian," aged twenty-four, of Armenian ethnicity, resident of Paris, arrived in Ellis Island on a ship named *Saint Paul*, which departed from Southampton; and three days later, on 25 August 1920, another "Solomon Telarian," aged twenty-four, of Armenian ethnicity, resident of Paris, arrived at the island on a ship named *Olympic*, which departed from Cherbourg, France.[55] The glitch in the archives fascinatingly reproduces the doubling that seems to have characterized Tehlirian's life at the time.

It is admittedly quite difficult to reconcile this later version of Tehlirian's story with the figure he cuts in the trial as a man who seems genuinely haunted by memories of a massacre of which he was the only survivor. One wonders about the source of the story of deportation and massacre he told as his own during the trial. Did he make it up, or did he borrow it? Was it entirely a product of his imagination, or could it be a story that he heard from someone else, say, one of the orphans he received during his service in Russia? Could it be that he was haunted by the testimonies of these orphaned children to the extent that he adopted their stories and adapted them to his own loss? Bearing witness to the testimony of others, being the immediate receiver of the testimony of survivors is "actually participat[ing] in the reliving and reexperiencing of the event."[56] Writing of his experience of working on the Video Archive for Holocaust Testimonies at Yale, psychoanalyst Dori Laub suggests that "the listener (or the interviewer) becomes the Holocaust witness *before* the narrator does" in this reoccurrence of the event, as the encounter between listener and survivor "makes possible something like a repossession of the act of witnessing" (85). But in being the primary witness to the event through witnessing its reoccurrence and reliving, the listener also becomes "part of the struggle to go beyond the event and not be submerged and lost in it" (76). This is not to say that one will necessarily manage to prevail over that struggle.

While there is a veritable disjuncture between how convincing Tehlirian was deemed in his trial and the fact that his story was otherwise, it is not entirely possible to explain this disjuncture away by attributing it to his cunning or theatrical skills. If we are to take into account the loss that he did suffer, we might ask what it might mean for one's relatives to disappear without a trace in a series of events later relayed by survivors in unthinkable narrations. This line of inquiry may begin to bridge the disjuncture between Tehlirian's credibility at the trial and his other story, and afford a new perspective on the haunting itself. As Avery Gordon suggests, "Disappearance is an exemplary instance in which the boundaries of rational and irrational, fact and fiction, subjectivity and objectivity, person and system, force and effect, conscious and unconscious, knowing and not knowing are constitutively unstable."[57] The epistemological instability effected by loss as disappearance is a liminal experience that is akin to the structure and operation of haunting. This combination of loss as disappearance, and witnessing as listening (as the immediate receiver of survivor testimonies) may provide an insight to Tehlirian's haunting that was deemed credible in his trial by character witnesses, experts, and, finally, the jury. In the trial, just as the character witnesses and psych-experts testified to Tehlirian's haunting through their statements, the members of the jury did the same by returning a not guilty verdict. In exploring the politics of this particular political trial, the key question is not so much whether Tehlirian's haunting was genuine or not, but what it meant for other trial participants to share Tehlirian's ghosts, by verifying the haunting, and thus partaking in it.

The Politics of Haunting

Writing on the proverbial drama of the parental ghost appearing to the son to demand vengeance, Ross Poole addresses the nuance between the political and the personal significations of the ghost in William Shakespeare's play *Hamlet*. He indicates that due weight is rarely given to the political meaning of the ghost in its stage productions, or its theoretical interpretations.[58] In its first few appearances, the ghost in *Hamlet* is "a public existence, and not a private experience" (129), it appears as the warrior king clad in combat armor, and it is visible not only to Prince Hamlet but also to the sentinels and Horatio. Contesting Hegel's reading of the play in *Aesthetics*, Poole suggests that the ghost in its early appearances "is not *just* 'an objective form of Hamlet's inner presentiment,'" it is also "an 'objective form' of the presentiments of those others to whom it appears" (130). This significance shifts dramatically in Act III during the bedroom scene between Hamlet and Gertrude—in this final appearance, the ghost is visible to Hamlet only, not to his mother, and this time, the specter of the father is clad in night attire. Hamlet is trapped in an Oedipal return. Poole concludes that "a political story has been reduced to a domestic drama" (133).

Following in the steps of this reading of *Hamlet*, we could propose that the political is, to a certain extent, a sharing of ghosts. The politicization of the Tehlirian trial was an effect of such a ghostly convergence: The singular ghost of Tehlirian's mother came to represent and ushered into the courtroom the many ghosts of the Armenian genocide; and possibly other ghosts, too, given that it was held in the wake of the great war. In "The 'Uncanny,'" published in the immediate aftermath of the war, Sigmund Freud ruminates on the swift uptake of ghosts, and of the belief that "the dead can become visible as spirits," even in a "supposedly educated" milieu, including by some of "the most able and penetrating minds among our men of science."[59] Freud explains this modern inclination to be haunted in terms of a primitive remainder, the entrenchment of old beliefs and the primordial fear of the dead that is "still so strong within us and always ready to come to the surface on any provocation" (242), and "ready to seize upon any confirmation" (247). Whereas Freud's analysis is based on a civilized/primitive dualism which he holds on to even as he problematizes it, contemporary theorists of ghosts point out that we are prone to hauntings precisely because of the violence of civilization—because "indignities and damages continue under cover of civilization";[60] and "deep 'wounds in civilization' are in haunting evidence."[61] The shared haunting in Tehlirian's trial can be interpreted as the collective recognition of the unthinkable, that this level of atrocity is humanly possible. The specter gives form to what is "really real";[62] it becomes a figure that contains the impossible recognition of what we now call genocide.

Ironically, even though the ghost played a central role in politicizing the proceedings, it was initially introduced in an attempt to depoliticize the crime. The discrepancy between Tehlirian's admissions during his police interrogation and his trial testimony[63] is of significance in this regard: During his police interrogation Tehlirian admitted to intentional killing with vengeful premeditation, whereas in the trial he introduced the figure of his mother's ghost as a way to indirectly deny premeditation. We find an explanation for his change of testimony in Tehlirian's memoirs. According to this text, it had to do with his encounter with a fellow prisoner after his police interrogation, who explained to him that murder committed with political motivations will incur the death sentence, whereas killing for personal reasons would be treated with more leniency in German courts.[64] I have not encountered any firm indicators of such an operative distinction between political and personal moti-

vations in German criminal law of the time,[65] and perhaps the issue had more
to do with the question of premeditation—likely assumed to exist in a "political" crime, whereas not necessarily in a personal "crime of passion." It is nevertheless interesting to consider this differentiation between the political and
the personal that Tehlirian's memoirs indicate he heeded. In an attempt to shift
the focus from the political to the personal, Tehlirian speaks of his mother's
ghost. The quintessential "political crime," the assassination of a (former) statesman by someone who is a stranger to him, was to become personalized
through the figure of a ghost, who establishes an intimacy, a link of private
vengeance between the assassin and his victim. Tehlirian's trial appearance
was very much in line with this strategy of keeping it personal, as he limited
his account of the Armenian deportations and massacres to what he presented
as his eyewitness testimony of the sufferings of his own family.

But note also that this particular ghost constantly oscillates between the
personal and the political. It is introduced as a personal ghost but is swiftly
taken up by the men of law. It then multiplies to effect a representation, or
more accurately, a spectral presence of the Armenian genocide in the trial,
only to be restored to Tehlirian's personal "mental state." The ghost steals
the show: It expropriates the agency for Talat Pasha's assassination and ab-
solves Tehlirian of his guilt by coming to stand in for the first genocide of
the century. But in the end Talat's responsibility for the genocide is figured
not as historical fact, but only as personal belief. It may be said that the
ghost works to destabilize the distinction between the personal and the political in the trial, foreshadowing the ways in which criminal justice in the
aftermath of atrocity would come to be assigned therapeutic functions such
as closure and reconciliation.

Tehlirian's commitment to keep politics out of the trial was shared by the
prosecution and the presiding judge, according to historical records. Tessa Hofmann provides an account of the prosecutorial strategy and the position of
the judge by drawing on previously unearthed case records and files document-
ing the correspondence between the Foreign Office, the Ministry of Justice,
the attorney general, the chief public prosecutor, and the trial prosecutor regarding how the Tehlirian case should be handled. In a plea to the Ministry
of Justice written about one week before the beginning of the trial, the chief
public prosecutor expresses the worries of the Foreign Office regarding the approaching trial. The escalation of the trial into a "mammoth political case"
could create disturbances on the public front "as well as in German-Turkish
relations."[66] The correspondence expresses fear that the defense may question
the stance of the German government on the Armenian atrocities, and suggests that this would be undesirable especially at a time when Germany was

busy trying to suppress the Polish insurrection in Upper Silesia (44–45). The chief prosecutor adds: "Of even greater concern from the political point of view is a line of inquiry during the trial, which would consider (Talat) Pasha's general political role and his German connections" (45). Representatives of the Foreign Office met the trial prosecutor Gollnick one day before the trial to discuss these concerns, and the presiding judge was similarly briefed according to Hofmann's research (46). The authorities initially entertained the idea of excluding the public from the trial to keep its politics under control, but then decided that this strategy might backfire. Instead they tried to contain the trial by restricting the time and the facts: "Only subjective and medical questions were to be raised" (46).

Hofmann's conclusion is that the prosecutor and the presiding judge indeed handled the case extremely tactfully, to render it "conspicuously unpolitical" (49). She concludes, "It was no true victory for political justice, but rather just a first and involuntary step in the right direction" (50). Note that Hofmann writes this in the Dashnak-supported journal *Armenian Review,* to break the perhaps unwelcome news that the Tehlirian trial was not exactly the idealized moment of rupture that later Armenian nationalist mythologizing held it out to be: the legal recognition of the plight of Armenians on the world stage, justice done and justice seen. According to Hofmann's account, there were other, more parochial political considerations at work, which required the depoliticization of the proceedings. The trial's politicization may indeed have been "involuntary," as Hofmann puts it, but this does not make it any less consequential. In fact, it is highly significant that the politics of the trial emerged, operated, and cohered beyond the individual and institutional strategies and damage limitation exercises invested in it. The figure of the ghost determined not only the legal outcome of the trial but also its legal and political afterlives, as I discuss in some detail in the next chapter.

This is not to say that there were no felicitous performatives of expediency: That the German authorities planned to play down the political significance of the trial did not prevent them from capitalizing on it for their own political ends. The transcript specifically betrays an attempt to absolve Germany of any liability for the Armenian deportations and massacres. Historians differ on the question of Germany's complicity in the plight of the Armenians; some accord a decisive level of responsibility, whereas others limit it to quiet complicity at the top echelons.[67] Certainly at the time of Tehlirian's trial, Germany was widely seen as blameworthy, in part due to Entente propaganda campaigns to this effect.[68] Therefore, the need to emphasize Germany's innocence emerged then and again in the Tehlirian trial. Notably, it was flagged at the very beginning of the trial by the defense counsel, who, when arguing for the necessity to introduce testimony on the Armenian massacres, said, "Believe me, gentlemen, it is in the interests of the German government that nothing be left out" (ST 4). Concerning the interests of the German government, it seems, the defense and the prosecuting authorities were very much in agreement.

Germany's innocence provided a point of consensus even for witnesses otherwise entirely in disagreement with one another. It united, for example, the testimonies of Liman von Sanders and Johannes Lepsius, though they contradicted one another on nearly every other issue.[69] But the issue came to the fore most crucially during the closing speech of one of the defense counsel. After congratulating himself and his team for not turning the trial into a political trial, Kurt Niemeyer made this argument on behalf of acquitting Tehlirian:

> During the war, German military and other establishments, both in this country and beyond its borders, passed over in silence and then tried to cover up the atrocities committed against the Armenians. This was done in such a manner as to imply that our German government actually condoned these atrocities. Certainly, up to a point, individual Germans tried to put an end to the atrocities, but to the Turks the implications were clear. They thought, "It is impossible for these events to take place without the consent of the Germans. After all, we are their allies and they are so much stronger than us." Therefore, in the East and all over the world, we Germans have been held responsible with the Turks for the crimes committed against the Armenians. There is a wealth of literature in the United States, Great Britain, and France whose purpose is to show that the Germans were really the Talats in Turkey. If a German court were to find Soghomon Tehlirian not guilty, this would put an end to the misconception that the world has of us. The world would welcome such a decision as one serving the highest principles of justice. (ST 162)

We do not know whether this argument played a role in the jury decision. We can, however, surmise that in responding to the proceedings with a not guilty verdict, the jury, composed of average Berliners, may have sought to dissociate from the harrowing atrocities they had listened to. The decision, which functions as a condemnation of Talat's responsibility in the genocide, may be interpreted as a collective attempt to put (at least some of the) ghosts to rest.

The transcript of Soghomon Tehlirian's trial provides a partial record of the ghosts that flocked into the courtroom following the introduction of the singular ghost of the assassin's mother. In the foregoing analysis, I have tried to trace the various operations of the ghost within the trial: what it enacted, what it effected, what it revealed, what it concealed, and how it recast the genocide itself as spectral. In the next chapter, I move on to a consideration of the fore-lives and afterlives of the Tehlirian trial, in an attempt to trace its spectral lega-cies. I inquire into the processes of law and violence that came to haunt the Tehlirian trial, and the processes of law and violence that the trial came to haunt, exploring the spectral operations of political violence through legal procedure.

5

Spectral Legacies

Legal Aftermaths of the Armenian Genocide

It has become commonplace to appeal to law in the wake of catastrophic violence. The discourses and industries of human rights, international criminal
law, and transitional justice have mainstreamed the notion that law can serve
a crucial memorial function and provide closure by means of the public fora
it creates and the conclusiveness of the verdicts it reaches. Along with other
post-Holocaust trials, the International Military Tribunal at Nuremberg is held
up and celebrated as a key precedent in the attribution of a range of didactic,
pedagogic, memorial, and therapeutic functions to legal processes, and to other
similar public occasions that partake of law's instruments, methods, and media, such as truth and reconciliation commissions and public inquests. As I
have indicated in my discussion of the 1960s critical literature on Nuremberg
in Chapter 1, such precedenting requires a number of legalistic disavowals and
denials of the ways in which law and violence are always already entangled,
and how law is not only conditioned but also characterized by the force/vio-
lence at its origin. I have proposed that theories of performativity as they bear
on critical legal thought can provide a conceptual idiom and framework that
is attuned to such entanglement, allowing us to trace the specters of political
violence in the spectacles of law.

Alongside and in response to the now dominant conception of the relationship of law, violence, and memory, a body of critical literature has been
emerging, questioning the ability of law to master political violence and to provide effective closure.[1] In this chapter, I offer a consideration of the fragmentary and oblique legal aftermaths of the 1915 Armenian genocide along this
critical vein. As an event that precedes the Holocaust, and one that has not
achieved as clear and conclusive a legal framing as the latter, this earlier genocide

of the twentieth century complicates easy presumptions about law's mastery over violence, as it highlights law's co-implications with violence in distinctive ways. But rather than attempting a comprehensive and exhaustive treatment of the legal aftermaths of the Armenian genocide, my analysis here is fragmentary, and in this sense similar to its object. It proceeds through tracing the fore- and afterlives of the 1921 Berlin trial of Soghomon Tehlirian, the subject of the preceding chapter. I present a sketch of the legal processes and violent events that the Tehlirian trial was haunted by, and the legal processes and violent events that it came to haunt, and then move on to consider one such event in more detail in the latter half of this chapter. This is the 2007 assassination of Armenian Turkish journalist Hrant Dink in Istanbul, which was understood by a number of public commentators as a potential "vendetta" for the assassination of Talat Pasha by Tehlirian. But if Dink's assassination brought back the specter of Talat's assassination, it also brought back, and much more palpably, the specters of the Armenian genocide, with Dink often figured, in numerous memorial protest events held since his death, as one more victim of the genocide. Significantly, law is also implicated in this spectral return: Both the process of judicial harassment leading to Dink's assassination and its labyrinthine legal aftermath speak of the ways in which genocidal violence continues to haunt the legal order as its unspeakable foundation. Here, the "unspeakable" is not literal, it is not that which literally cannot be brought to language, but rather the bringing to language of which occasions the return, repetition, and renewal of its violence. This violence takes the form of denial, both in the sense of the denial of the right to existence, and in the sense of negationism, the denial of the factuality of the genocide. As I discuss in this chapter and in further detail in the next chapter, law is implicated in denial in both senses.

I take recourse to the language of haunting and spectrality in this chapter, not only because the Tehlirian trial literally and quite spectacularly featured a ghost, as I have detailed in the preceding chapter, but also because the notion of haunting allows us to capture the strange temporalities of law in its relation to violence, or the ways in which time is "out of joint" in the entanglements of law and violence. The language of performativity thus merges with that of spectrality, but this is not an artificial grafting. As I proposed in Part I, and particularly in Chapter 3, law's misfires can often be traced to its performative institution and the force/violence that conditions and perpetually haunts it, but that also remains sealed off from it as its unspeakable. Concerning the performative institution of law, Jacques Derrida writes in "Force of Law," "There is here a silence walled up in the violent structure of the founding act; walled up, walled in,"[2] and later, in glossing Benjamin's "Toward the Critique of Violence," adds:

> The very violence of the foundation or positing of law (*Rechtsetzende Gewalt*) must envelop the violence of the preservation of law (*Rechtser-haltende Gewalt*) and cannot break with it. It belongs to the structure of fundamental violence in that it calls for the repetition of itself and founds what ought to be preserved, preservable, promised to heritage and to tradition, to partaking. (272)

The iterability that characterizes and governs a legal order must thus be understood as yielding a haunted structure, in its mixing of foundation with preservation. In *Specters of Marx*, written a few years after "Force of Law," Derrida returns to the question of ghosts and haunting in both more extensive and nuanced ways. Although the concerns of this later text primarily lie elsewhere, its conceptualization of spectrality can be brought to bear on the implications of the earlier text. In *Specters*, Derrida suggests that spectrality throws time out of joint, and that the specter of the past and the specter of the future cannot be differentiated once and for all.[3] As I attempt to demonstrate in my discussion of the fore- and afterlives of the Tehlirian trial, this strange temporality has a critical bearing on conceiving of the co-implications of law and violence, law's relationship to its own historicity, and by extension, on the question of law's ability to attain mastery over past political violence.

In *Specters* Derrida puns on ontology to propose "hauntology" as a way of knowing that involves, but is more than, and is indeed the condition for the possibility of ontology. The concept is offered as if in jest, without spelling it out as a methodology in detail, yet Derrida writes of the necessity of introducing "haunting into the very construction of a concept. Of every concept."[4] Although not yet naming it as such, "Force of Law" also begins to broach the notion of hauntology as "a quasi-logic of the ghost which, because it is the more forceful one, should be substituted for an ontological logic of presence, absence or representation" (259). Hauntology thus calls for a particular attunement to ghostly returns, so as to assist in formulating a sense of "how the past lives indirectly in the present, inchoately suffusing and shaping rather than determining it."[5] I thus offer this hauntological account of the lives of the Tehlirian trial with a view to making sense of the legal and political dead ends, impasses, and attendant injuries that contemporary attempts at the legal recognition of the Armenian genocide continue to produce. I begin by locating the Tehlirian trial within a history of political trials by seeking its "cross-legal" connections, in Shoshana Felman's formulation, considering the ways in which it refers to or "recapitulates the memory" of, "repeats and reenacts,"[6] and also, crucially, pre-enacts other trials, including those that never came to be.

Legal Returns

In a veritable sense, the trial of Soghomon Tehlirian was haunted by the Ottoman Special Military Tribunal held in Istanbul after the war and its 1919 judgment that had sentenced Talat to death for his responsibility in the Armenian deportations and massacres. The postwar Ottoman trials against the leaders of the wartime government, held between 1919 and 1922, are significant, though their legacy has not been explored exhaustively, because of various limitations on scholarship on the subject. For Turkish nationalist historiography, one key limit has been an ideological one. The regime that instituted the tribunal was toppled within a few years, thus rendering the trials infelicitous. The final administration of the Ottoman state, the postwar government in Istanbul, was supplanted by the Ankara government of the Kemalist forces that led the war of independence, which in turn resulted in the founding of the Republic of Turkey in 1923 as the successor state to the Ottoman Empire. The new republic did not uphold the legacy of the Istanbul tribunal; to the contrary, the condemned Unionist leaders would soon come to be celebrated as national heroes, as they still are. For example, Talat's remains were repatriated in 1943 and buried on the site of the Monument of Liberty which sits atop the highest hill in central Istanbul, now abutting the new mammoth complex of the Istanbul Palace of Justice. In Turkish nationalist historiography, the trials of Unionist leaders held in the immediate aftermath of World War I are repudiated as treasonous exercises in political justice and therefore not taken seriously in their substance. Another main reason why the Ottoman Special Military Tribunal has not been studied exhaustively is that its entire archive is lost, including

> the papers of the commission of inquiry established in November 1918, the papers from the investigations carried out by the courts-martial themselves, the case files for the approximately 63 cases filed at these courts, the minutes of the court sessions, the testimonies of both the witnesses and defendants, and the investigation papers regarding dozens of persons and events that did not make it to trial. All of this—*all* of it—has disappeared without a trace and without a clue as to its fate or whereabouts.[7]

Existing studies of the tribunal are mainly based on thirteen indictments and verdicts that were published in the official gazette at the time.[8] The indictments and verdicts refer to and cite the items of documentary evidence that were included in the case files, but as the latter are lost, historians have to suffice with these citational traces.

The trials of the Unionist leaders and functionaries held before the Ottoman Special Tribunal can be identified as successor regime trials that were meant to provide legitimacy to the new regime through an incrimination of the policies of the previous regime, that is, the wartime Unionist government. The importance of this tactical aspect has to be appreciated within the proceedings' immediate political context: They were instigated at a time when the Ottoman Empire was anxious to placate the victors of the war in the midst of negotiations that were underway from January 1919 for a peace agreement. Thus to some extent, the trials can be seen as part of Ottoman authorities' attempt to distance themselves from their predecessors so as to gain legitimacy vis-à-vis the Entente and secure leniency. This is one of the reasons why in contemporary Turkish nationalist historiography, the trials are often dismissed as farcical, cruel exercises in political justice imposed and orchestrated by the Entente.[9] It would, however, be misguided to overemphasize the international realpolitik aspects of these trials at the expense of recognizing other political dynamics that were operative at the time.[10] It must be understood, for example, that the Unionist Party had made many political enemies during the tumultuous decade that it governed, except for brief interruptions, from 1908 until the end of World War I. What characterized the postwar and pre-republic Ottoman government in Istanbul was not mere opportunistic sycophancy and eagerness to please the Entente, but also a genuine outrage vis-à-vis the actions of the previous government, including its genocidal policies.

We encounter signs of this outrage in the parliamentary debates and publications of that era.[11] One such primary source in English is a pamphlet published by the National Congress of Turkey in 1919, titled *The Turco-Armenian Question: The Turkish Point of View*, written essentially as a plea to the Entente not to punish the entire Turkish population for the atrocities against the Armenians. Insofar as the pamphlet takes recourse to a narrative of unreasonable territorial claims of ungrateful Armenian revolutionaries and their treasonous wartime conduct, it can be seen as recording an early incarnation of the current official arguments of the Turkish state. However, what is unusual compared to today's official stance is that this narrative is offered not as a defense of necessity, and thereby a justification, but rather as an articulation of mitigation. More significant, the fact of the genocide, or to put it less anachronistically, mass murder and dispossession as government policy, is not contested. The pamphlet states: "The guilt of the Unionist organization which conceived and deliberately carried out this infernal policy of extermination and robbery is patent. Its leaders rank among the greatest criminals of humanity."[12] It may also be noted that it was not only anti-Unionist politicians who understood the atrocities against Armenians to be state policy and were opposed to it as such. For example, the Unionist politician Mehmet Cavid Bey, who served as minister of finance in numerous cabinets between 1909 and 1918, noted in his diaries his conviction that the ongoing atrocities against Armenians were organized and condoned by Talat, and that it was "an attempt not only to destroy the political representation but also the living presence of an entire ethnic group."[13] This diary entry by Mehmet Cavid Bey written sometime between August and September 1915, ends with the chilling premonition that "I'm afraid that Talat, who has so far managed to evade the wrath of Abdülhamid's spies, of the Greeks, the Bulgarians and of Ottoman dissidents, will end up being the target of an Armenian bullet" (136). That the author of these lines was also convicted in the Military Tribunal and sentenced to fifteen years imprisonment can be interpreted as testifying to the partisan character of the court.

The political trials that were held before the Ottoman Special Military Tribunal can be considered early legal processes concerning what would later come to be categorized and codified as crimes against humanity and genocide.[14] Historians have noted that the procedure employed in the tribunal suggests that the evidentiary standard that it upheld was high, producing a record that proves to be of historic value.[15] This ties in with the tribunals' legacy in relation to the Tehlirian trial: the specific evidence against Talat in the Ottoman court-martial indicated not only that he had knowledge and awareness of the extent of atrocities that were going on around the deportations, but also that he had personally ordered the annihilation of the deportees. Whereas the latter incrimination was based on witness testimonies, the evidentiary basis for the former was documentary.[16] Thus Talat's trial in the Ottoman tribunal proves a significant node in considering the ways in which the Tehlirian trial came to be haunted: The earlier trial had not only publicized a body of evidence directly incriminating Talat vis-à-vis the Armenian deportations and massacres but also convicted him and sentenced him to death. Therefore, it is as if the Berlin trial immunized the assassin as the legal executor of this earlier death sentence.

The Tehlirian trial was also haunted by the trial that never was. On 24 May 1915, exactly one month after the beginning of the genocide, Great Britain, France, and Russia issued a joint declaration stating,

> In view of these new crimes of Turkey against humanity and civilization, the Allied governments will hold personally responsible all the members of the Turkish Government, as well as all officials who have participated in these massacres.[17]

The reference to the "new crimes" against humanity and civilization here was without precedent,[18] but the Allied governments were clearly conjuring a future judicial process in their emphasis on personal accountability. Indeed, the idea of prosecuting state leaders for war crimes was quite prevalent already at the beginning of World War I. After the war, it was brought to the table at the Paris Peace Conference, one of the consequences of which was Article 227 of the Treaty of Versailles, pertaining to bringing the German emperor before an international tribunal. As for Ottoman authorities, we can look at Article 230 of the Treaty of Sevres, which stipulates the establishment of an international tribunal for the "massacres committed" in Ottoman territory during the war. The said tribunal was never formed, and eventually the Treaty of Lausanne covered the perpetrators with the shield of amnesty. It is in this sense that the trial that never was haunts the Berlin trial, possessing it, and turning a murder trial into a trial about the genocide.

Perhaps more significant, the Tehlirian trial haunts, in advance, the trial to come. It is astonishing in hindsight that this was a trial about a genocide, held in Germany just over two decades before the Nuremberg trials. But there are also important biographical threads that connect the two historical moments. It is now known that Raphael Lemkin, the jurist who coined the word "genocide" in 1944, was captivated by the Tehlirian trial as a young man about to start law school. Lemkin must have followed the Tehlirian trial through the media accounts that spectacularized the proceedings. In his draft autobiography published posthumously, Lemkin notes that he discussed the trial extensively with his professors during his studies at Lwow University, and identifies it as one of the key events that shaped his thinking around mass atrocity, the crime of genocide, and international law:

> Tehlirian, who upheld the moral order of mankind, was classified as insane, incapable of discerning the moral nature of his act. He had acted as the self-appointed legal officer for the conscience of mankind. But can a man appoint himself to mete out justice? Will not passion sway such a form of justice and make a travesty of it? At that moment, my worries about the murder of the innocent became more meaningful to me. I didn't know all the answers but I felt that a law against this type of racial or religious murder must be adopted by the world.[19]

Lemkin's conceptualization of the problem with the Tehlirian trial in this brief passage is notable: There was justice in Talat's assassination, but the law could not do justice to the justice that inhered in the act of killing, other than by framing it in terms of temporary insanity and thereby misnaming it. Further, the "justice" of the acquittal threatened law itself insofar as it ceded the monopoly of violence to a "self-appointed legal officer for the conscience of mankind." Lemkin's solution is that the monopoly must somehow be restored: "A law against this type of racial or religious murder must be adopted by the world." Thus the Tehlirian trial is inscribed and incorporated as the (autobiographical) precedent of what would eventually be codified as genocide. It may be noted that Lemkin also cites as "precedent" the 1927 Paris trial of Sholem Schwartzbard who assassinated Ukrainian politician Symon Petliura in an act of vengeance for his responsibility in the 1919–20 pogroms against the Jews. Like Tehlirian, Schwartzbard was acquitted in a sensational trial that publicized the victim's culpability for mass atrocity.

Another among the young law students paying close attention to the Tehlirian trial was Robert Kempner, who attended the proceedings as an observer. Kempner would later participate in the investigation and prosecution of Adolf Hitler for the 1923 Beer Hall Putsch, and he would be exiled following Hitler's rise to power, only to return to Germany as part of the US prosecutorial team for the International Military Tribunal at Nuremberg. In a 1980 article, Kempner wrote of the Tehlirian trial's legal historical significance in somewhat exaggerated terms:

> For the first time in legal history, it was recognized that other countries could legitimately combat gross human rights violations caused by a government, especially genocide, without committing unauthorized intervention in the internal affairs of another country.[20]

Kempner thus monumentalizes the Tehlirian trial as something that it never was, or, something that it wasn't exactly.

In both Lemkin's and Kempner's reflections on the Tehlirian trial, we see the attempt to incorporate it into a triumphant legal history of international justice. Perhaps a key aspect of the Berlin trial in this regard was that it was prefiguratively occupied with the question of specific intent, which would only later be codified as a key element of the crime of genocide. In examining the expert witnesses on the deportation and massacres of Ottoman Armenians, Tehlirian's lawyers explicitly attempted to establish that the annihilation of the Armenian deportees was state policy, and not merely circumstantial or accidental. As I discussed in some detail in the preceding chapter, this effort was dissipated at a critical point during the hearings, when the question of the facticity of specific intent was abandoned for the sake of finding a personal motive: It was sufficient to have ascertained that the defendant believed that there was specific intent. Then again, even if the court shied away from a finding vis-à-vis the facticity of specific intent, the ghostly, formless, shadowy appearance that this question assumed in the hearings came to acquire something of a legacy in international criminal law, albeit mainly through biographical threads.[21]

Atemporal Histories of Terror

While the men of law thus attempt to incorporate the trial of Soghomon Tehlirian into a triumphant legal history of international justice, various threads and traditions of political violence have proven as, if not more, hospitable to the revenants of this trial.[22] One thread here pertains to state violence. In the aftermath of Talat's assassination, German newspapers featured debates about what happened in 1915. Two moments are notable in this range of publications: In trying to justify Talat and the deportations, one Middle East correspondent held up the specter of what the British did in the Boer War, namely an early use of concentration camps, and argued that the Armenian deportations were similarly justified out of military necessity.[23] The second is an article written after the trial by the former German chief of general staff of the Ottoman army, Bronsart von Schellendorf, in testament to Talat's genius as a statesman. Outraged by the decision of Tehlirian's acquittal, which he read as an incrimination of Talat, von Schellendorf also argues the primacy of military necessity, but not with reference to past events such as the Boer War: Imagine, he suggests instead, if in today's Germany all Polish insurgents were removed from Upper Silesia and placed in concentration camps, or, he says, if all communists were deported from Germany, would not, he asks "a storm of applause roar through the whole of Germany?" as if conjuring the events of the next world war.[24] As these two moments indicate, the logic of haunting, the inability to distinguish the ghosts of the future from those of the past, has a particularly strong purchase on the question of political violence.

Tehlirian's deed and trial are also cited as potential "precedents" by Hannah Arendt in *Eichmann in Jerusalem*, as part of her consideration of Israel's jurisdiction over Adolf Eichmann. One of the jurisdictional objections that Eichmann's defense counsel had put forth was that the District Court of Jerusalem could not try Eichmann because he had been illegally kidnapped from Argentina and brought to Israel in a clear breach of international law. Arendt agrees that the kidnapping of Eichmann was indeed against international law, but also notes that no legal alternative existed to kidnapping, given Argentina's "impressive record for not extraditing Nazi criminals,"[25] as well as various technical reasons including the lack of an extradition treaty between Argentina and Israel, and the fact that Eichmann's crimes had already fallen under the statute of limitations under Argentine law. Arendt then adds that there was only one real alternative to kidnapping, and we may note this wasn't legal either: "Instead of capturing Eichmann and flying him to Israel, the Israeli agents could have killed him right then and there, in the streets of Buenos Aires." Noting her surprise that the preferability of this course of action was most vehemently argued by those who were outraged by the illegality of the act of kidnapping, she suggests that "those who proposed it forgot that he who takes the law into his own hands will render a service to justice only if he is willing to transform the situation in such a way that the law can again operate and his act can, at least posthumously, be validated" (265). This is when Arendt turns to the cases of Soghomon Tehlirian and Sholem Schwartzbard as "two precedents in the recent past" that fulfilled justice in precisely these terms, by bringing their acts before the law. The idea that Eichmann's outright assassination would be a less messy alternative to his kidnapping to be brought to trial in Israel mirrors the initial British argument in the immediate aftermath of World War II that it was a better option to summarily execute the Nazi criminals rather than bringing them before an international tribunal. Here, the appeal of the extralegal option (assassination or summary execution) stems, counterintuitively, from a form of legalism, because what drives these arguments is a concern to keep the law untainted by not so legal origins such as illegal kidnapping in the case of Eichmann, or victor's justice in the form of political trials in the case of Nuremberg. Thus Arendt's response to this odd form of legalism in citing the cases of Tehlirian and Schwartzbard must be read as a reminder that the law is always already implicated in unsanctioned violence.

Consider, however, a recent uptake of Arendt's discussion of the cases of Tehlirian and Schwartzbard as potential "precedents" for the justness of extralegal assassinations. Roger Berkowitz, director of the Hannah Arendt Center for Politics and Humanities at Bard College, and the winner of the Heinrich Böll Foundation's 2019 Hannah Arendt Prize for Political Thought, takes recourse to Arendt and the specter of a political trial that never was in order to argue that the assassination of Osama bin Laden by US military agents could be legally justified, if such justification were to be sought. Notably, the trial that Berkowitz invokes counterfactually is not that of bin Laden, but of the members of the special operations unit that killed bin Laden. It is a somewhat circuitous argument, but Berkowitz refers to Arendt's discussion of the "precedents" of Schwartzbard and Tehlirian and their acquittals. In Berkowitz's rendering, Arendt

> argues that to take the law into one's own hands can promote justice, at least under particular circumstances; he who "takes the law into his own hands," she writes, "will render a service to justice only if he is willing to transform the situation in such a way that the law can again operate and his act can, at least posthumously, be validated." Revenge, in other words, can be just when done in certain ways—namely, when the avenger submits the justice or injustice of his act to the legal verdict of a jury.[26]

So Berkowitz argues, while we should not shy away from celebrating bin La-den's (that's "Osama" to the author) killing by "whatever means it was accom-plished" (351), perhaps it would have seemed more like the just assassination it was, had the American Navy SEALs that assassinated him voluntarily sub-mitted themselves to a jury trial, "before an American jury because one can-not imagine them receiving a fair trial in Pakistan and because a trial before a judge in the Hague would lack the judgment of a jury and the possibility of jury nullification upon which the SEALS' claim of justice must rest" (349). Putting aside the glaring limitations of a legitimacy sought in an all-American jury nullification for such a case, we may note that in marshaling Arendt and her discussion of Schwartzbard and Tehlirian as potential "precedents" to just assassinations by state agents, Berkowitz conveniently leaves out Arendt's strong conclusion to the contrary in *Eichmann in Jerusalem*:

> It is more than doubtful that this solution would have been justifiable in Eichmann's case, and it is obvious that it would have been *altogether unjustifiable if carried out by government agents*.[27]

This miscitation by the distinguished Arendt scholar may have been due to mere oversight, but it is very much in keeping with the general tendency of contemporary liberalism's distorted uptake of the 1960s critical thought on po-litical trials, as I have discussed in Chapter 1. What is further noteworthy is the re-precedenting that the case of Soghomon Tehlirian is subjected to in this particular version of post-9/11 hawkish liberalism, with a swaggering confi-dence that even unbridled sovereign acts of vengeance can be presented as lawful, if need be.

The specter of Soghomon Tehlirian's trial continues to roam around. Like every ghost, the ghost of this trial that we encounter today is an impoverished and distorted version of the life, the live event it once was, inflected through various chauvinisms, or various modalities of resentment, enmity, frustration, grief, longing, and desire. This is traced particularly easily in the fictionalized retellings of the trial: In a novel by Turkish writer Mim Kemal Öke, who de-picts almost all Armenians as ungrateful, back-stabbing bandits and all Turks as magnanimous, tolerant peace-seekers, Tehlirian's mother appears toward the end of the trial, not as ghost but in flesh and blood, and explains to the court that she has long disowned her son Soghomon because he killed his own older brother, who refused to collaborate with the Dashnak fighters against the Ot-toman Army. The melodramatic narrative has it that Soghomon then testified against a Turkish soldier for his brother's murder in a hearing held by Talat himself, who had sensed he was lying but, being a man of justice, would honor a Christian's word as much as a Muslim's, and therefore sentenced the

Turkish soldier to death. Soghomon then felt he had to kill Talat because his piercing and accusing gaze had become the stuff of his nightmares.[28] In Armenian American writer Lindy Avakian's similarly imaginative reconstruction, Tehlirian is portrayed as nothing less than a superhero—vigorous, muscular, and ultra-virile. He doesn't say much in his trial except protesting when the judge identifies his country of origin as "Turkey": *"No, Sir!"* There is consternation in the court until his counsel leaps to his feet: "If it please the court, I believe I can explain my client's answer. As an Armenian he recognizes neither Soviet nor Turkish domination of his country. He was born in Erzinga, Armenia. The defense respectfully asks the court to recognize the defendant's birthplace as Erzinga, Armenia, rather than Turkey."[29]

The fictional retellings involve much fantasizing about sovereignty and sovereign agency in the trial. The same can be said for the ways in which the trial is understood in retrospect. In the Turkish nationalist imaginary, the acquittal of Talat's killer in Berlin serves as proof of the old ally Germany's betrayal, hypocrisy, and injustice. For example, when Angela Merkel and the Christian Democrats submitted a motion in 2005 to the German Parliament that called for Turkey to apologize to Armenians, a senior columnist in a popular daily suggested that perhaps Merkel should apologize to the Turks on behalf of German judges for the injustice that was perpetrated in Tehlirian's trial.[30] This kind of rhetoric about the trial is often thrown around, with parochial historical vision (i.e., as if Tehlirian's acquittal was the only problem with Weimar courts) and without regard to certain key facts (i.e., that it was a jury trial).

In the Armenian nationalist imaginary, Tehlirian's acquittal is a triumph of truth and a victory for justice: As a momentary recognition on the world stage of the genocidal violence of 1915, it is a memory that is held dear. But this acquittal seems to also serve as vindication for acts of political violence that are legitimized in terms of retribution for 1915. Tehlirian was a source of inspiration for the Justice Commandos of the Armenian Genocide (JCOAG) and Armenian Secret Army for the Liberation of Armenia (ASALA) killings of Turkish diplomats from the mid-1970s to the mid-1980s.[31] These were assassinations through which, in the words of Fatma Müge Göçek, "The unexamined past thus suddenly and unexpectedly came to *haunt* the present."[32] The timing of the publication of the Armenian Revolutionary Federation's English edition of the Tehlirian trial transcript, the year 1985, is significant in this sense, and the foreword to the publication actually highlights this link between Tehlirian and ASALA/JCOAG assassinations. Signed by "Armenian Revolutionary Federation, Varantian Gomideh, Los Angeles," the foreword mentions the "recent trials of Armenian political prisoners around the world who have, as Tehlirian did in 1921, forced the Armenian Cause onto the streets and courts of world capitals." Tehlirian's trial, it is suggested, was the first case during which the horrors of 1915 were "introduced as evidence to justify political violence in the face of neglect by world governments" and concludes: "Over six decades later, those same facts—compounded by Turkish denials—have motivated a new generation of survivors to use a variety of means in seeking justice and retribution for the Armenian people."[33] This formulation of "a new generation of survivors" in a nod toward the new assassins is noteworthy, as it evokes a heritage of haunting, a lineage of haunted hunters. We may also note that it was this wave of attacks on Turkish officials that prompted the Turkish government to properly develop an official stance of hyperproductive denialism.[34]

A similarly sinister return of the 1921 Berlin drama may have been the assassination of Armenian Turkish journalist Hrant Dink in 2007. Dink, the editor-in-chief of the Istanbul-based Armenian Turkish bilingual weekly newspaper *Agos*, was murdered close to his office on the sidewalk of a busy, central street in Istanbul, in broad daylight, shot in the back of his head—just like Talat. Dink's lawyer Fethiye Çetin, who went on to represent his family in the murder trial, noticed in the case file that Yasin Hayal, an ultranationalist young man arrested soon after the killing and eventually convicted of soliciting Dink's murder, had been obsessed with the assassination of Talat and the acquittal of his killer. Dink's assassination followed a period during which he was subjected to judicial harassment and hounded by ultranationalist mobs protesting him at his trials, among them a certain "Talat Pasha Committee," established to organize denialism around the Armenian genocide. Such resonances and threads of connection between the two killings have been noted in the Turkish print media, including by historian Taner Akçam, who suggests that Dink's murder was revenge for Talat's assassination.[35] I dedicate the remainder of this chapter to an analysis of the events leading up to Dink's assassination as well as the legal aftermath of his killing. While law's ability to provide closure and serve a memorial function has become something of a truism in post-Holocaust industries and discourses of justice, the case of Hrant Dink, as yet another spectral trace of the Armenian genocide, crystallizes some of the ways in which the law is equally, if not more, capable of effectively producing not only violence but also oblivion.

Process unto Oblivion

Hrant Dink's assassination on 19 January 2007 was the culminating point of a persecution campaign that went on for three years, and involved overt and covert threats by official bodies and belligerent individuals, a series of unmistakably political prosecutions, a scandalous conviction for "denigrating

Turkishness," and ultranationalist mobs protesting outside the offices of his newspaper *Agos* and hounding him in courthouses. The campaign against Dink began in February 2004 when he published in his newspaper *Agos* the claim that the national hero Sabiha Gökçen was of Armenian descent, and that she had been orphaned during the 1915 deportations and massacres. Gökçen was not only the world's first woman war pilot but also the adopted daughter of Mustafa Kemal Atatürk, the "founding father" of the Turkish republic. In another context, a claim of this sort may have been no more than a minor footnote to history. But its implications regarding the nationalist mythopoetics of the Turkish republic and its founding were rather enormous. Two weeks later, on 21 February 2004, the mainstream daily *Hürriyet* ran an uncharacteristically carefully worded story about the claim published in *Agos*. On the following day, the General Staff of the Turkish Armed Forces, the highest echelon of the Turkish army, made a harsh public statement repudiating the claim, and accusing those who disseminate it of ulterior motives against national unity and national values. Although it was unexceptional for the army to take the liberty to express its political position concerning current affairs, it was nevertheless a rare occasion for it to comment on a news article that did not strictly feature itself.[36] The day after the army's statement, on 23 February, Dink was summoned to the Istanbul deputy governor's office and "warned" by two people who were introduced to him as "friends" of the then deputy governor. Six and a half years after this compulsory meeting, and three and a half years after Dink's assassination, the National Intelligence Organization finally admitted that the two people who threatened Dink in the deputy governor's office were its senior operatives and that this "meeting" with Dink was organized upon the demand of the General Staff of the Turkish Armed Forces. While attacks on press freedom in Turkey have taken various forms over the past several decades, the summoning of a journalist to appear before senior intelligence operatives on the order of the army was unheard of.[37]

Soon after these threats, in early March 2004, Dink was prosecuted on charges of "denigrating Turkishness." Notably, the charges were pressed not for the article about Sabiha Gökçen, presumably because that would have risked reigniting public debate about the possibility of her being an Armenian orphan, bestowed the claim a spectacular platform in the form of a public courtroom, and further risked the legal verification of the claim. Instead, Dink was prosecuted for a single sentence lifted out of a series of eight articles that he had written on "Armenian Identity," which he had published in his newspaper earlier in February 2004, before the piece about Gökçen came out. Dink's article series was an elaborate critique of Armenian diasporic identity.[38] The gist of the sentence that was isolated for the prosecution was that Armenians in the diaspora would do well to get over their obsession with Turkey and its denial of the genocide, instead to move on to form strong bonds with the Republic of Armenia. Dink suggested that the diasporic Armenian hatred of Turks was of a kind that poisoned the blood. Cleansing their blood of this hatred, he suggested, would help diasporic Armenians to move on to form a much-needed, genuine relationship with Armenia. But the actual sentence itself was, admittedly, badly formulated. What he wrote can be translated verbatim as "the clean blood that will replace that poisoned blood when it's rid of the Turk," but if taken out of context, it could also be read to mean "the clean blood that will replace that poisonous blood which will be let from the Turk." In other words, if entirely isolated from its context of meaning, this sentence could be misread as a call for bloodshed, for the killing of Turks; moreover, if one were to extend the misreading, the sentence could be understood as characterizing Turkish blood as poisonous. What further must have allowed the insistence on the toxic misreading was that Dink's sentence explicitly mimicked the famous finale of Atatürk's 1927 Address to the Turkish Youth, recognizable to anyone who went through any formal education in Turkey.[39] The nationalist bravado of the original must have helped distort Dink's meaning, and the fact that this famous statement of the founder of the republic appeared remixed in an Armenian Turkish writer's article about diaspora Armenians and their relationship to the Republic of Armenia must have struck as scandalous in itself. Indeed, one of the complaints filed with the prosecutor's office by a private citizen that effectively initiated Dink's prosecution for "denigrating Turkishness" referred to the scandalous "parody" of Atatürk's Address, and claimed that Dink was "attempting to disturb the peace by promoting racism, and by rousing the specters of ASALA terrorist organization and of Dashnakism, with the aim to provoke rebellion and terrorism among Armenian citizens who live peacefully in our beautiful country." The prosecution, then, was prompted by the claim that Dink was out to stir up old ghosts. In one sense, this wasn't entirely inaccurate, given Dink's extensive and courageous efforts to render the Armenian genocide addressable in Turkey's public sphere. But it included a fatally toxic lie about which ghosts were being called on, and for what purpose.

A number of inexplicable things happened during Dink's trial for "denigrating Turkishness." First, the court accepted all applicants for third-party participation in the case. Turkish criminal procedure does allow *partie civile* participation for those who claim to have been harmed by the alleged offense, and yet the common practice for courts is to greatly restrict participation to direct victims or, in cases of homicide, their family members. In this case, the court accepted the participation of a group of far-right lawyers and activists who claimed to have taken personal offense at their Turkishness being denigrated by Dink in the article he published. Allowed full representation in the trial, these people then went on to create a lynch mob atmosphere in and around the courtroom. This was not the only oddity. Following the request of the defense counsel, the court commissioned an expert report on whether the said offense had been committed; but then, in another bizarre move, it went on to completely ignore the report's findings and recommendations in its decision. The detailed report written by three academics chosen by the court itself had strongly argued that the single sentence did not constitute an offense when considered within its general context of meaning, and that the indictment was based on a gross misreading of that sentence. In convicting Dink and thus ignoring the report that it itself commissioned from its own sources, the court deviated from common practice in such cases, which is to decide on the basis of expert reports where available. Another peculiar aspect of the trial was the unwarranted delays that the court effected between receiving the expert testimony and passing its judgment, raising suspicions of political interference.[40]

When the case went to the ninth chamber of the Court of Cassation, the supreme court of appeal, the chamber upheld Dink's conviction, despite the argument of the public prosecutor to the contrary. In other words, in the appeal before the high court, both parties, the appellant (Dink) and the state (the public prosecutor allocated to the Court of Cassation as the representative of the people against Dink) agreed that the conviction was unsafe, and yet the Court of Cassation ignored their arguments, and upheld the lower court's conviction. The public prosecutor then further appealed the case to the General Council of the Court of Cassation, where it was dismissed in July 2006, sealing Dink's conviction and leaving no further avenues of redress other than the European Court of Human Rights (ECtHR). These decisions signaled, at best, a severe difficulty in reading comprehension starting right at the top of the judiciary, but more likely, direct political interference in the legal process and lack of judicial independence and impartiality. The ECtHR, to which Dink had applied shortly before his assassination, eventually, that is, more than three years after his death, found that not only had Dink's right to freedom of expression been breached, but also that the judicial harassment and the legal verdicts that he had been subjected to "had made him a target for extreme nationalists."[41]

Judicial harassment and legal processes did play a crucial role in the lead-up to Dink's assassination. In the foregoing brief overview of the immediate background of the killing, we can further discern the involvement of certain key state agencies in making Dink a target: the military, the intelligence agency, and the office of the governor of Istanbul. Information that surfaced in the immediate aftermath of the assassination allows us to add the police force and the gendarmerie to this mix, and implicates the army and the intelligence agency even further. This web of potential culpabilities corroborated what was an immediate and seemingly generally shared sense of the murder as state-sponsored. Within a few hours of the assassination, around ten thousand people had spontaneously gathered in Istanbul's central Taksim square and marched to the location of the assassination, with the time-honored slogan "the murderer state will be held to account,"[42] which continues to be chanted in memorial rallies for Dink and protests held outside the courthouses where the trial has been taking place. The latter context for the slogan is particularly aporetic, given the complicity of law in Dink's assassination. Indeed, perhaps the most difficult aspect of the aftermath of Dink's death is that justice must be sought in the same legal system and the same courts as those that paved the way for his killing.

Fourteen years after the assassination, in March 2021, the Dink murder trial culminated in an unsatisfactory second verdict. The trial first began in July 2007, a first verdict was reached by the court in January 2012, the Court of Cassation ordered a retrial in May 2013. Among the reasons for the high court's retrial decision was the inappropriateness of what had been the most controversial finding of the lower court: that the killing did not involve a criminal organization. The key significance of this initial ruling was that it denied what everybody knew: It disavowed the seemingly sprawling network of officials around the immediate culprits and limited culpability solely to the latter, casting the assassination as the deed of a handful of misguided youth motivated by ignorance and extreme nationalism. The finding of no organization in the first trial was partly due to a logic of discontinuity, disconnection, dissociation, and fragmentation that seemed to permeate the entire investigation and prosecution. The defendants were considered in isolation from their established and suspected connections with state agents and institutions, and any attempts to pursue a wider set of culpabilities were thus preempted. Of the police and gendarmerie officers who were implicated in the process, only a few were prosecuted, and not as part of the main trial in Istanbul concerning Dink's assassination, but in separate, isolated hearings in other cities.[43] Although the investigating prosecutors identified a number of officers within the gendarmerie and the police force who could be held liable for negligence, abuse of office, destroying, obscuring, tampering with, and fabricating evidence relating to the case, the courts refused to proceed with their prosecution.

The logic of discontinuity and dissociation was also quite stark in how the evidence was handled: Key CCTV footage of the incident was seized by the

Istanbul police and went missing under their watch; the gunman's communi-
cations on his mobile and over the internet immediately before and after the
assassination were never properly disclosed or investigated; certain suspect
figures caught by CCTV cameras at the time of the incident were not traced.
The court's written requests from official bodies such as the Intelligence Service and the High Council for Telecommunications were either left unanswered, or responded to with incomplete, incorrect, or entirely irrelevant
information. The lower court's refusal to identify the assassination as the deed
of an organization was thus the culminating point of this general operation of
dissociation. Notably, as the judges announced their finding of no organization
on the last day of the hearings, they forgot to pass verdict on one of the defendants. This lapsus memoriae, slip of the memory, served as a clearly recognizable symptom of the court's disavowal of what everybody knew. Something
was indeed missing in the verdict, and this was the role of the state in the assassination. The lapsus, performed by the court at the most crucial and highly
publicized moment of the trial, literalized the glaring absence by displacing
it. It too knew that something was missing. In turn, the performative disavowal
of state involvement served as a perverse avowal of the tradition of state-
sponsored killings.

The aporia of having to seek justice within the same legal order that facilitated Dink's killing was powerfully captured in a submission to the lower court
by the lawyers representing Dink's family in the murder proceedings. The
lawyers made this submission just before the court reached its first verdict.
They introduced the document into the case file, but also took turns to read
the hundred-page document to the court in its entirety. This was first and foremost a call on the court to extend and deepen the scope of its inquiry. The
submission worked against the court's logic of dissociation by providing a detailed account of the persecution campaign that culminated in Dink's assassination, flagging the involvement of state institutions and officials. The
document also served as a meticulous record of all of the procedural breaches
and errors involved in the investigation and the prosecution of the murder,
including the numerous failings of the court to which it was submitted. The
submission thus implicated the court, in no uncertain terms, in the overall
design of injustice that the family perceived, whereby the criminal justice process was understood to operate as an extension of the crime itself. The submission stated that the trial unfolded before the family as if it were a scripted
play, fully proofed to ensure that impunity remained the rule and that even
the accidental cracks were swiftly covered over by the various official bodies.[44]
The submission thus indicted the court simultaneously as it petitioned it for
justice. Its aporetic structure crystallizes the very aporia of the legal aftermath
of Dink's assassination.

But the submission goes even further than this and suggests that culpability for Dink's murder lies with the state itself, and then proceeds to calmly explain this claim. It is proposed that Hrant Dink's murder is located at the
intersection of Turkey's two entrenched state traditions: the tradition of political assassinations and that of Armenophobia.[45] The former is elaborated with
a chronological account from the late-Ottoman rule of the Committee of
Union and Progress up until the present, covering many instances of political
killings, so-called unknown perpetrator (but evidently state-sponsored) assassinations and massacres of the past decades. The latter, Armenophobia, is
explained by a genealogical account that begins with its reconsolidation in the
aftermath of the Russo-Ottoman War of 1877–78, incorporates the 1915 genocide, and traces its reconfigurations in the official ideology and legality of the
new republic. The explicit reference to the genocide (spelled out as such in
the document and thus read out to the court) is introduced in passing, calmly
and without fanfare, as if it were a noncontroversial designation on which there
is general consensus.

What does it mean to identify the culprit as "the state itself" in a criminal
court of the very state that is being accused? How can the suggestion that state
traditions have created the crime under consideration even begin to compute
within the logic of criminal procedure? How can a court register the claim
that the state represents not only a history of law but also a tradition of its trans-
gression? The Dink family's submission to the court reveals the aporia of de-
manding accountability for state crimes in a criminal legal setting, as well as
the difficulty of pinpointing a state that manifests itself not in its institutions
and services, nor in its legitimized forms of violence, but in its extralegal violence. The contextualization of the crime that the submission offers is irre-
ducibly incommensurable with legal procedure. Indeed, at times, the
submission reads as if it has no concern for whether it is registerable by the
court. Here, then, is an unusual rupture strategy,[46] not on behalf of the defense, but on behalf of the victim of the offense. The submission serves as an
"objection that cannot be heard," not because it challenges the foreclosure of
the political by the court, but because it goes to the heart of law-instituting
violence and identifies its legacies, including in the court's own practice and
operation itself.[47] Against the trial's operations of discontinuity and dissociation, it presents a counter-memory, a careful tracing of continuities of state
violence.

Following the Court of Cassation's May 2013 verdict ordering a retrial, the
case was reopened in September 2013. Then, finally in December 2015, owing
to the extensive efforts of the lawyers of Dink's family as intervening parties in
the case, a separate trial was launched, indicting a number of senior and ju-
nior public officials implicated in Dink's assassination and in obstructing the

provision of effective justice in the aftermath of the killing. The following month, in January 2016, the trial of the public officials was combined with the main trial. It wasn't clear whether this process was going anywhere for its first several months, until Turkey was hit by a coup attempt in July 2016. The coup attempt was allegedly organized by the Pennsylvania-based Turkish cleric Fetullah Gülen and his movement, a sprawling community of followers, who had been key allies of Tayyip Erdoğan's government until only a couple of years before, and had been allowed if not actively encouraged to secretly organize within key official bodies including the police and the judiciary. In the wake of the coup attempt, the number of defendants in the Dink trial grew further, due to an overeager wave of arrests mainly targeting members of the gendarmerie. In April 2017, a new indictment was issued in the Dink murder case, it listed Fetullah Gülen himself as the first on the list of defendants, and attributed the assassination of Dink to the Gülenist movement, characterizing it as the first action with which the organization launched its effort to overthrow the government. In other words, the resistance within the legal system to prosecuting Dink's assassination as a state-sponsored crime that implicated an organized network of extralegality across state institutions was partially suspended only due to convenience. Now that a new enemy had been identified as having infiltrated state institutions, the Dink trial could be used as an instrument of convenience for sake of the purge of this enemy who could be scapegoated with the assassination. And yet, as the March 2021 verdict shows, the legal process was not to go any further than the limits allowed by this convenience. For example, despite numerous well-founded and carefully elaborated requests by the lawyers intervening on behalf of Dink's family to hear the testimony of the intelligence officers who had been ordered by the army to threaten Dink in the Istanbul deputy governor's office in 2004, the court refused to call on these officials as witnesses, let alone as potential suspects. Thus the potential involvement of the intelligence service and, by implication, the armed forces in the process leading to Dink's assassination was consigned to legal oblivion.

There are several other ways in which the trial was engineered to produce oblivion: The panel of judges appointed to the retrial has changed four times in a case that has a voluminous file that would be difficult to master even if the same panel of judges were overseeing the process from its beginning to its end. The judges who decided the verdict did not hear the live testimony of the witnesses, the defendants, or the intervening parties. It is also highly likely that they have not caught up on the case file. An interim application to the Constitutional Court by Dink's family in 2019 in an attempt to reverse the omissions of the ongoing process in pursuing the full net of culpability came to naught. The high court ruled that this may be considered only after the process comes to a conclusion, and only after it goes to another appeals court.

Left to its own devices, law defers and forgets. It forgets to pass judgment on the defendant who stands before it. It forgets the evidence of the role of an organized network across state institutions in the production of the extralegal killing of a public figure who attempted to speak of the genocidal violence at its founding. Then it forgets that it forgot this evidence, but only when and to the extent that it is convenient to remember, and only momentarily and fragmentarily. When it remembers, it remembers only so as to be able to forget better. When it is reminded and asked not to forget, it rules to defer the remembering so that the forgetting will be deeper and darker.

"Genocide" as Counter-Memory

On the day of his funeral, Hrant Dink was commemorated by two hundred thousand people who marched some eight kilometers from the location of his killing to the cemetery where he was buried. Some had pinned on their chests a small piece of paper with the portrait of Dink, and below it, the year of his birth and the year of his death separated by a dash. At first glance, this seemed like a standard funeral badge, an object that has become common in urban ceremonies in Turkey over the past couple of decades. It has also become something of a battered cliché to use the infinity symbol "∞" in place of the year of death, to indicate that the deceased will live on in memory, forever. But in Dink's funeral march, one realized on second take that these badges were neither standard nor cliché. The span of Dink's life was represented not as "1954–2007," nor as "1954–∞" but as "1954–1915." This particularly powerful utilization of the rhetorical device of *hysteron proteron*, the inversion of ordinary temporal order, combined with the depiction of now as then is indicative of the strange logic and temporality of haunting. The time of haunting is time out of joint, as Jacques Derrida reminds us. For Derrida, haunting helps us see through the "doubtful contemporaneity of the present to itself." What he calls the "spectrality effect" "consists in undoing this opposition, or even this dialectic, between actual, effective presence and its other."[48] The temporal rupture depicted on these badges had various immediate resonances, ranging from the recognition of the state-sponsored nature of the killing to the understanding that Dink had been eliminated for working against genocide denialism so effectively so as to threaten to destabilize the official version of history concerning the Armenian "deportations." Most pertinently the badges said that the genocide was not over, that it was not even past. A similar trope that is often used in rallies held in memory of Hrant Dink ever since is

"1,500,000 + 1"—the former figure in reference to the estimated number of victims of the Armenian genocide, and the latter to Dink himself.

These figurations of the continuity of the Armenian genocide in Dink's assassination contain and make manifest an understanding that has become particularly pronounced in the aftermath of Dink's death: that the denial of the genocide is its perpetuation. The denial of genocide is its perpetuation, because the production of denial is an integral part of genocide. In one sense, the crime of genocide itself can be understood as a crime of denial, as captured by this formulation in an Advisory Opinion issued by the International Court of Justice on 28 May 1951:

> The origins of the Convention show that it was the intention of the
> United Nations to condemn and punish genocide as "a crime under
> international law" involving a denial of the right of existence of entire
> human groups, a denial which shocks the conscience of mankind and
> results in great losses to humanity.[49]

Then again, the denial in genocide is not only limited to the denial of the right of existence but also incorporates the denial of this denial. So the production of denial is an integral part of genocide also in the sense that built into the operation of genocide is the denial and destruction of its own factuality. We find a most staggering formulation of this insight in the work of philosopher and literary critic Marc Nichanian, who suggests with bitter irony that genocide is the "first philosophical machine of the twentieth century":

> The genocidal machine is, in its essence, a denegating and negationist
> machine; because those who invented it had already perfectly under-
> stood everything about the coming reign of the archive, consequently
> its operations can never become a fact. . . . The genocidal-denegating
> machine is dedicated to destroy *the very notion of fact*. Such is its most
> radical finality.[50]

What the inventors of this machine understood in perfectly understanding "the coming reign of the archive" was the way in which legal and historiographic methods of validation would come to determine "fact" as such, and that these methods partook of the same logic of destruction. We find an earlier formulation of this idea in a passage by Derrida in the postscript to "Force of Law" from which Nichanian borrows the title phrase of his book, "historiographic perversion." Here Derrida writes of how, in the "final solution," the Nazi regime,

> kept the archive of its destruction, produced simulacra of justificatory
> arguments, with a terrifying legal, bureaucratic, statist objectivity and

(at the same time, therefore) produced a system in which its logic, the logic of objectivity, made possible the invalidation and therefore the effacement of testimony and of responsibilities, the neutralization of the singularity of the final solution; in short, it produced the possibility of the historiographic perversion that has been able to give rise both to the logic of revisionism (to be brief, let us say of the Faurisson type) as well as a positivist, comparatist, or relativist objectivism (like the one now linked to the *Historikerstreit*) according to which the existence of an analogous totalitarian model and of earlier exterminations (the Gulag) explains the "final solution," even "normalizes" it as an act of war.[51]

The logic of objectivity is the logic of objectification and instrumentalization. We need not take recourse to the "Who, after all, speaks today of the annihilation of the Armenians?" quote questionably attributed to Adolf Hitler to capture the continuity between the Armenian genocide and the Holocaust. The continuity is there in the shape of the terror. The terror of genocide is that it is the "final solution" to a "question" that is posed as such, in such a way so as to bureaucratically reduce an entire group to a problematic object that in turn necessitates an objective resolution. This was formulated in precisely these terms already in 1916 in a diplomatic cable to the German chancellor by Germany's ambassador to the Ottoman Empire, Count Wolff Metternich, who wrote of the Ottoman government's "purpose to resolve the Armenian question by the destruction of the Armenian race."[52]

In speaking of the ways in which the denial of the genocide is its perpetuation, the memorial figurations of the continuity of the Armenian genocide in Dink's assassination (1954–1915; 1,500,000 + 1) may in one sense be deemed indicative of a captivity to the repeated return of the traumatic event.[53] But they are importantly also powerful means of articulating and thereby attempting to disrupt the ways in which law-positing violence is repeated and reenacted in law-preserving violence. Indeed, just as in Walter Benjamin's discussion of the death penalty as the spectacle by which law-positing violence makes itself known through law-preserving violence, in the assassination of Dink the genocidal origins of the republic "burst into the status quo, manifesting themselves in a fearsome manner."[54] But the various memorial-protest events held since Dink's assassination attempt to ensure that this obscene manifestation of originary violence is not the sole meaning of Dink's assassination, if one may provisionally suspend the shame of speaking of meaning in such a senseless killing. In an article written on the occasion of the centenary of the genocide, which was also the year he took office as one of Dink's successors as the editor in chief of *Agos*, Yetvart Danzikyan observes that Dink's murder had two meanings. It meant "both that 1915 still continues on one level, and paradoxically also that it can no longer continue."[55] In relation to the latter, he offers the accurate observation that it was in the wake of Dink's assassination that more and more people in Turkey's public sphere began to speak of the "Armenian Genocide" without qualifiers. This was because, he writes, "They knew one thing: What was there left to lose? Wasn't an enormous price already paid?" (250). Danzikyan ends his essay with the following note: "Whenever I, the writer of these lines, say the Armenian Genocide, in this article and others, in TV appearances, I experience a disquietude that is difficult to describe. There should not have been such a heavy price to be able to say this" (251).

The judicial harassment that Dink was subjected to was, as we have seen, instrumental in this "heavy price." He was subjected to this harassment precisely for his attempts to render the Armenian genocide speakable in Turkey's public sphere. Both Dink's murder and the legal aftermath of his murder, engineered to produce oblivion, crystallizes how genocidal violence haunts the legal order as its unspeakable foundation. Dink attempted to bring this unspeakable to the language of public discourse by probing the "silence walled up in the violent structure of the founding act,"[56] and seeking the cracks in the wall, such as by publicizing the "minor detail" that Atatürk's adopted daughter and national hero Sabiha Gökçen must have been an orphan of the genocide. Dink's attempt occasioned the return, repetition, and renewal of the violence of founding in his assassination. But as Danzikyan's essay indicates, there is more here, in that the designation "Armenian Genocide" itself has since become something of a memorial site. Its utterance today in Turkey's public sphere, exponentially more frequent than before Dink's killing, memorializes Dink, and with him the victims of the 1915 genocide: 1 + 1,500,000, as it were.

In its counter-memorial iterations, the utterance "Armenian Genocide" thus works as an attempt to performatively resignify the event beyond its historiographic and legalistic capture, which reduces it to a matter of, as Nichanian puts it, "the three essential elements that constitute any self-respecting genocide: the intent, the organization, and the execution. The precise intention, the centralized organization, the systematic execution."[57] Insofar as it is driven by an objective logic of validation that was foreseen and forestalled by the inventors of the genocidal-denegating machine, this legalistic capture of "genocide" repeats and perpetuates the destruction of the factuality of genocide. As Nichanian states, "Each of the extermination projects conducted over the course of this century has been—among other things, yet perhaps essentially—a challenge directed at law" (20). Legal methods and procedures of validation partake in the same logic of objectivity, the "legal, bureaucratic and statist objectivity" that when taken to its limit produces "solutions" and "resolutions" such as the genocides of the twentieth century. Even when we bracket out the unsavory recognition that law is often instrumentalized to facilitate genocidal violence (some argue that such law is never law as such, as it is not the "law" of the "Rule of Law"), law must be understood as always already implicated in genocidal violence in that it assists the inscription of genocidal violence with its own invalidation. Law produces erasure, forgetting, and oblivion, but no closure. It can, however, occasion the emergence of powerful sites of counter-memory. It cannot but make space for the kind of counter-account that Dink's family's 2011 submission to the court presented. And it cannot prevent the liberation of the designation of "genocide" from its legalistic capture and its re-signification as a site of counter-memory.

I have attempted in this chapter to trace the co-implications of law and violence by seeking the specters of the Tehlirian trial in legal and violent events that preceded and succeeded it. As a consideration of the fragmentary legal aftermaths of the Armenian genocide and its atemporal histories of violence, my account also touched on the significance of biographical threads, as well as the erasures, misreadings, misrepresentations, and the black, white, and gray lies that inevitably attend the work of "precedenting" in international law. I paused on the assassination of Hrant Dink as one event that bears the trace of the Tehlirian trial, and an all too untimely spectral formation, a haunting presence that comprises a particularly telling amalgam of past political and legal violence. Both the violent event itself and its legal aftermath powerfully speak of the continuities of law-positing violence in law-preserving violence. What we can further discern in the legal aftermath of this assassination is the seemingly inevitable failure of law to either break free from this cycle of continuity or to shift gears altogether to serve a memorial function. Those who invest in the redemptive pedagogic, historiographic, didactic, memorial, and therapeutic functions of law may say that such a conclusion is foregone in a domestic context, where the assassination in question brought back the ghosts of the genocidal violence that founded the very legal order. But things are not so straightforward, as we will see in the next chapter, in the consideration of the first trial before the European Court of Human Rights concerning the denial of a genocide other than the Holocaust, namely the Armenian genocide outside of its "domestic context." Indeed, even with "memory laws," or laws formulated with an explicit memorial function, it is possible to end up in denial.

6

Law of Denial

The Armenian Genocide before the European Court of Human Rights

When the French National Assembly passed a draft bill to criminalize the denial of the Armenian genocide in 2006, Hrant Dink declared that if this bill were to come into effect, he would travel to France to breach it by publicly denying the genocide.[1] At the time of this statement, Dink had been in the spotlight in Turkey for his efforts to render the Armenian genocide publicly addressable. As detailed in the preceding chapter, he had received explicit death threats from Turkish ultranationalists who held protests in front of his office building, and he was subjected to a campaign of judicial harassment that took the form of a series of criminal investigations and prosecutions for "denigrating Turkishness" and other crimes of expression. In his attempts to undo the strange amalgam of silences and hyperproductive denials surrounding the Armenian genocide in the public and official discourses in Turkey, Dink was both particularly effective as a magnetic and compelling spokesperson and particularly vulnerable as a member of Turkey's now minuscule Armenian population.

Why did Dink object to France criminalizing the denial of the Armenian genocide, when he had been criminalized in Turkey for speaking of the genocide and for working to render it speakable? Why would he take the risk of being prosecuted as a negationist in France, when he had taken so many risks for the sake of the public avowal of the Armenian genocide in Turkey? Dink's own explanation of his position on the French bill was couched in terms of freedom of expression: Just as one had to resist criminalization for speaking of the genocide in Turkey, one had to resist criminalization for denying the genocide in France. It would, however, be a mistake to interpret Dink's position as a form of free speech absolutism that is willfully blind to the contexts of political, structural, and objective violence in which ostensibly "free" speech circulates and onto which it latches.[2] To the contrary, Dink objected to the bill precisely because of a certain political acuity—he thought it would aggravate existing conflicts by reinforcing and further entrenching polarized positions on the issue.[3] Indeed, the immediate political context of the bill, namely France's questionable opposition to Turkey's joining the European Union, and the popular resentment that this produced in Turkey at the time, meant that the bill, rather than serving the purpose of doing justice to the genocide itself, offered the genocide up as a new weapon in a contemporary conflict. Thus instead of rendering the genocide addressable, not just as historical fact but also in terms of its presences today so that reconciliation and reparations may be in sight one day, the draft bill made the genocide unaddressable in brand-new ways by engineering a new political present for it, re-politicizing its acknowledgment and denial according to a contemporary battle map, and potentially contributing new circuits and patterns of violence to its repertoire—for example, by pointing out Turkey's Armenian minority population as a target for the resentment that had been building up in the EU accession process.[4]

Doing justice to the past requires a political and theoretical attunement to the ways in which law, in purportedly attempting to address past political violence, inscribes itself into contemporary contexts of violence. This may be limited to an analysis of how law is an effect of and affects the political, or in the above example, how certain political expediencies contribute to the formulation of memory laws, and how these laws in turn can become instrumentalized, ostensibly against their "general spirit," to aggravate existing political conflicts. However, we may further refine this attunement in a critical register, suspending our common assumptions about the "general spirit" of memory laws, to instead question what it is about memory laws that renders them particularly vulnerable to political instrumentalization. In the above example, the attempted imposition of a universalized truth about the Armenian genocide, laudable as it may be in itself, interpenetrates with, and becomes subsumed by the longue durée of a European universalism that is exclusionary, interventionist, and often experienced by Europe's others as hypocritical.[5] What is it that so easily lends memory laws to political agendas and temporalities that are seemingly beyond their own purview?

There has been a reanimation of debates concerning the legal regulation of public memory in Europe.[6] A key catalyst for this was the 2008 European Union Framework Decision, which called for each member state to criminalize "publicly condoning, denying or grossly trivializing crimes of genocide, crimes against humanity and war crimes."[7] Just as in the earlier episodes of scholarship on the subject, which had mainly clustered around high-profile cases of so-called revisionist historians, in this more recent body of work there is a general consensus on the political histories that have rendered memory laws necessary, desirable, or at least understandable. The common points of reference here are World War II, the Holocaust, and the consequent international legal processes, including the emergence of a new regime of human rights. Generally, the current entanglements of denialist or other forms of provocative speech with hate speech are evaluated against this background. With the history of law thus backgrounded, the questions that come to the fore in this literature tend to revolve around issues such as the challenge of assimilating the legal imposition of historical truths in liberal democratic frameworks, the problem of balancing the need to protect freedom of expression with the need to prevent hate speech, the question of the proportionality of using criminal law to regulate public memory, and the potential backlash and antagonization that such regulation could create. However, for a more refined analysis, it may be not only worthwhile but also necessary to foreground the background, and to reflect on the legal effects of the political histories that are understood to justify contemporary memory laws. This would be a task of attempting "to identify . . . what is forgotten in law, and to understand the law's mode of justifying what is forgotten," in the words of Emilios Christodoulidis, who writes of the need to find ways of resisting what he calls "law's immemorial," that is, "the logic of a certain concealment of *what* is forgotten and of *that* it is forgotten."[8] Such a shift of perspective is vital for addressing the ways in which law's claim of mastery over past political violence is undermined by frequent reversals of that relationship of mastery—reversals that enable the violence of the law, including its symbolic violence, to become easily incorporated into *longues durées* of political violence, rather than mastering them, settling them, or providing closure.

This chapter aims to pursue such a critique, taking as its immediate focus the European Court of Human Rights (ECtHR) case of *Perinçek v. Switzerland*, with occasional forays into debates around the criminalization of Armenian genocide denialism in France. The *Perinçek* case concerned Switzerland's imposition of criminal sanctions on a visiting Turkish politician who publicly denied that the Armenian genocide was a genocide. At the ECtHR, the applicant claimed that Switzerland thus breached his right to freedom of expression. The case concluded in 2015 after producing two judgments, first by the Second Chamber, and then by the Grand Chamber of the ECtHR.[9] However, although they both found for the applicant, the Chamber judgment and the Grand Chamber judgment had very different lines of reasoning, and notably different conceptions regarding the relationship between law and history. I proceed in this chapter by tracing the shifting status of "history" and "historians" in these two judgments, and paying attention to the deferrals, disclaimers, and ellipses that structure law's relation to history and historiography. An insight that the Perinçek case provides is that insofar as "genocide" remains a legal term of art with a very narrow definition, its denial, when couched in legalistic terms, effects law's inadvertent complicity with the politics of genocide denial. In other words, the Perinçek case can be read as the substantiation of Marc Nichanian's important observation that "all genocidal projects of the twentieth century have been first of all challenges to law."[10] As an act that contains within it the destruction of its own factuality, genocide preempts and forestalls the legal methods and procedures of validation that it would be subject to: "The genocidal will, in other words, is that which wants to abolish the fact in and through the very act that establishes the fact" (11). But this insight can be pushed even further to interrogate law's own denials that emerge from its performative structure and augment this complicity. In the Perinçek case, I identify these denials as produced by what remains unresolved in law's understanding of historicity (most importantly its own historicity as a performative sedimentation), and by its conflicted interpretation of its own role vis-à-vis the task of historiography. I trace how these denials proliferate law's symbolic violence, rendering it unable to respond to historical violence without inscribing itself into a history of violence—a process regarding which it remains in denial.

The Envoy

First, a note on the protagonist of the ECtHR case. Doğu Perinçek is a socialist-turned-ultranationalist politician who has been on Turkey's political scene for more than half a century. He first emerged as a socialist student leader affiliated with the Workers Party of Turkey (Türkiye İşçi Partisi) in the late 1960s while he was completing his doctorate in law—a qualification that would come to have some significance at the ECtHR. Perinçek then became the founder and leader of a Maoist party that has had various official names over the past decades but is generally referred to as the Aydınlık (Enlightenment) group, after the title of their periodical. Following the 1971 and 1980 coups d'état, Perinçek spent a total of seven years in prison for his role as the chairman of this party. In the late 1990s, his party made a conspicuous shift in its political profile and took a distinctly statist and ultranationalist turn. This led to complete reversals of the party's positions on critical issues such as the Kurdish right to self-determination, the legitimacy of the Turkish army's invasion of Cyprus in 1974, and indeed, the criminality of the deportations and massacres of Ottoman Armenians during World War I.[11] As part of this shift, the party began to make alliances with a number of far-right groups and figures. One outcome of these associations was the prosecution and conviction of Perinçek and a number of his fellow party members in the infamous Ergenekon trial (in session 2009–13), also known as Turkey's "deep state" trial, where defendants were effectively accused of state-sponsored crimes against the state.[12] Perinçek was sentenced to aggravated life imprisonment for founding and leading an armed terrorist organization, attempting to overthrow the government by force, inciting an armed uprising against the government, and obtaining classified documents, among other offenses, and spent six years in prison from 2008 to 2014.[13]

One alliance that Perinçek's party made with the far right in the lead-up to the Ergenekon process was the so-called Talat Pasha Committee, formed to serve as a platform for genocide denial, and named after the Ottoman statesman widely deemed the architect of the 1915 Armenian genocide. It was as part of this campaign that Perinçek and his allies traveled to several cities in Switzerland in 2005 to deny the genocide publicly, in order to test Switzerland's memory laws. They managed to provoke a criminal legal response: Perinçek was convicted under a Swiss law that forbids the denial of "a genocide," formulated in these vague terms because the legislators were keen to avoid Holocaust exceptionalism, even though it was Holocaust denialism that initially triggered the legislative debates.[14] Perinçek's conviction was upheld through two appeals, first by a cantonal court, then by the federal court. Perinçek applied to the ECtHR with a number of claims, the most important being that his conviction constituted a breach of his right to freedom of expression under Article 10 of the European Convention on Human Rights. The Turkish government was granted representation as a third party intervener. The Second Chamber ruled in Perinçek's favor in December 2013, and on Switzerland's request the case was referred to the Grand Chamber. At this stage, various additional third party interveners were allowed, including the Armenian and French governments, Turkey's Human Rights Association, the Istanbul-based Truth Justice Memory Center, and a number of other NGOs and private persons. Importantly, due to his involvement in the Ergenekon case in Turkey, Perinçek had been subject to a travel ban that would have barred him from attending the Grand Chamber hearing of the ECtHR in Strasbourg in January 2015. However, less than two weeks before the hearing, Perinçek's travel ban was lifted by a court, expressly to allow him to attend the hearing in Strasbourg. In its ruling, the Istanbul heavy penal court stated:

> The hearing at the ECtHR is not just about the personal views of the defendant on the Events of 1915, but about whether or not the ECtHR

is going to accept the official theses of the Turkish state concerning the 1915 Armenian event.[15]

Thus, although on trial in Turkey for state-sponsored crimes against the Turkish state, Perinçek was sanctioned as an envoy for the Turkish state to represent its position on historical state crimes.

The fact that Perinçek's case went all the way to the ECtHR Grand Chamber was a significant political victory for the so-called Talat Pasha Committee: This successful legal provocation entailed the ECtHR's spectacular instrumentalization in denialism in the centenary of the Armenian genocide. The high profile of the case allowed Perinçek and his allies to claim in their media campaign that this would be the case that decides whether or not there was a genocide. The campaign was effective: The ECtHR Grand Chamber hearing was widely covered in the Turkish media as *the trial* that would "put an end" to the so-called "hundred-year-old genocide lie." It also received coverage internationally, mostly owing to Amal Clooney's celebrity presence at the hearing as part of the team representing Armenia. The Grand Chamber published its judgment on 15 October 2015, also ruling in Perinçek's favor and finding a breach of Article 10 by Switzerland. Back in Turkey, Perinçek and his party celebrated the judgment, claiming in bold PR campaigns: "We put an end to the genocide lie."

The Judge, the Historian, and the Politician

While the *Perinçek* case was obviously never meant to and did not result in a judgment about the facticity of the Armenian genocide, Perinçek's application did exploit a number of indeterminacies concerning what can be legally acknowledged as historical fact, and it is precisely this on which the political instrumentalization of the case turned. These indeterminacies can be understood as pertaining to that which remains unresolved in law's relationship to history, and more specifically, law's self-exposure to a riddle that it is ultimately unable to solve: Who decides the facticity of "historical fact"? Is it the judge (i.e., a competent court), the historian (i.e., a general scholarly consensus over facts), or the politician (i.e., a statement of recognition by a political body)? This is a riddle that runs through the *Perinçek* case, and bedevils in particular the 2013 judgment by the Second Chamber. Especially noteworthy is the way in which the judgment, in its inability to alter the terms of the question or to properly suspend it, falls into the trap of this riddle, producing a series of denials of its own, which in turn bind it to the denialist agenda on which it was meant to deliver judgment. Two dynamics intertwine to produce this consequence: first, the Second Chamber judges' inability to dissociate themselves from the markedly legalistic arguments of the applicant, and second, the effects of what may be interpreted as a form of Holocaust exceptionalism in ECtHR's jurisprudence.

The Second Chamber judges had to respond to Perinçek's thoroughly legalistic argument. Perinçek argued that when he said "The Armenian genocide is an international lie," he was not denying the reality or the factuality of the massacres and deportations of Armenians in 1915 and the following years— he admitted that these took place. What he took issue with was the designation of these deportations and massacres as genocide. He argued that genocide is a legal designation, defined by international law; therefore, questioning, indeed denying, the applicability of this legal designation to the events in question should not be subject to sanction. Note that Perinçek's argument is not a new one in the arsenal of denialism pertaining to the Armenian genocide:[16] Unlike Holocaust denalism which tends to target the facts themselves and the evidentiary framework (i.e., "there were no gas chambers"), Armenian genocide denialism often resorts to this more legalistic argument.[17]

This legalistic or "interpretative denial"[18] is enabled by the fact that "genocide" is a legal term of art that was coined three decades after the events in question, and has a very narrow application, requiring a specific intent "to destroy, in whole or in part, a national, ethnical, racial or religious group." The argument goes that unlike the Holocaust, which was recognized at the International Military Tribunal in Nuremberg against the major war criminals, there has been no judgment by a competent court that has established the deportations and massacres of Ottoman Armenians in 1915 as a "genocide." Thus went Perinçek's argument at the ECtHR: The fundamental difference between his case and other ECtHR cases concerning denialism was that the latter concerned the Holocaust, which "had been categorized by the Nuremberg Tribunal as a crime against humanity."[19] Here, a sleight of words obscures an inconvenience that the legal history of the word "genocide" poses for a strictly legalist approach. It was not "genocide" but indeed "crimes against humanity" that figured as a legal category in the IMT process, which preceded the 1948 UN Convention of the Prevention and Punishment of the Crime of Genocide by two years. The IMT indictment evoked the word "genocide" only once, and used it merely descriptively rather than as a legal category,[20] whereas the final judgment did not even mention it once.[21] In other words, strictly speaking, the Holocaust was not legally categorized as a "genocide" at Nuremberg, and thus this legalistic brand of interpretative denialism, if argued *ad absurdum*, would involve taking issue with the legal characterization of the Holocaust itself as a genocide.[22] Another inconvenience posed by the legal history of the term "genocide" is that, even though the UN Genocide Convention was undoubtedly triggered by the Holocaust, its preamble avoids attributing an exceptional legal status to the Holocaust, instead noting "that at all periods of history genocide has inflicted great losses on humanity."

The interpretative denialism regarding the Armenian genocide further exploits the "specific intent" requirement of the legal category of genocide as articulated in the 1948 Convention and in its later iterations, utilizing the fact that unlike the Nazi regime, the Ottoman authorities did not diligently keep but instead worked to destroy the documents and archives of the evidence of their "intent to destroy, in whole or in part, a national, ethnical, racial, or religious group." Indeed, the legal category's requirement of a "specific intent" has, to some extent, shaped the contemporary historiography of the Armenian genocide, with historians avowedly attempting to trace the genocidal intent in the archives, looking for traces of evidence of Talat Pasha's criminal intention as they work against state-sponsored denialist research.[23] Thus, Perinçek in his application submitted

> that "genocide" was a clearly defined international crime . . . which required any one of the specified acts to have been "committed with intent to destroy, in whole or in part, a national, ethnical, racial or religious group" (*dolus specialis*) [and according to the International Court of Justice] that the onus was on the applicant party to prove an allegation of genocide and that the requisite standard of proof was high.[24]

The challenge that this legalistic denial posed for the Chamber judgment was compounded by the fact that *Perinçek* was the first case at the ECtHR concerning the denial of the Armenian genocide. The court's jurisprudence on denialism has developed mainly through cases involving the denial of the Holocaust, or revisionism of facts and events surrounding the Nazi regime and its collaborators.[25] Significant for *Perinçek* is a formulation that has emerged in relevant ECtHR case law concerning "clearly established historical facts," the negation of which is excluded from the protection of Article 10 governing the right to freedom of expression, on the basis of Article 17 which prohibits the abuse of rights. In ECtHR decisions and judgments, the usual form this formulation takes is that what is being denied or "revised" is deemed to or deemed not to "belong to the category of clearly established historical facts— such as the Holocaust—whose negation or revision would be removed from the protection of Article 10 by Article 17."[26] The rule has come under scrutiny in legal scholarship for building an "exceptional regime" in ECtHR's jurisprudence by affording Article 17 a content-based "guillotine effect" in Article 10 applications.[27] More pertinently for our discussion, the category of "clearly established historical facts" effects the legal reinscription and reproduction of a form of Holocaust exceptionalism, so that although proffered as exemplary ("such as"), the Holocaust becomes paradigmatic. As Laurent Pech writes,

> While the court uses the plural, the sole Holocaust has been found to constitute a clearly established historical fact, and the court has yet to precisely explain when exactly a historical fact does become "clearly established."[28]

Indeed, once the jurisprudence begins to revolve around a notion of "clearly established historical facts," the riddle inevitably imposes itself: Is it the judge, the historian, or the politician who shall determine when a historical fact becomes clearly established? Pitted against this category of "clearly established historical facts," for which the Holocaust provides the singular example, are facts which are deemed to be subject to "ongoing debate between historians," a category that the Chamber judgment borrows[29] from previous case law.[30] As Pech writes, "The question then becomes: how can a court determine when a debate between historians has ended?"[31] ECtHR's case law leaves this question unanswered.

It is important to note that Armenian genocide denialism also often capitalizes on this notion of the interminability of historical debate. "Let's set up a joint Turkish-Armenian panel of historians," Turkish officials exclaim.[32] "#LetHistoryDecide" reads a skywriting for the denialist campaign over New York City on the 101st anniversary of the genocide. "I have 90 kilos of documents in evidence!" Perinçek gleefully claims at the Grand Chamber hearing, and complains that the Swiss courts were unwilling to consider this archive that would prove that the genocide is no genocide.[33] These are perfect examples of what Nichanian refers to as "historiographic perversion." As we have seen, for Nichanian the perversion is symptomatic of a much deeper problem concerning the "truth of the facts" in the aftermath of genocide. Nichanian understands the interminable deferral of historical judgment on the question of "genocide" as a product of the genocidal machinery itself. The genocidal act is one that necessarily, by its nature, effects an epistemic crisis: As an act of negation, "genocide is destined to annul itself as fact."[34] Writing in the aftermath of a trial in which the defendant, the orientalist historian Bernard Lewis, took recourse to the same brand of interpretative denial as Perinçek's, Nichanian states:

In the genocidal and denegating will, it is not the qualification of the events that is in question. . . . In the last resort, what is at stake is the factuality of the fact, its reality. At stake is the universal procedure of validation. But the events have been invalidated from the start, in their very eventiality. *That is what constitutes the genocidal fact* (30, emphasis in the original)

For Nichanian, "perverse historians play with this or ginary invalidation, they wager on it, they repeat it and extend it" (30), and thus the deferral to historical inquiry (e.g., #LetHistoryDecide) is in itself productive of denialism.

As Nichanian shows in his discussion of the case, the judgment in the civil action brought against Bernard Lewis in France in 1994 is interesting to consider in terms of the tug-of-war that law stages between the judge and the historian on the question of who has jurisdiction over historical facts. The action against Lewis was the final point of the controversy triggered by his statements in a *Le Monde* interview effectively trivializing the Armenian genocide. In the trial he argued along the interpretative/legalistic denialist line and stated that what he denied was not the fact that one and a half million Armenians perished during the deportations, but that these events should be characterized as genocide. The High Court of Paris ruled against Lewis and found him liable for damages, while clarifying that this was not on the basis of the necessity to characterize the massacres and deportations of 1915 as a genocide. The court took recourse to the usual disclaimer on the matter, stating that "the courts do not have as their mission the duty to arbitrate or settle arguments or controversies these events may inspire and to decide how a particular episode of national or world history is to be represented or characterized." Instead, the verdict was based on the finding that Lewis "concealed information contrary to his thesis" and "failed in his duties of objectivity and prudence by offering unqualified opinions on such a sensitive subject," and thereby "unfairly rekindled the pain of the Armenian community."[35] In the Lewis judgment, the combination of the court's rejection of jurisdiction over history and its finding of a failure of objectivity constituted a central indeterminacy: The judge deferred to the historian on the question of veracity, while passing judgment on the historian's methods of verification, which in turn was meant not to be interpreted as a reclamation of the jurisdiction over veracity. Let us also note the emphasis on the "sensitivity" of the subject and the offense of having "rekindled the pain" of the Armenian community—we have seen this movement from the question of historical fact to that of psychological effect in the trial of Soghomon Tehlirian, and we will see it again in the final ECtHR judgment in *Perinçek*.

The indeterminacy that we see in the Lewis judgment on the question of who decides veracity finds a renewed articulation in the Second Chamber judgment in *Perinçek*. The judgment is clearly lured by the appeal of the legalism of the applicant's argument; in fact, it seems to have bought it wholesale. Notably, when Perinçek argued the "no judgment by a competent court" line, he suggested that he could not have expected to be prosecuted for challenging the legal designation, especially not as a doctor of law, with his "legally-oriented mind."[36] The judges of the Second Chamber indeed do seem to have perceived the appellant as a peer of sorts, a fellow jurist. In the brief summary of the judgment it is twice stated that Perinçek "is a doctor of law"; in the full text of the judgment, the fact that Perinçek has a PhD in law comes up now and again, signaling an identification and thus slight unease.[37] Thus Perinçek flirts with the Second Chamber judges: I'm like you, a doctor of law, I can take issue with legal designations and interpretations. The judges requite Perinçek's advances; the recognition of Perinçek as a doctor of law, and the identification of the issue at stake as the freedom to debate a legal characterization, determines the gist of the judgment of the Second Chamber: He is a doctor of law, he is one of us, he is free to publicly discuss and debate the appropriate legal characterization of this or that act.

What compounds this approach, as I have indicated, is an exceptional status granted to the Holocaust, as the judges take caution to distinguish the *Perinçek* case from cases involving Holocaust denialism. According to the judgment of the Second Chamber, the case is distinct in three ways: First, Holocaust deniers were denying the facts and not their legal characterization; second, their denial "concerned crimes perpetrated by the Nazi regime that had resulted in convictions with a clear legal basis"; and third, "the historical facts challenged by the applicants in those cases had been found by an international court to be clearly established."[38] Apparently, what makes "fact" is a finding by an international court, with a clear legal basis. Here, the basic fact that the legal bases of the charges and convictions in Nuremberg, a "successor trial" in Otto Kirchheimer's taxonomy, owed their "clarity" not so much to the "thereness of law" as Judith Shklar might put it, but rather to military victory, is written out of history.[39]

Even though the judgment repeatedly takes recourse to the usual disclaimer on its task not being to settle matters of history (e.g., "The Court further reiterates that while it is an integral part of freedom of expression to seek historical truth, it is not the Court's role to settle historical issues"),[40] it cannot quite bring itself to grant this power to anyone else either. In its response to Switzerland's argument that there is a general academic consensus that the events of 1915 constituted genocide, the judgment comes out as skeptical:

It is even doubtful that there can be a "general consensus," particularly
among academics, about events such as those in issue in the present
case, given that historical research is by definition subject to controversy and dispute and does not really lend itself to definitive conclusions or the assertion of objective and absolute truths.[41]

To paraphrase, the court, in effect, says: We have nothing authoritative to say
about history; that is up to the historians. But we can say that historians in turn
can have nothing conclusive to say about history because by definition historical research does not lend itself to the assertion of objective and absolute truths.
The matter rests undecided and can therefore be endlessly questioned, especially by a doctor of law who is taking issue with the legal characterization as
such regarding events whose historical status has not been judged as objective
history, that is, as "clearly established facts" by law, which in turn can't have
anything authoritative to say about history unless explicitly enlisted and competent to do so, because that's up to the historians, who in turn can have nothing
conclusive to say about history. . . . The combined effect of legalism, Holocaust
exceptionalism, and historical skepticism in the Chamber judgment produces
an endless deferral which both empowers the judge with jurisdiction over history more than the historian, but at the same time functions as a disavowal of
that jurisdiction so that the deferral itself comes to effect denial. Inadvertently,
the judgment performs the very function that it was enlisted for by the applicant, namely, casting doubt on the factuality of genocide.

How can this particular form of denial-by-deferral be countered? Styled as
an archive of the self-evidence of the Armenian genocide, the dissenting opinion penned by two of the Second Chamber judges takes recourse to documentation, evidence, proof. But it is important to be cognizant that such
archival recourse is always already enlisted and disempowered by the logic of
denialism. The very engagement in the effort of validation fails to recognize
that the opponent is "playing another genre,"[42] and fuels the obscene hyper-
productivity of denialism: "90 kilos of documents!" Perinçek exclaims; "200
kilos of working documents," Faurisson claims. Marc Nichanian has a different proposal. For him, memory laws are precisely what is needed for countering denial-by-deferral. Writing against the background of intensified controversy
concerning the Gayssot Act, which criminalizes the denial of the Holocaust
in France, and responding to contentions that the act unjustly usurps the historian's jurisdiction, Nichanian argues for the necessity of such laws in the
following terms:

There had to be a law to recognize something that no one had
recognized until then, because no one had needed to recognize it,

namely, that—in the extreme conditions of humanity . . . *only the law can tell the fact.* . . . The law should certainly not intervene in the interpretation of an event. Yet it has no choice but to intervene in order to posit a fact as such, there where the fluctuation of the very notion of fact could lead to generalized insanity.[43]

Thus for Nichanian, in the face of an epistemic crisis that is caused by the extreme conditions of the violence of the genocide, which is in turn aggravated by the endless historicist deferral of determination, by keeping the object open to disputation and re-contextualization, law has to play a decisive and interventionist role. It must say, this is the fact, this is genocide, denying it is illegal.

However, we may need to question whether this appeal to the performative power of law to institute the fact by naming alone can fully resonate in a scene of law. Legal performatives cannot quite operate in the mode that Nichanian proposes, that is, explicitly and unapologetically instituting facts by naming alone. The common register for law's performativity is not, and cannot be "it is because I say so," but it is rather, "it is, because it self-evidently is." In other words, as I have discussed in some detail in Chapter 2, it is necessary for law to pass its performatives off as constatives, propping up this disguise by a scaffolding of self-evidence and conventionality. Tellingly, the wording of the Gayssot Act actually excludes Nichanian's rationale for it. The Act criminalizes the negation of "crimes against humanity" as defined by the IMT Charter and as established by international and French courts on that basis. Thus previous performative legal moments, here the retrospective institution of "crimes against humanity" by the IMT Charter and subsequent trials, are rendered not only constative, but also non-negatable, by recourse to their own definitional authority in a circular self-referentiality.[44]

In this spirit, a recent review of the Gayssot Act by the French Constitutional Council[45] refused to allow the Armenian genocide within its scope, even though the French National Assembly publicly recognized the genocide in 2001 by passing a bill to this effect, and the court could have relied on that as a basis to take as given the "truth of the fact" of genocide. Earlier, the French Constitutional Council, in responding to a proposed bill criminalizing Armenian genocide denialism on the basis of the 2001 political recognition, declared the bill unconstitutional, stating that "a legislative provision with the purpose of 'recognizing' a crime of genocide cannot in itself have the normative scope attaching to the law."[46] While there is indeed a normative difference between a law (or "legislative provision") that recognizes a crime and thus memorializes it, and a law that criminalizes the denial of a crime, the significant point here is that a politically produced legal recognition of genocide as fact (i.e., a remembrance law enacted by a parliament) does not legally resonate as weighty a sign of self-evidence as a finding by a competent court as to the fact of genocide. In this context, Emilios Christodoulidis's argument in "Law's Immemorial" finds a specific articulation. He writes:

> Law's memorial events cannot stand independent of law, . . . memory is always-already institutional memory and . . . thus it cannot break free of the "trappings" of the institution because both time and eventhood are determined institutionally . . . and this undercuts . . . the attempt to call upon the institution of law itself to articulate and guarantee the truth of a memory that is purportedly independent of it.[47]

The "trappings" of law's self-referentiality reinscribes, in this case, the Armenian genocide as immemorial, despite the political institution of its recognition as a law.

The Swiss judgments that convicted Perinçek had actually sufficed with a barely disguised and indeed political rather than legal performative institution of genocide as fact. The Swiss judgments avowed that the matter was technically officially unsettled: There had not been an international tribunal recognizing the Armenian genocide; the majority of states had not passed laws recognizing the genocide; and the Federal Council of Switzerland itself had advised the National Council against officially recognizing the genocide. Nevertheless, they relied on the existence of what they referred to as a "broad consensus within the community [i.e., the Swiss public] which is reflected in the political declarations and is itself based on a wide academic consensus as to the classification of the events of 1915 as genocide."[48] The public opinion says so, therefore it is. But it was precisely this political category of consensus that became a problem at the ECtHR, especially in the judgment of the Second Chamber, which dedicates a section to this notion, titled "Method adopted by the domestic authorities to justify the applicant's conviction: the notion of consensus."[49] The judgment finds the said method "questionable."[50]

Judging the Presence of the Past

One way of countering legalism's denial-by-deferral is to ask for law's withdrawal, to argue that if the Court claims not to have jurisdiction over history, then the Court must remain silent vis-à-vis history. This was the gist of Armenia's submission to the Grand Chamber as a third party intervener. Rather than arguing for Switzerland or against Perinçek, Armenia intervened to "correct the record" and "correct certain misjudgments of fact."[51] It agreed with "Pe-rinçek and the government of Turkey that the Court is not required to determine whether the massacres suffered by the Armenians amounted to genocide"[52] and took the Second Chamber to task for exceeding its stated jurisdiction and hence indirectly casting doubt on the facticity of the Armenian genocide. Although Perinçek's counsel Laurent Pech "could not identify any relevant legal arguments for settling the pending case in Armenia's submission,"[53] the Grand Chamber's judgment shows that this intervention was audible, because the judgment is extremely cognizant of what it does and does not say about history.

In coming to the same conclusion as the Second Chamber that there should not have been criminal sanctions imposed on Perinçek for his utterances, the Grand Chamber in its reasoning consciously avoids any pronouncements to do with the historical record. It achieves this by addressing the judgment to the present life of the denialist utterances, that is, the present life of the history that is being denied: The focus is shifted away from the constative content of denialist utterances to their perlocutionary effects. This happens in two movements. The first is the kind of movement we have seen at a critical point in the trial of Soghomon Tehlirian and in the judgment of the Paris court on Bernard Lewis: The issue is transformed into a matter of perception and psychic injury. The judgment speaks of how "many of the descendants of the victims of the events of 1915 and the following years—especially those in the Armenian diaspora—construct [their] identity around the perception that their community has been the victim of genocide."[54] It then acknowledges that freedom of expression may be interfered with to protect that identity. Here we have a shift from history to memory, insofar as past violence is handled as a sedimentation in the form of ethnic identity. The judgment recognizes the presence of this particular formation of memory rather than deeming it a matter of past violence whose historical, factual, legal status is yet to be settled. The Grand Chamber's conclusion in this regard is that Switzerland's "interference with the applicant's right to freedom of expression can thus be regarded as having been intended 'for the protection of the . . . rights of others.'"[55] Nevertheless, the Grand Chamber decides that a criminal penalty was "not necessary in a democratic society" to that end. So there is the recognition of a wounded identity and its rights, but criminal sanctions are seen as disproportionate to protect this memory. We may, of course, question the desirability of this paternalistic formulation around the woundedness of an identity. Further, the ultimate resolution that the court brings to its own formulation is contiguous with the more sardonic forms of free speech absolutism that call for the protection of the "right to be insulted."

171 LAW OF DENIAL

Second, the Grand Chamber considers the present danger of these utterances for the public and "democratic society" in general. Here the ruling depends, again, on a crucial distinction between Holocaust denialism and the present case. However, this distinction is quite different from what we find in the Chamber judgment, which had depended on a dubious notion of "clearly established historical facts" to distinguish the Holocaust from the Armenian genocide. The Grand Chamber judgment states that Holocaust denialism is rightly criminalized by a number of European states, but that this is less about the question of facticity than the question of the present life of Holocaust denialism:

> For the Court, the justification for making [Holocaust] denial a criminal offense lies *not so much in that it is a clearly established historical fact* but in that, in view of the historical context in the States concerned . . . its denial, even if dressed up as impartial historical research, must invariably be seen as connoting an antidemocratic ideology and anti-Semitism. Holocaust denial is thus doubly dangerous, especially in States which have experienced the Nazi horrors and which may be regarded as having a special moral responsibility to distance themselves from the mass atrocities that they have perpetrated.[56]

Thus history is figured not in terms of clearly established facts and objective truths, but rather in terms of the crises it effects in its present life. Rather than exposing itself to a maddening riddle and bogging itself down in a crisis of verification in which the IMT at Nuremberg serves as a desperate grip on "fact," the court withdraws from that realm altogether to consider instead the ways in which the past populates the present. This is an imaginative move in terms of both capturing and countering strategies of denialism without rendering law fully vulnerable to instrumentalization by those strategies.

Nevertheless, denial proves necessary to the judgment, albeit in a different form, traceable in the way the ECtHR distinguishes the present life of the Armenian genocide from the present life of the Holocaust when discussing whether interference with the right to freedom of expression was "necessary in a democratic society." The Grand Chamber's reasoning for the distinction proceeds in two main steps: First, the link between the Holocaust and current European states does not exist between the events of 1915 and Switzerland.[57] Second, the impact of this history may be considered for present-day Turkey, but Switzerland was not considering this when convicting Perinçek, and none of the submissions clearly establishes the relevance of the applicant's denial of "genocide" for that particular domestic context.[58] In making this analysis, the Grand Chamber glosses over the important submissions of a number of third party applicants, including a submission by the International Federation for Human Rights and a joint submission by Turkey's Human Rights Association, the Istanbul-based Truth Justice Memory Center, and the International Institute for Genocide and Human Rights Studies. These argued that there is a direct link between Perinçek's statements and the climate of hostility against Armenians in Turkey. In rejecting the relevance of that argument, not so much by debating and disputing it, but by rendering it inaudible, the Grand Chamber effects its own denial. By distinguishing the present life of the denial of the Armenian genocide from the Holocaust in this particular way, the court seems to be saying: Their ghosts are not our ghosts; they cannot be understood to haunt the present in the same way. Further, by excluding the present Turkish context from consideration, the Grand Chamber also denies the relevance and the potential violence of its own judgment for that context. In Turkey, the judgment was indeed distorted and flaunted as the victory of Turkey's official theses in Europe. Perinçek's party claimed, "We put an end to the lie of genocide," during their propaganda campaign for the November 2015 general elections. The official website of the Ministry of Foreign Affairs currently repeatedly miscites the Grand Chamber judgment as legitimating "Turkey's theses" on the events of 1915. And all this was entirely foreseeable. Ironically, through the ECtHR's moves to distinguish this case from Holocaust denialism, the old European borders get reestablished: Their ghosts are not our ghosts; our judgment does not bear on their world. Although there is some weight to the argument that ECtHR's jurisprudence has to be "highly context-specific"[59] when considering whether an interference with the right to freedom of expression is necessary in a democratic society, what the judgment cannot take stock of or respond to is the court's own enlistment as a key infrastructure in the context to which it understands itself as merely responding.

What can legal judgment make of denial when it has been provoked and rendered necessary by a denialist agenda? How does denial contaminate judgment? How does it operate through judgment? How does it condition judgment? Such lines of inquiry into the entangled operations of judgment and denial bear on the question of law's implication in temporalities of violence in a case like *Perinçek*, where judgment has to grapple with the injurious presence of a past that is seen as settled neither by history nor by law. If legal judgment is often a necessity that has to address itself to a moment of crisis, this moment is never one of pure presence. In this particular case, it was a particularly rigid and intractable sedimentation of the past, an interbedding of law, history, and violence that also imposed itself as an epistemic crisis. Thus the legal figuration of this "moment" in the ECtHR judgments not only says much about what legal judgment can make of sedimented temporalities of violence but also determines how legal judgment places and replaces itself within that sedimentation—whether it works as a force of dissipation or a further layer in the sedimentation. It is in this sense that in addressing itself to the crisis of history and memory, legal judgment not only figures temporality but also configures itself onto a plane of temporality that is only partially of its own making.

We may need to ask, what is the task of legal judgment in the face of a hyperproductive denialism, which is never merely about silent negation but rather a proliferation of "interpretations" and "archives" that colonizes as its infrastructure and medium official fora, legal and historical "scholarship," and even human rights courts? The register of such judgment cannot be legalism, since the only closure that legalism produces tends to be in the form of a closing in on itself—an obliviousness to its own context and effects, other than its legal context and legal effects. Nor can it be historicism, as the tendency to endlessly contextualize and recontextualize plays into the hands of denialism. What may be needed is a form of judgment that is critically and self-critically attuned to the juxtapositions of law, history, and violence, starting with an awareness and avowal of the potential of its own violence—this is a register that calls for further articulation.

Conclusion

The substantive work of this book began with a close reading of three works published in the early 1960s on political trials. I argued that the writings of Otto Kirchheimer, Hannah Arendt, and Judith Shklar marked a shift in the literature on political trials, as each work in its own way went beyond the classic approach that more or less sufficed with being scandalized by the combination of "political" and "trial." Instead, these thinkers crafted thoughtful accounts of the relationship between politics and law, and of the materializations of this relationship in a trial. Those that triggered Kirchheimer's, Arendt's, and Shklar's studies were, of course, trials held in the aftermath of the Holocaust. The necessity of some kind of politico-legal response to this extreme form of political violence stood out against a background of various unsavory practices in political justice, some recent and some old, that had left nothing much redeemable of "the use of legal procedure for political ends." This combination of necessity and controversy can be understood to account for the tangible urgency and the keen thinking of the political discernible in their works. In turn, that acuity, I have tried to show, is linked to an incipient recognition of the various ways in which legal proceedings operate performatively. I took this as my point of departure in formulating a framework for studying political trials that draws on and reworks theories of performativity, particularly the thread that runs from ordinary language philosophy to deconstruction.

The irreducible potential for failure, resignification, and subversion is a key element of the performative theory of political trials I develop over Chapters 2 and 3. As I discussed in the first chapter, that was a defining feature of political justice for Kirchheimer, who identified the ways in which numerous counterforces may materialize in the course of a trial, working over and against designs of sovereign expediency. Kirchheimer traces this potential for failure to the various forms of incalculability inevitably produced by legal procedure itself, so it is legal conventionality that contains the possibility to trouble and subvert the political calculations and wills invested therein. As we have seen, the potential for failure (or for infelicity, including misfires, misinvocations, misexecutions, and so on) also has a central status in the lineage of performative theory that I work with. In bringing theories of performativity to bear on the thinking of the politics of trials, I sought to achieve a richer picture of the ways in which legal performatives may fail, misfire, be resignified, or, indeed, take shape despite not being backed by a clear will or intention. This is the work of not only the vicissitudes of conventionality but also the involvement of bodies that "arise as such" in speech, the vagaries of circumstances. and the tribulations of authority. My analysis thus resonates with and builds on important contributions in critical legal theory concerning the co-implications of law and force/violence, and the question of how to conceptualize the role of law's own historicity and materiality in such co-implication.

The performative theory of political trials in Part I is offered as a general framework for making sense of the politics of political trials, and my hope is that it may afford openings for others. The work in Part II can be read as my own attempt to trace the implications of this theoretical framework for a constellation of trials concerning the Armenian genocide. As with most conceptual apparatuses in relation to the messy realities on which they are brought to bear, this "application" yields both less and more, and in any case is not intended as a paradigmatic offering. In attending to a fragmentary archive of the legal aftermaths of the Armenian genocide ranging from the 1921 trial concerning the assassination of Talat Pasha by Soghomon Tehlirian to the 2015 *Perinçek* case before the Grand Chamber of the European Court of Human Rights, I have sought to identify the role of law (including legal history, legal language, instruments, and mechanisms) in contributing to, if not producing, the ongoing intractability of the violence of this genocide that is now more than a century old. I have done so by tracing the various permutations of the co-implication of law and violence in this particular archive through close readings of cases. Given that the Armenian genocide is a ghostly precursor to the Holocaust in legal history, this is an archive that also troubles the easy closures and concealments effected by mainstreamed narratives of political justice that begin with trials concerning the Holocaust.

Indeed, today, the trials of the Holocaust, and particularly the Nuremberg trial, have gone through what may be understood as a "precedenting" that has had the effect of subsuming the more critical evaluations of political justice.

At the end of Chapter 1, I noted how later studies that draw on Kirchheimer, Arendt, and Shklar to address political trials from a liberal perspective tend to jettison the urgency and abandon the critical thinking of politics and law that permeates their writings. This kind of uptake may not be entirely surprising for mainstream legal and political scholarship, particularly in the aftermath of the attacks of 9/11, as ghastly formations of hawkish liberalism have besieged scholarship on the intersections of law, violence, and war. But the urgency for a sharpened thinking of the political in political trials proves dispensable in critical theoretical work as well. Consider the wonderfully innovative study of Shoshana Felman, *The Juridical Unconscious*. The book includes two chapters on the Eichmann trial, throughout which Felman is engaged in an intimate conversation with Arendt. One of Felman's arguments is that Arendt failed to recognize that the Eichmann trial "consist[ed] in a juridical and social reorganization of [the public sphere and the private sphere] and in a restructuring of their jurisprudential and political relation to each other."[1] According to Felman, the theme of, as well as the occasion for, this restructuring of the relationship between the public and the private was victimhood. For Felman, the Eichmann trial owed its historic value to the fact that it was a victims' trial:

> [The] historically unprecedented revolution in the victim that was operated in and by the Eichmann trial is, I would suggest, the trial's major contribution not only to Jews but to history, to law, to culture— to humanity at large. . . . A Jewish past that formerly had meant only a crippling disability was now being reclaimed as an empowering and proudly shared political and moral identity. . . . Victims were thus for the first time gaining what as victims they precisely could not have: authority, that is to say, semantic authority over themselves and over others. (126–27)

Felman thus praises the Eichmann trial as rearticulating the Israeli body politic as a nation of victims and survivors. The point is important and has been made and reiterated by others:[2] The trial was the first time that the stories of survivors found a public voice in Israel, where their suffering had been silenced and suppressed until then for sake of a nationalism that projected muscular invulnerability. Thus in Felman's account we see the recognition and articulation of the performative operation of the trial vis-à-vis the national, as well as the diasporic, public sphere. And yet, note that this laudatory account of the 1961 trial's performative politics was published in 2002, two years into the second Intifada. Palestinians are confined to a single footnote[3] in Felman's celebration of the Eichmann trial as the political event that secured a rearticulation of Israeli identity as one of empowered victimhood. Note also that in her careful conversation with Arendt, in which she finds Arendt to be lacking in political vision in failing to appreciate the political significance of the Eichmann trial, Felman does not seem to notice the prescience of Arendt's veritable horror in the face of what she figures as something of a monstrosity of victimhood produced by the Nazi atrocities. "Just as inhuman as [the Nazis'] guilt is the innocence of the victims," Arendt writes in her famous letter to Karl Jaspers, "we are simply not equipped to deal, on a human, political level, with a guilt that is beyond crime and an innocence that is beyond goodness or virtue."[4] As I have elaborated in the first part of this book, it may well be that Arendt did in fact keenly appreciate the reorganization of the political that the Eichmann trial effected, including the implications of a politicization of victimhood that to this day continues to fortify the sovereign violence of a nation-state.

Notably, Felman begins her book with reference to an address by the US President George W. Bush following the attacks of 11 September 2001. Quoting Bush's "Whether we bring our enemies to justice or bring justice to our enemies, justice will be done," Felman interprets this as the promise of a trial to come and couches her response in a civilizational discourse:

> As a pattern inherited from the great catastrophes and the collective
> traumas of the twentieth century, the promised exercise of legal
> justice—of justice by trial and by law—has become civilization's most
> appropriate and most essential, most ultimately meaningful response
> to the violence that wounds it.[5]

This passage is followed by an endnote, a disclaimer in which Felman suggests that as thoughts articulated in the aftermath of the attacks when the United States had already launched a "war on terror," her point here "is not political but analytical" (182n7). "Whatever the political and moral consequences" of the war, which Felman suggests "cannot be predicted or foreseen with total certainty or with a total clarity of moral vision," the promise by "America" of "justice by trial and by law" exemplifies "Western civilization's most significant and most meaningful response precisely to the loss of meaning and disempowerment occasioned by the trauma" (182n7). The renunciation of a "clarity of moral vision" vis-à-vis military warfare in the twenty-first century and the civilizational rhetoric in Felman's disclaimer are indicators that the analytical and the political not only should not, but actually cannot, be divorced in attending to the intersections of law and politics.

Felman cannot be faulted for failing to foresee that Bush Jr.'s "justice will be done" in the aftermath of 9/11 would come full circle with Barack Obama's

announcement that "justice has been done" following the extrajudicial execution of Osama bin Laden ten years later. We saw in the course of my discussion in Chapter 5 the argument that prominent Arendt scholar Roger Berkowitz
makes for justifying this execution by misciting Arendt and utilizing her for
an argument for "assassinating justly." This is an example of scholarship that
takes a certain ideological hegemony for granted and addresses the overlap between politics and law from within that hegemonic position. Indeed, Berkowitz imagines himself as responding to "one discordant clang amidst the
harmony of praise" for bin Laden's assassination,[6] the clang being the objections that came from a number of Western human rights lawyers. The analysis says much about its acoustic milieu: impenetrable to those speaking from
outside the empire of a hegemonic (albeit "liberal democratic") consensus, and
impatient with the dissonant voices that speak from within. It also teaches us
that contemporary liberalism normalizes its hegemony partly through the foreclosure and monopolization of the significance of the political in the coincidence of law and politics.

The version of the so-called war on terror launched in the aftermath of
9/11[7] has led to its own violent formations of political justice, perhaps most
spectacularly in the obscene legal execution of Saddam Hussein following a
political trial, and the off-scene extralegal assassination of Osama bin Laden.
But this renewed war on terror has also intensified a certain trend whereby the
more routine and less spectacular kinds of state violence take *hyperlegal* forms,
rather than emerging through traditional legal procedure or manifesting in
extralegal violence, and this trend is occasionally reflected in today's political
trials. Legal scholar Nasser Hussain defines hyperlegality as part of a "larger
methodology of governance"[8] that is characteristic of the late modern state but
has roots in colonial administrative practices. In formations of hyperlegality,
the combination of "a proliferation of new laws and regulations, passed in an
ad hoc or tactical manner, and diverse administrative procedures" produce a
"bureaucratic legalism" (516) and "a web of administrative legality."[9] Guantánamo is a key example of hyperlegality in Hussain's account—both the camp
itself, but also the larger set of violent formations of the war on terror that Guantánamo stands in for. Even though "Guantánamo" featured prominently as a
paradigm in "state of exception" analyses in the first decade of this century,
Hussain points out that what we have here is not so much exceptionality in
the sense of an absence of law or a space outside law, but rather a space "between laws, in the interstices of multiple legal orders" (738) that operates
through "an abundant use of technical distinctions, differing regulations, and
multiple invocations of authority" (740). Such sites of hyperlegality are not so
much lawless but rather "lawfull," in that they are actually full of law, as

regimes of exceptionality are built into legal processes and procedures, effecting their multiplication. Also important is Hussain's indication that hyperlegality had already been defining forms of governance in peacetime in liberal democracies, especially in spaces such as prisons and national borders, where mixtures of executive decrees and legislative authorizations, the activation of special powers based on bureaucratic determinations and classifications of persons, the use of special commissions and similar hybrid administrative-legal operations have produced a "diffuse condition of exceptional laws of all sorts found throughout the administrative apparatus of the state" (741).

I call on the work of Nasser Hussain here because this inscription of exceptionality or emergency within conventional legal forms can be discerned in political trials today, particularly in cases that effect the criminalization of protest. Consider the flood of prosecutions following the August 2011 riots that erupted in England after the police killing of Mark Duggan. There has been much debate on the political significance of these riots and on whether they even had any, as they were described as opportunistic "consumer riots," including by left-leaning commentators who bemoaned the widespread and systematic looting, which they saw as a clear sign of depoliticization.[10] Unlike previous urban riots in England such as the 1981 Brixton uprising that did register as *political* protest despite the looting and even led to a government-sponsored public inquiry, the 2011 riots are often reduced to mere criminality in public discourse. This depoliticization was perhaps most felicitously effected by "the shock and awe of the criminal justice system"[11] that was unleashed on the rioters, with more than three thousand prosecutions that resulted in over two thousand convictions and lengthy prison sentences, even for minor transgressions that normally would not lead to arrest or criminal sanction, such as the theft of a bottle of water.[12] Of those prosecuted, more than half were under the age of twenty: 26 percent were aged eighteen to twenty, and another 27 percent were juveniles, aged eleven to eighteen.[13] The cases were handled with "prosecutorial zeal and judicial abandon," as ordinary protections for youth offenders were suspended, sentencing guidelines were abandoned, and heavier charges were pursued.[14] Courts went into overdrive, holding all-night and weekend sessions, refusing bail, handing out excessive custodial sentences, and dispensing what has been referred to as "emergency justice,"[15] or indeed, "conveyor-belt justice."[16]

A similar trend of punitive hyperlegality has been identified in the federalization of criminal prosecutions following the summer 2020 Black Lives Matter protests in the United States. As described in detail by a report published jointly by the Movement for Black Lives and CLEAR Clinic at CUNY School of Law, many involved in the protests were indicted under federal charges instead of state-level charges, and were thereby subjected to more severe laws, a higher rate of convictions, and longer prison sentences with no chance of parole.[17] The report understands the move to federalization as a tactic in the government's attempt to disrupt the protest movement, and notes that the extension of federal jurisdiction to cases that in fact bore no federal interest involved creative arguments by prosecutors. In one case, the prosecutors claimed federal jurisdiction for a felon in possession of a firearm charge, because the firearm in question was a makeshift Molotov cocktail that incorporated an empty liquor bottle that had been manufactured in another state. The argument was that the case was of federal interest because the bottle had crossed state lines at some point in its material life, regardless of whether the defendant had done so (22).

Another contemporary set of political trials that prominently bears the imprint of this creep of administrative legality is the Academics for Peace affair in Turkey, when hundreds of signatories of a petition were individually prosecuted on charges of "making propaganda for a terrorist organization."[18] The January 2016 petition addressed the then ongoing episode of armed conflict between the Kurdistan Workers' Party (PKK) and Turkish forces in the form of an urban war in city centers and residential neighborhoods of Turkey's Kurdish populated towns; the petition called attention to the grave human rights breaches by security forces that effected the collective punishment of the residents of these towns; and it called on the government to cease the hostilities and resume the peace negotiations. Even though there was just the one petition, there were more than eight hundred individual trials launched against signatories between 2017 and 2019, and the number of trials would have eventually matched the number of signatories (more than two thousand) had the Constitutional Court not thrown out the cases. I prefaced this book with an account of the first hearing in my own trial for signing this petition: All prosecuted under the same copy-paste indictment, we were to be churned out of the courts with prison sentences arbitrarily varying from fifteen to thirty-six months, unless we "chose" the "option" to request a "suspension of the pronouncement of verdict." If granted by the court, this request would in turn suspend the sentence. But it would also mean accepting having committed the crime as charged, and require submitting to the condition not to commit such a "crime" for five further years to avoid prison. In other words, the option was between imprisonment and a five-year gag order. Meanwhile, hundreds of signatory academics working in universities in Turkey were subjected by their institutions to disciplinary investigations, preventive suspensions, and forced resignations. Others were dismissed outright as terrorism suspects by "decrees having the force of law," a hybrid legal-administrative instrument that became a routine governance device during the state of emergency that was declared in response to the July 2016 coup attempt. The decree-laws were issued, often at midnight, by the cabinet, led by the president. Despite carrying the force of law and thereby implying a claim to generality if not universality, the decree-laws individually named each academic who would be dismissed from their post and banned from public service with immediate effect. When the criminal cases were thrown out by the July 2019 Constitutional Court decision, this did not halt the wheels of administrative violence: The same court decided that it could not reach a judgment on decree-law dismissals, which needed to be referred to the newly set up "Inquiry Commission on the State of Emergency Measures." In turn, this temporary special commission took two years and three months after the July 2019 Constitutional Court decision, to only begin to summarily and arbitrarily dismiss these applications for reinstatement.

While classic literature on political trials tends to emphasize their spectacular character, the history of the judicial harassment of social movements and protest groups teaches us that political trials do not always take the form of singular spectacle-events. Today, this is especially pronounced where trials of dissenters are routinized as part and parcel of regimes of hyperlegality. Such prosecutions attempt the criminalization of protest, but they also do more: The legal procedure serves as a mechanism of discipline, and punishment before conviction. Defendants are held in limbo with the threat of criminal sanctions, pressured into refraining from further public speaking and acting, while movements are forced to re-channel resources away from their primary struggles to solidarity work with the prosecuted—this is seen today in the criminalization of acts of solidarity with or humanitarian assistance for illegalized border crossers, particularly in Europe and the United States.[19] In other contemporary political prosecutions of dissenters in which allegations include recourse to violence, this can foreclose the support of international human rights organizations, which are cornered into compromised positions so as to not lose "credibility" and their audience with the governments in question. Then again, the legalized capture in political trials is never total. Even when deployed as a fine-tuned instrument of repression in a judicial context stable enough to mask it as due process, the trial remains a site of struggle.

This is also the case for trials concerning state-sponsored violence. Readers may interpret my insistence on the co-implications of law and violence in this book, particularly pronounced in Part II, as leading to an argument for withdrawal from law as a site of struggle. I do not intend to go there. Instead, in exploring the performative operations of trials, I have sought to identify the conditions of and potentialities for the emergence and crystallization of coun-

terforces, willed and unwilled, working with and against the rituals and rep-
etitions of the legal forms. My hope is that this positioning will have come
across in my theoretical discussion of the potentials for performative resignification and subversion in Part I, and in my discussion of empirical examples of
the use of legal forms for counter-mobilization, counter-memory, and counter-
narration in Part II. In any case, it would be insensible to call, in the pages of
an academic book, for a total disengagement from existing institutional structures, especially at a time when we witness an incredible range of struggles
that engages with legal mechanisms, methods, forms, and fora in resourceful
ways.

We see this creative ferment in interventions that seek accountability in and
beyond the courtrooms, engaging with trials as intervening third parties, observers, and campaigners in attempts to reclaim and reshape their political significance. In Germany, the 2013–18 trial of Beate Zschäpe and other associates
of the neo-Nazi organization National Socialist Underground (NSU) for a series of racially motivated murders and other offenses was diligently monitored
and recorded by NSU-Watch, an alliance of anti-fascist organizations. This co-
lossal voluntary effort was undertaken not because high hopes were invested
in the criminal legal process, but with the full knowledge that the justice this
trial would yield was going to be significantly circumscribed and merely car-
ceral. The observers knew that the official trial record (dictated by the judge
in the form of notes and minutes as per German criminal procedure, and not
a verbatim transcription) would be limited and that it likely would not register
important clues that might nevertheless arise during the live trial about the
crucial political questions that the case raised. These were questions about institutional racism and the role of state agents in sustaining and supporting
far-right terrorism, but also about neo-Nazi organizing in contemporary
Germany—how large is it, who is involved, and how is it that they avoid interference? The trial was thus treated by the NSU-Watch as a live archive, only
temporarily accessible, but one that would potentially air and expose details
that might never again publicly surface or be officially recorded. The NSU-
Watch in Germany inspired the Golden Dawn Watch in Greece, where an
alliance of anti-fascist organizations similarly monitored and publicized a five-
year trial against sixty-nine members of Golden Dawn. Since Golden Dawn
was a far-right political party that had commanded a voter base, even holding
seats in the Hellenic Parliament for seven years, the trial monitoring process
was carried out with added emphasis on ensuring that the mobilization outside
the courtroom would constitute the political will that kept the trial on course.
In Turkey, feminists have long used trials concerning violence against women
as key sites of mobilization. Seeking and sometimes securing third-party

representation in the trials, and demonstrating outside the courtrooms, they have managed to *politicize* myriad cases of femicide, domestic violence, and sexual violence, precisely by calling out, intervening in, and obstructing law's complicity with perpetrators of violence against women.[20]

We currently also see a fascinating range of political practices that mimetically engage with forms pertaining to legal proceedings. Initiatives and organizations such as Forensic Architecture, Forensic Oceanography, Bellingcat, SITU Research, and others working in "counter-forensics" produce research that turns the forensic gaze on patterns and instances of systemic and state violence, including police violence, military violence, corporate violence, and environmental devastation. Characteristic of this work is an exceptionally resourceful approach to evidence, as investigators use whatever source of data is available to produce painstakingly meticulous reconstructions of the event under consideration. Often, the primary aim of these counter-investigative evidentiary practices is to help get a foot in the door of the courtroom—to initiate legal proceedings, to intervene in ongoing processes, or to reinitiate them where they have come to an unsatisfying conclusion. The resultant requirement to be legally legible has of course a bearing on the methods employed for the investigations as well as on how these investigations are presented: They have to risk reproducing the aesthetics and rhetoric of official legal verification mechanisms. As I have discussed in Chapters 5 and 6, and as others have pointed out, these mechanisms are not neutral and can often serve to effectively annihilate rather than substantiate the factuality of state-sponsored violence. While counter-forensics and the strategic litigation initiatives they support may thus remain problematically indexed to the legal forums that they may not actually be able to penetrate or shift, there are often other critical openings that these practices afford. To put it in the terms that this book has traded in, the counter-forensic engagement with legal forms can be described as a performative practice that contains the possibility of subversion and resignification. Indeed, one key gesture we find in this genre of work is the often explicit attempt to reclaim and rethink the *forum* in forensics anew and beyond the courtroom, as that space where the public may gather together to collectively exercise judgment.[21]

Relatedly, people's tribunals constitute another currently prominent genre of political practice that engages with legal forms performatively. These initiatives tend to draw on a tradition of people's tribunals (also referred to as citizens' tribunals or tribunals of opinion) often traced back to the 1967 Russell Tribunal on war crimes in Vietnam. Recent examples include the World Tribunal on Iraq held in various cities across continents from 2003 to 2005 and organized by a network that emerged from the global anti-war movement of that period;[22] the Russell Tribunal on Palestine also held in various cities from 2010 to 2012;[23] the International Monsanto Tribunal held in 2016 in The Hague;[24] and the Tribunal Unravelling the NSU-Complex organized by a co-alition of migrants' organizations and anti-fascist groups in Germany since 2017.[25] As Chowra Makaremi and Pardis Shafafi have suggested in a recent overview of research on people's tribunals,[26] they can be understood as "labo-ratories of resistance" that provide occasions to grapple with and creatively ad-dress essential questions to do with the politics of trials, including questions of legitimacy, authority/authorization, and the relationship between the form and substance of doing justice.

These are some examples of a rich array of contemporary practices that at-tempt to creatively mobilize the potentials of the legal form beyond the limits with which it is inscribed, in seeking accountability for state-sponsored vio-lence, insisting on the archival function of legal proceedings, investing them with counter-archival practices, reclaiming their verificatory powers, and re-imagining their forms and forums. Instead of a withdrawal from legal meth-ods, mechanisms, sites, and institutions as sites of political struggle, practices such as these remind us how important it is to stay with the trouble and to keep questioning law's limits and counterproductive potentials for redress for state-sponsored violence. In this sense, there is something crucial to retain of the critical acumen of the 1960s literature on political trials, which endeavored to take account not only of the violence of the acts that were on trial, but also the violence of the law that attempts to address those acts through the trial.

This book has been my uptake of the 1960s critical legacy. The attempt to pursue more rigorously its incipient formulations vis-à-vis the performativity of trials has led me to a number of considerations pertaining to the overlap between law and politics. These considerations included the ways in which a trial's performance makes and unmakes its performativity; how the sovereign performatives of a trial can be undermined by not only the unconscious fears and desires embodied by its participants but also by law's structural uncon-scious; how specters may disrupt spectacles; how law can be enlisted by a de-nialist agenda to produce its own denials; and more generally, the ways in which law-preserving violence coincides with law-positing violence in the trial. This, then, was one attempt to rethink the "political" in political trials.

Acknowledgments

This book was in the making for longer than I shall admit in print, and though I will inevitably omit some in this note, I cannot deny the debt of gratitude I have accumulated over the years to many, many people. The work here has greatly benefited from the generous and spirited guidance of Costas Douzinas and Elena Loizidou at Birkbeck School of Law. Some of the ideas began taking shape under the luxurious mentorship of Ross Poole at the New School—I cherish the traces of our extended conversations in the folds of my thoughts and of these pages. I am very lucky to have been bestowed with the time and attention of an amazing cohort of judicious readers: Emilios Christodoulidis, Avery Gordon, James Martel, and Müge Gürsoy Sökmen read and commented on earlier full drafts; Meltem Ahıska, Alexis Alvarez-Nakagawa, Eirini Avramopoulou, Özlem Biner, Eric Bogosian, Eray Çaylı, Hannah Franzki, Tara Mulqueen, Marc Nichanian, İz Öztat, Mayur Suresh, Alice von Bieberstein, and Yeşim Yaprak Yıldız read and offered generous feedback on parts.

My research for this book was supported by Patricia Tuitt, Stewart Motha, Marinos Diamantides, and Peter Fitzpatrick, who opened up various forms of institutional space for it at Birkbeck. There, it was also vitally held up by the camaraderie of Hannah Franzki, Tara Mulqueen, Sara Paiola, Mayur Suresh, Lisa Wintersteiger, Soo Tian Lee, Paola Pasquali, and Beto Yamato. Elsewhere, Awol K. Allo, Valerie Kerruish, Uwe Petersen, and Karin van Marle hosted valuable encounters where I could let the work breathe and speak and be spoken to. I also thank Anna Boecker, Angela Harutyunyan, and Barbara Kraml, who have so kindly assisted with historical resources.

I am grateful to my parents, Yaprak Zihnioğlu and Gürhan Ertür, not only for the various forms of critical sustenance they offered as I worked on this book, but also for the gift of their genuine engagement. My mother delved into the Ottoman newspaper archives for me on numerous occasions, and handed me the keys to a miraculous space during the first year of the pandemic, when space was everything I needed to be able to revise. My father always lent his ear and always with the joy of thinking together, prompting for more and asking to hear further, and also knowing when not to ask at all. This book is dedicated to them, and to others who brought me up to ask after justice in its nebulous forms—I hope it lives up in some ways to the measure of their struggle, care, and wisdom.

The book owes its material existence to the supportive presence and guidance of my editor, Richard Morrison, and his colleagues at Fordham University Press. I am grateful to Teresa Jesionowski for her sensitive and keen-eyed editorial work. The book owes its final shape to my hadjis who made it much more preferable for it to be judged by its cover: My immense gratitude to Lawrence Abu Hamdan for proposing and gifting the cover image—a photograph from the 2021 exhibition of his work *The Witness-Machine Complex*, which restages the mechanism used by simultaneous translators at the Nuremberg trials to pace the speakers on the stand. Nabla Yahya designed the cover; I am indebted to her for being so generous with her time and talent.

I am very grateful to those who wove magical webs of friendship around me during the various periods of intensive work on this book, so that I could throw myself out of it and not crash. In the earlier stages in London, they were Nicole Wolf, Billur Dokur, İrem İnceoğlu, Ruth Novaczek, Danilo Mandic, Jelena Stojkovic, Lawrence Abu Hamdan, Nora Razian, Garine Aivazian, and later, Özlem Biner, Ulele Burnham, Karim Aïnouz, and Mario Brandão. On the island formerly known as Prinkipo, they were Meltem Ahıska, Ayça Çiftçi, Timuçin Gürer, and "Fiti" Ahmet Öğüt. At large they are İz Öztat, Mine Kurtuluş, Merve Kayan, Tolga Karaçelik, Çiğdem Öztürk, and Banu Karaca.

There is a pre-history to this project that was the World Tribunal on Iraq—those involved in organizing it may discern its traces across these pages. There were too many of us to name, but I wish to thank those that I learned so much from in that collective endeavor of organizing, thinking with urgency, acting in concert, and trying to stage a version of justice: Ayşe Berktay, Müge Gürsoy Sökmen, Hilal Küey, Hülya Üçpınar, Ayça Çubukçu, Anthony Alessandrini, Koray Çalışkan, Anjali Kamat, Leili Kashani, Aslı Bâli, Peter Weiss, John Burroughs, Suzy Salamy, Claudia Garriga-López, Biju Matthew, Samera Esmeir, Sinan Hoşadam, John Baldwin, Emrah Göker, Rasha Salti, Hamid Dabashi, Zeynep Dadak, and Enis Köstepen.

But the one person who made this book possible just short of writing it for me is Alisa Lebow. The range and amount of intellectual and emotional labor she poured into it over the many years of its making is in fact incalculable. I am forever grateful for the sparkling intelligence, the love, the joy, the humor she brings to it all.

Notes

Introduction

1. Jacques Derrida, "Performative Powerlessness: A Response to Simon Critchley," *Constellations* 7, no. 4 (2000): 467.

2. Hannah Arendt, *Eichmann in Jerusalem: A Report on the Banality of Evil* (New York: Penguin, 1963), 4.

3. Pnina Lahav, "The Eichmann Trial, The Jewish Question, and the American-Jewish Intelligentsia," *Boston University Law Review* 72, no. 3 (1992): 558.

4. Arendt, *Eichmann in Jerusalem*, 4–5. In this section further page references to this work will be given parenthetically in the text.

5. See, for example, Gerhard Mueller, "Problems Posed by Publicity to Crime and Criminal Proceedings," *University of Pennsylvania Law Review* 110, no. 1 (1961): 7; Leora Bilsky, *Transformative Justice: Israeli Identity on Trial* (Ann Arbor: University of Michigan Press, 2004), 92–93.

6. Arendt doesn't even pose the problem with the Eichmann trial as one of "bad theater" as opposed to "good theater" (cf. Catherine M. Cole, *Performing South Africa's Truth Commission: Stages of Transition* [Bloomington: Indiana University Press, 2010], 2), but rather as a problem of theatricality pure and simple. Something of what Jonas Barish termed the "antitheatrical prejudice" is clearly in evidence here (Jonas Barish, *The Antitheatrical Prejudice* [Berkeley: University of California Press, 1981]). And indeed, Arendt is taking recourse to what happens to be a very common trope: Theatricality is an accusation that is often encountered in prose on trials, especially those deemed to be political trials.

7. Philip Auslander, "Legally Live: Performance in / of the Law," *Drama Review* 41, no. 2 (1997): 9–29; Linda Mulcahy, "The Unbearable Lightness of Being? Shifts Towards the Virtual Trial," *Journal of Law and Society* 35, no. 4 (2008): 464–89;

Kathryn Leader, "Closed-Circuit Television Testimony: Liveness and Truth-Telling," *Law Text Culture* 14, no. 1 (2010): 312–36.

8. Julie Stone Peters, "Legal Performance Good and Bad," *Law, Culture and the Humanities* 4, no. 2 (2008): 198.

9. The original formulation by Lord Hewart was "a long line of cases shows that it is not merely of some importance but is of fundamental importance that justice should not only be done, but should manifestly and undoubtedly be seen to be done" (R v Sussex Justices, Ex parte McCarthy [1924] 1 KB 260).

10. Peters, "Legal Performance Good and Bad," 185.

11. J. L. Austin, *How to Do Things with Words*, rev. ed. (1955; Cambridge, MA: Harvard University Press, 1975), 14.

12. Judith Butler, *Excitable Speech: A Politics of the Performative* (New York: Routledge, 1997), 16.

13. Plato, *Apology of Socrates*, trans. Thomas G. West (Ithaca, NY: Cornell University Press, 1979); Xenophon, *Apology and Memorabilia I*, trans. Matthew D Macleod (Oxford: Oxbow, 2008). In Ancient Athens, the charge of impiety had been utilized in political trials of the previous decades, see Richard A. Bauman, *Political Trials in Ancient Greece* (London: Routledge, 1990). In Socrates' trial, the charge included three specifications: not believing in the gods of the city, introducing new divinities, and corrupting the youth (Thomas C. Brickhouse and Nicholas D. Smith, *Plato and the Trial of Socrates* [New York: Routledge, 2004], 79).

14. See, for example, Brian Harris, *Injustice: State Trials from Socrates to Nuremberg* (Stroud: Sutton, 2006); Sadakat Kadri, *The Trial: A History from Socrates to O. J. Simpson* (London: Harper Perennial, 2005).

15. See, for example, Ron Christenson, *Political Trials: Gordian Knots in the Law*, rev. ed. (New Brunswick, NJ: Transaction Publishers, 1999); Ron Christenson, ed., *Political Trials in History: From Antiquity to the Present* (New Brunswick, NJ: Transaction Publishers, 1991).

16. Meletus was the first to accuse Socrates according to Plato's dialogue *Euthyphro* (Plato, *The Collected Dialogues*, ed. Edith Hamilton and Huntington Cairns [Princeton, NJ: Princeton University Press, 1961]). In the *Apology*, he appears as one of the three accusers. Most criminal proceedings in Ancient Athens at the time were initiated by private individuals. The accusing individual would draw the indictment and if the charges were deemed admissible by a magistrate (*arkhon*) following a preliminary inquiry (*anakrisis*), the trial would take place before hundreds, and in some cases thousands of jurors. The civilian accuser would play the role of the prosecutor in the trial. Thus in Socrates' trial Meletus was both plaintiff and prosecutor. For a detailed discussion of procedure in Ancient Athens, see Douglas M. MacDowell, *The Law in Classical Athens* (London: Thames and Hudson, 1978), 24–40, 237–54.

17. Or "pure flippancy" according to the Hamilton and Cairns edition (13).

18. Plato, *Apology*, 26e–27a.

19. Xenophon, *Apology*, para. 26.

20. The Rosenbergs did not advance an overtly political defense in their trial; however, we can appreciate with the benefit of hindsight the political significance

of their refusal to divulge any incriminating information while obediently answering every question and seemingly accepting the court on its own terms. See Sam Roberts, "Father Was a Spy, Sons Conclude with Regret," *New York Times*, 26 September 2008, http://www.nytimes.com/2008/09/17/nyregion/17rosen bergs.html.

21. Plato, *Apology*, 30d.

22. Elizabeth A. Wood, *Performing Justice: Agitation Trials in Early Soviet Russia* (Ithaca, NY: Cornell University Press, 2005), 22–23.

23. Catherine M. Cole, *Performing South Africa's Truth Commission: Stages of Transition* (Bloomington: Indiana University Press, 2010), 56. Jacques Derrida makes the same point in his "Admiration of Nelson Mandela, or The Laws of Reflection," *Law & Literature* 26, no. 1 (2014): 9–30.

24. Jacques Vergès, *De la Stratégie judiciare* (Paris: Minuit, 1968). However, what Vergès has baptized the strategy of rupture does not seem to have originated with him. We can identify a predecessor in the figure of communist lawyer Marcel Willard, who founded L'Association Juridique Internationale and advocated throughout the 1920s and 1930s a similar strategy of refusing to engage with the courts in the terms laid down by the accusation and instead using the courtroom as an arena, a stage for propaganda (Liora Israël, "From Cause Lawyering to Resistance: French Communist Lawyers in the Shadow of History (1929–1945)," in *The Worlds Cause Lawyers Make: Structure and Agency in Legal Practice*, ed. Austin Sarat and Stuart A. Scheingold [Stanford, CA: Stanford University Press, 2005], 147–67). Willard's approach was based on a letter by Vladimir Lenin, written in 1905 in response to members of Russia's Social Democratic Labour Party who had been arrested the previous year and had consulted him as to how to proceed with the defense (ibid., 149). Further, Lenin seems to have derived his wisdom on defense strategy from the revolutionary trials of the previous decades in Russia (Wood, *Performing Justice*, 23). Thus a preliminary genealogy of Vergès's rupture strategy takes us through Willard and Lenin, back to the late nineteenth-century Russian political trials.

25. "Interview with Notorious Lawyer Jacques Vergès," *Spiegel*, 21 November 2008, http://www.spiegel.de/international/world/interview-with-notorious-lawyer -jacques-verges-there-is-no-such-thing-as-absolute-evil-a-591943.html.

26. Vergès was known for his role as defense counsel in trials that were already of political significance, involving political defendants and / or political crimes. His clients included Algerian FLN militants, Nazi war criminal Klaus Barbie, international Marxist-Leninist terrorist Ilich Ramírez Sánchez (aka Carlos the Jackal), and more recently, up until his death in 2013, he was counsel for the former Khmer Rouge head of state Khieu Samphan.

27. Bilsky, *Transformative Justice*; Shoshana Felman, *The Juridical Unconscious: Trials and Traumas in the Twentieth Century* (Cambridge, MA: Harvard University Press, 2002).

28. Felman, *Juridical Unconscious*, 9. In this section further page references to this work will be given parenthetically in the text.

1. Theorizing Political Trials

1. Otto Kirchheimer, *Political Justice: The Use of Legal Procedure for Political Ends* (Princeton, NJ: Princeton University Press, 1961); Hannah Arendt, *Eichmann in Jerusalem: A Report on the Banality of Evil* (1963; New York: Penguin, 1994); Judith N. Shklar, *Legalism: Law, Morals, and Political Trials* (Cambridge, MA: Harvard University Press, 1964).

2. Article 6(c) of the Charter of the International Military Tribunal (IMT) (1945) specifies crimes against humanity as "murder, extermination, enslavement, deportation, and other inhumane acts committed against any civilian population, before or during the war; or persecutions on political, racial or religious grounds *in execution of or in connection with any crime within the jurisdiction of the Tribunal*, whether or not in violation of the domestic law of the country where perpetrated" (emphasis mine). In the judgment, "crimes against humanity" figured in this contingent and peripheral definition, i.e., only in connection to war crimes or crimes against peace. It was thus limited to acts committed between 1939 and 1945: "To constitute crimes against humanity, the acts relied on before the outbreak of war must have been in execution of, or in connection with, any crime within the jurisdiction of the Tribunal. The Tribunal is of the opinion that revolting and horrible as many of these crimes were, it has not been satisfactorily proved that they were done in execution of, or in connection with, any such crime." (International Military Tribunal, "Judgment of the IMT for the Trial of German Major War Criminals: The Law Relating to War Crimes and Crimes Against Humanity," 30 September and 1 October 1946, Avalon Project, Yale Law School, https://avalon.law.yale.edu/imt/judlawre.asp).

3. I use this shorthand here and in the rest of the book to refer to the Trial of the Major War Criminals before the IMT.

4. Kirchheimer, *Political Justice*, vii. In this section further page references to this work will be given parenthetically in the text. Later studies on political trials tend to follow Kirchheimer's taxonomical approach, proposing their own criteria for classifying political trials. See, for example, Barbara J. Falk, "Making Sense of Political Trials: Causes and Categories," in *Controversies in Global Politics & Societies* 8 (Toronto: Munk Centre for International Studies, University of Toronto, 2008); and Jens Meierhenrich and Devin O. Pendas, "'The Justice of My Cause Is Clear, but There's Politics to Fear': Political Trials in Theory and History," in *Political Trials in Theory and History*, ed. Jens Meierhenrich and Devin O. Pendas (Cambridge: Cambridge University Press, 2017), 1–64.

5. In the Kastner trial, an elderly Hungarian Jew was accused of defaming the Zionist leader Rudolf Kastner by alleging that he had collaborated with the Nazis. As the court sought to establish whether his claims against Kastner had merit, the defendant became the de facto accuser during the course of the trial. Thus his acquittal amounted to a symbolic conviction of Kastner, who appealed the decision, but was assassinated before the court reached a ruling. For a fascinating discussion of the politics of the Kastner trial, see Leora Bilsky, *Transformative Justice: Israeli Identity on Trial* (Ann Arbor: University of Michigan Press, 2004), 19–82.

6. Kirchheimer's use of the term "judicial space" does not incorporate any actual spatial or architectural analysis, referring solely to the discretion to judge independently.

7. For a more contemporary analysis of this failure, see Danilo Zolo, *Victors' Justice: From Nuremberg to Baghdad* (London: Verso, 2009).

8. Jacques Derrida, "Declarations of Independence," *New Political Science* 7, no. 1 (1986): 7–15.

9. For example, in her *Transformative Justice*, legal scholar Leora Bilsky compellingly reads a theory of political trials into *Eichmann in Jerusalem*, by drawing on Arendt's prior work in *The Human Condition* and later work on judgment. For other close engagements with Arendt's book in making sense of politics of trials, albeit with a tendency to forget the centrality of the question of legal violence for Arendt, see Shoshana Felman, *The Juridical Unconscious: Trials and Traumas in the Twentieth Century*, (Cambridge, MA: Harvard University Press, 2002) and Yasco Horsman, *Theaters of Justice: Judging, Staging, and Working through in Arendt, Brecht, and Delbo* (Stanford, CA: Stanford University Press, 2011).

10. *Hannah Arendt*, directed by Margarethe von Trotta (2012).

11. See Introduction.

12. Bilsky, *Transformative Justice*, 11.

13. Hannah Arendt, *Responsibility and Judgment*, ed. Jerome Kohn (New York: Schocken, 2003), 22.

14. Ariella Azoulay and Bonnie Honig, "Between Nuremberg and Jerusalem: Hannah Arendt's *Tikkun Olam*," *Differences* 27, no. 1 (2016): 49.

15. Judith Butler, *Parting Ways: Jewishness and the Critique of Zionism* (New York: Columbia University Press, 2012), 161.

16. For in-depth discussions of these issues from that time, see Hans W. Baade, "The Eichmann Trial: Some Legal Aspects," *Duke Law Journal* 10, no. 3 (1961): 400–420; L. C. Green, "The Eichmann Case," *Modern Law Review* 23, no. 5 (1960): 507–15; Jacob Robinson, "Eichmann and the Question of Jurisdiction," *Commentary* 30, no. 1 (July 1960): 1–5; and Yosal Rogat, *The Eichmann Trial and the Rule of Law* (Santa Barbara, CA: Center for the Study of Democratic Institutions, 1961), 23–32.

17. Pnina Lahav, "The Eichmann Trial, The Jewish Question, and the American-Jewish Intelligentsia," *Boston University Law Review* 72, no. 3 (1992): 558.

18. See Rogat, *The Eichmann Trial and the Rule of Law*, for an intriguing critique of these three pedagogical aims of the trial.

19. David Ben-Gurion, "The Eichmann Case as Seen by Ben-Gurion," *New York Times*, 18 December 1960, sec. SM, 7.

20. In a telling anecdote, Arendt recounts how the prosecutor invited witness after witness to testify to the horrors that the Jewish people suffered in the Holocaust, without a view to whether the evidence presented had anything to do with the deeds of the accused. When the judges objected to irrelevant testimonies, the prosecutor would insist and plead with them to let him complete his "general picture." At one point, the presiding judge was pushed to exclaim "we are not

drawing pictures here" (Arendt, *Eichmann*, 120). In this section further page references to this work will be given parenthetically in the text.

21. "Justice demands that the accused be prosecuted, defended, and judged, and that all the other questions of seemingly greater import . . . be left in abeyance. Justice insists on the importance of Adolf Eichmann, son of Karl Adolf Eichmann" (5).

22. This is how Arendt introduces the case for the defense: "The facts for which Eichmann was to hang had been established 'beyond reasonable doubt' long before the trial started, and they were generally known to all students of the Nazi regime. The additional facts that the prosecution tried to establish were, it is true, partly accepted in the judgment, but they would never have appeared to be 'beyond reasonable doubt' if the defense had brought its own evidence to bear upon the proceedings. Hence, no report on the Eichmann case, perhaps as distinguished from the Eichmann trial, could be complete without paying some attention to certain facts that are well enough known but that Dr. Servatius [defense counsel] chose to ignore" (56).

23. By way of a succinct demonstration of this point, Arendt flags "the Nuremberg Charter's definition of 'crimes against humanity' as 'inhuman acts,'" and its translation into German as "*Verbrechen gegen die Menschlichkeit*—as though the Nazis had simply been lacking in human kindness, certainly the understatement of the century" (275).

24. Her use of "we" in these passages ostensibly refers to the three judges, but see Judith Butler, "Quandaries of the Plural," for an excellent analysis of the vicissitudes of this "we."

25. It may be noted that the official judgment did not actually incorporate sentencing remarks; these were spoken by the presiding judge in a final hearing, and unlike Arendt, he addressed Eichmann in the third person until the very last sentence informing the defendant of his right to appeal: "This Court sentences Adolf Eichmann to death, for the crimes against the Jewish People, the crimes against humanity and the war crime of which he has been found guilty. . . . This is the Sentence. You are entitled to appeal against the Judgment and the Sentence" ("The Trial of Adolf Eichmann, Session 121 (Part 1 of 1)," *The Nizkor Project*, http://www.nizkor.com/hweb/people/e/eichmann-adolf/transcripts/Sessions /Session-121-01.html). In contrast, Arendt's sentencing remarks are final: "And just as you supported and carried out a policy of not wanting to share the earth with the Jewish people and the people of a number of other nations—as though you and your superiors had any right to determine who should and who should not inhabit the world—we find that no one, that is, no member of the human race, can be expected to want to share the earth with you. This is the reason, and the only reason, you must hang" (279). A postscript follows the death sentence in the book, but in the *New Yorker*, where the text first appeared in print, the layout made the address even starker as what immediately followed these words was the signature of the author: ". . . This is the reason, and the only reason you must hang.—Hannah Arendt."

26. See Bilsky, *Transformative Justice*, and Butler, *Parting Ways*, for compelling readings of Arendt's report in this particular vein.

27. Eyal Weizman, "Introduction: Forensis," in *Forensis: The Architecture of Public Truth*, ed. Forensic Architecture (Berlin: Sternberg Press, 2014): 9.

28. The language of precedents and unprecedentedness does at times become questionable and somewhat misleading in Arendt's text. When Arendt insists on the "novelty" of the crime, does she mean to occlude the fact that crimes against humanity, as defined in Nuremberg, had numerous "precedents," for example in transatlantic slavery, in various colonial contexts, in the pogroms of the previous centuries, and in the Armenian genocide? Or does she highlight the "unprecedentedness" of the crime only in an attempt to rupture the trial's great epic narrative of the centuries of persecution faced by Jewish people? Arendt is critical of the Jerusalem court holding fast to precedents (and particularly Nuremberg as precedent) and considers that it was this legalistic conservatism that prevented the judges from doing justice to the unprecedented. But then why does she herself seek so many precedents in attempting to answer, on behalf of the court, the jurisdictional objectives put forth by the defense? In the course of her discussion, Arendt refers to the postwar trials in Nazi-occupied countries as precedents of the Eichmann trial; the kidnapping of Jewish German socialist Berthold Jakob by the Gestapo in Switzerland in 1935 as the only relevant precedent for the kidnapping of Eichmann; and the trials of Sholem Schwartzbard and Soghomon Tehlirian as a potential precedent (one which she raises only to dismiss) for the alternative to kidnapping Eichmann, namely assassinating him. I discuss this final point in more detail in Chapter 5.

29. Arendt, *Eichmann*, 269. It has been suggested that this and other passages in which Arendt acknowledges Israel's right to sit in judgment are signs of her failure to conclude definitively on whether a national or an international court would be the appropriate forum (Ayça Çubukçu, "On the Exception of Hannah Arendt," *Law, Culture and the Humanities* 15, no. 3 [2019]: 13–15). Then again, Arendt is quite clear in her insistence on the suitability of an international court. The "yes, but" formulation we find here is clearly not an "either/or." It can instead be read as the sign of a post-Zionist positioning that works with the founding of Israel as a fait accompli and thus recognizes the validity of its sovereign power (Arendt writes "In this respect . . . the trial resembled the postwar trials in Poland and Hungary, in Yugoslavia and Greece, in Soviet Russia and France, in short, in all formerly Nazi-occupied countries" [258]; and "The Eichmann trial, then, was in actual fact no more, but also no less, than the last of the numerous Successor trials which followed the Nuremberg Trials." [263]) while nevertheless insisting on the necessity to move past the parochialisms of national sovereignty.

30. Judgment, Attorney General v. Adolf Eichmann, District Court of Jerusalem, Criminal Case No. 40/61, 11 December 1961, para. 16.

31. Philippe Sands, *East West Street: On the Origins of "Genocide" and "Crimes against Humanity"* (New York: Alfred A. Knopf, 2016), 336.

32. Ibid., 380.

33. Shklar, *Legalism*, 1. In this section further page references to this work will be given parenthetically in the text.

34. Shklar goes so far as to claim that "the political function of law becomes particularly apparent in the pluralistic and constitutional political order of America, where class domination is relevant neither in theory nor in practice" (144).

35. For an interesting response to Shklar on why such disavowal is an inalienable part of legalism, and why it is particularly necessary in the case of practicing lawyers engaging in thoroughly political processes such as international criminal trials, see Tiphaine Dickson, "Shklar's Legalism and the Liberal Paradox," *Constellations* 22, no. 2 (2015): 188–98. Samuel Moyn makes the same point, suggesting that "legalism not only does work but must work as a noble lie: philosophers, and perhaps associated guardians, know it is false but allow its many votaries to proceed as if it were true because only the myth makes their conduct possible" (Samuel Moyn, "Judith Shklar versus the International Criminal Court," *Humanity* 4, no. 3 [2013]: 494).

36. Andrey Yanuaryevich Vyshinsky was the chief prosecutor for Joseph Stalin's Great Purge trials (1936–38).

37. In the London Conference that produced the Charter for the IMT, Justice Jackson spoke of the task as one of "codification" of war crimes. Shklar is very dismissive of this: "There is no security in relying upon agreements as if they were a part of an operative system of criminal law" (*Legalism*, 163).

38. As Christiane Wilke points out in her fascinating discussion of the Nuremberg Justice Case (the trial of fourteen former Nazi judges, prosecutors, and Department of Justice officials before a US military tribunal in 1947), the aim of "re-enthroning law in Germany" was explicitly articulated as a key rationale, at least for this later trial (Wilke, "Reconsecrating the Temple of Justice: Invocations of Civilization and Humanity in the Nuremberg Justice Case," *Canadian Journal of Law and Society* 24, no. 2 [2009]: 182). In this sense, Shklar can be understood as accepting the prosecutors' own rationale, and applying it retrospectively to the Trial of the Major War Criminals.

39. Slavoj Žižek, *The Sublime Object of Ideology* (London: Verso, 1989), 38.

40. Moyn, "Judith Shklar versus the International Criminal Court," 490–91.

41. Moyn, "Judith Shklar on the Philosophy of International Criminal Law," *International Criminal Law Review* 14, no. 4–5 (2014): 722.

42. Shklar, *Legalism*, 167.

43. Hannah Arendt and Karl Jaspers, *Correspondence 1926–1969*, ed. Lotte Köhler and Hans Saner (New York: Harcourt Brace Jovanovich, 1992), 54.

44. Arendt, *Responsibility and Judgment*, 23.

45. Ibid.

46. Bonnie Honig, *Political Theory and the Displacement of Politics* (Ithaca, NY: Cornell University Press, 1993), 76–125.

47. Mark Osiel, *Mass Atrocity, Collective Memory, and the Law* (New Brunswick, NJ: Transaction Publishers, 1997), 66.

48. Ibid., 46.

49. Eric A. Posner, "Political Trials in Domestic and International Law," *Duke Law Journal* 55, no. 1 (2005): 106.

2. The Form and Substance of Doing Justice:
Law, Performativity, Performance

1. Shoshana Felman, *The Scandal of the Speaking Body: Don Juan with J.L. Austin, or Seduction in Two Languages* (Stanford, CA: Stanford University Press, 2003).

2. Jacques Derrida, "Performative Powerlessness: A Response to Simon Critchley," *Constellations* 7, no. 4 (2000): 467.

3. J. L. Austin, *How to Do Things with Words*, rev. ed. (1955; Cambridge, MA: Harvard University Press, 1975), 14–15. Further page references to this work will be given parenthetically in the text.

4. Timothy Gould, "The Unhappy Performative," in *Performativity and Performance*, ed. Andrew Parker and Eve Kosofsky Sedgwick (New York: Routledge, 1995), 23–24.

5. J. L. Austin, "Performative-Constative," in *Philosophy and Ordinary Language*, ed. Charles Edwin Caton, trans. G. J. Warnock (Urbana: University of Illinois Press, 1963), 33.

6. J. L. Austin, *Philosophical Papers*, 2nd ed. (Oxford: Oxford University Press, 1970), 252.

7. Shoshana Felman writes, "The very performance of the performative consists precisely in performing the loss of footing: it is the performance of the *loss of the ground*" (Felman, *The Scandal of the Speaking Body*, 44); Jacques Derrida writing on performatives asks: "What would a mark be that could not be cited? Or one whose origins would not get lost along the way?" (Jacques Derrida, *Limited Inc* [Evanston, IL: Northwestern University Press, 1988], 12).

8. "A performative utterance will, for example, be in a peculiar way hollow or void if said by an actor on the stage, or if introduced in a poem, or spoken in soliloquy. This applies in a similar manner to any and every utterance—a sea-change in special circumstances. Language in such circumstances is in special ways—intelligibly—used not seriously, but in ways parasitic upon its normal use—ways which fall under the doctrine of the etiolations of language. All this we are excluding from consideration" (Austin, *How to Do Things with Words*, 22). As Parker and Sedgwick have noted Austin's "parasite" in this passage "has gone on to enjoy a distinguished career in literary theory and criticism" (Andrew Parker and Eve Kosofsky Sedgwick, Introduction to *Performativity and Performance*, 4), with commentators particularly focusing on the exclusion of theatricality. A close reading of Austin's oft-cited passage reveals, however, that it is not necessarily theater per se that he finds it necessary to exclude from consideration, but citational uses of language more generally. Further, Austin's seeming ascription of an ontological privilege to non-citational uses of language may also be read as a strategic move,

since the greater part of his project, his thorough and amusing discussion of infelicities, involves the exploration of how such "serious" uses of language can be hollow in their own particular ways. So it is as if the "non-serious" theatrical or citational is excluded so as to be able to better highlight the failures of utterances that populate the higher rungs of Austin's hierarchy.

9. John R. Searle, *Speech Acts: An Essay in the Philosophy of Language* (London: Cambridge University Press, 1969); *Expression and Meaning: Studies in the Theory of Speech Acts* (Cambridge: Cambridge University Press, 1979).

10. H. L. A. Hart and David Sugarman, "Hart Interviewed: H. L. A. Hart in Conversation with David Sugarman," *Journal of Law and Society* 32, no. 2 (2005): 273.

11. This he deems a topic "both contentious and practically important for everybody, so that ordinary language is on its toes: yet also, on its back it has long had a bigger flea to bite it, in the shape of the Law" (Austin, *Philosophical Papers*, 185–86).

12. Austin, *How to Do Things with Words*, 36.

13. For an elegant discussion of the language of texture in Austin, see Eve Kosofsky Sedgwick, *Touching Feeling: Affect, Pedagogy, Performativity* (Durham, NC: Duke University Press, 2003), 16–17.

14. The influence of Austin's speech act theory in Hart's first academic paper is tangible from the first sentences onward (H. L. A. Hart, "The Ascription of Responsibility and Rights," *Proceedings of the Aristotelian Society* 49 [1949]: 171–94). Hart accounts for this influence further in the introduction to his *Essays in Jurisprudence and Philosophy* (Oxford: Clarendon, 1983), 2–3. In turn, it has been suggested that the influence was mutual: "Herbert's legal input to seminars with Austin almost certainly contributed to the latter's development of his famous 'speech act theory'" (Nicola Lacey, *A Life of H.L.A. Hart: The Nightmare and the Noble Dream* [Oxford: Oxford University Press, 2004], 145). Although Austin himself dates the origins of his speech act theory to 1939 (*How to*, vi), that is, six years before meeting Hart, the recurrent references to the law in *How to Do Things with Words* and an explicit acknowledgment of Hart in a footnote for providing the term "operative" (as in, "operative clause") as the possible legal counterpart of the performative, do point to a fruitful exchange.

15. Hart and Sugarman, "Hart Interviewed," 274.

16. Austin, *How to Do Things with Words*, 19.

17. These verbs in this mode (first person singular present indicative active) also yield what Austin had defined earlier as the explicit performative. When I am not referring to Austin's particular discussion and classifications, I use illocutionary speech act and performative utterances interchangeably in the rest of this discussion.

18. Karl Olivecrona, "Legal Language and Reality," in *Essays in Jurisprudence in Honor of Roscoe Pound*, ed. Ralph A. Newman (Westport, CT: Greenwood, 1962), 151–91.

19. Karl Olivecrona, *Law as Fact*, 2nd ed. (London: Steven & Sons, 1971).

20. Olivecrona, "Legal Language and Reality," 175.

21. Olivecrona, *Law as Fact*, 231.

22. Alf Ross, "The Rise and Fall of the Doctrine of Performatives," in *Contemporary Philosophy in Scandinavia*, ed. Raymond E. Olson and Anthony M. Paul (Baltimore: Johns Hopkins University Press, 1972), 197–212.

23. See, for example, Dennis Kurzon, *It Is Hereby Performed: Explorations in Legal Speech Acts* (Amsterdam: John Benjamins, 1986).

24. See, for example, Deborah Cao, "Illocutionary Acts of Chinese Legislative Language," *Journal of Pragmatics* 41, no. 3 (2009): 1329–40.

25. See, for example, Veronica Rodriguez-Blanco, "Claims of Legal Authorities and 'Expressions of Intention': The Limits of Philosophy of Language," in *Law and Language: Current Legal Issues*, vol. 15, ed. Michael D. A. Freeman and Fiona Smith (Oxford: Oxford University Press, 2013), 79–99.

26. Timothy A. O. Endicott, "Law and Language," in *The Oxford Handbook of Jurisprudence and Philosophy of Law*, ed. Jules L. Coleman and Scott Shapiro (Oxford: Oxford University Press, 2002), 946.

27. In *Just Silences* (Princeton, NJ: Princeton University Press, 2007) Marianne Constable reads the Miranda warning given by the police to suspects in the United States as a speech act that effects a transformation in the circumstances of speech and notifies the suspect of this transformation. Understood as such, the Miranda warning serves as an opening to justice that takes account of the problematic speech conditions of pretrial interrogation, and preserves the trial as the proper site of speech and as the site of proper speech. In later work Constable (*Our Word Is Our Bond* [Stanford, CA: Stanford University Press, 2014]) inquires into claims of law as performative and passionate utterances, the latter being Stanley Cavell's development of Austin's idea of the perlocutionary act. This approach allows her to both appreciate the conventionality of legal speech acts, and to go beyond that framework to consider the unconventional legal appeals to right and justice, and the question of law's hearing.

28. Austin, *How to Do Things with Words*, 27.

29. Jacques Derrida, "Force of Law: 'The Mystical Foundation of Authority,'" in *Acts of Religion*, ed. Gil Anidjar, trans. Mary Quaintance (New York: Routledge, 2002), 241.

30. Walter Benjamin, "Toward the Critique of Violence," trans. Julia Ng, in *Toward the Critique of Violence: A Critical Edition*, ed. Peter D. Fenves and Julia Ng (Stanford, CA: Stanford University Press, 2021), 39.

31. Werner Hamacher, "Afformative, Strike," trans. Dana Hollander, *Cardozo Law Review* 13 (1991): 1133.

32. Benjamin, "Toward the Critique of Violence," 41.

33. Derrida, "Force of Law," 255–56.

34. Judith Butler, *Excitable Speech: A Politics of the Performative* (New York: Routledge, 1997), 147.

35. Judith Butler, "Performative Acts and Gender Constitution: An Essay in Phenomenology and Feminist Theory," in *Performing Feminisms: Feminist Critical Theory and Theatre*, ed. Sue-Ellen Case (Baltimore: Johns Hopkins University Press, 1990), 276.

36. Butler, *Excitable Speech*, 3.

37. Ritu Birla, "Performativity between Logos and Nomos: Law, Temporality and the Non-Economic Analysis of Power," *Columbia Journal of Gender and Law* 21 no. 2 (2011): 90.

38. Austin, *How to Do Things with Words*, 4.

39. Judith Butler, *Gender Trouble: Feminism and the Subversion of Identity*, rev. ed. (New York: Routledge, 1999), 55–73.

40. Quoted in Jacqueline Visconti, "Speech Acts in Legal Language: Introduction," *Journal of Pragmatics* 41, no. 3 (2009): 394.

41. There is a line of debate in legal theory in this vein, in response to Hart's work on ascription ("The Ascription of Responsibility and Rights") which was clearly inspired by Austin on performatives. Hart's early claim that legal language was primarily characterized by ascription of legal consequences to actions rather than descriptions of these actions was challenged by scholars such as P. T. Geach and George Pitcher who proposed that legal performatives, such as the passing of sentence, involved and were premised on factual referents, such as findings of fact in a trial (Frederick Schauer, "(Re)Taking Hart," *Harvard Law Review* 119, no. 3 [2006]: 855n5). Later, Hart agreed with his critics though without fully explaining why (Hart, *Essays in Jurisprudence and Philosophy*). See also Endicott, "Law and Language."

42. Derrida, "Declarations of Independence," 9–10.

43. The analysis of performativity we find in this text has found important resonances in critical legal thought; see, for example, the article by Jacques De Ville, teasing out the significance for constitutional theory of Derrida's emphasis on performativity: "Sovereignty Without Sovereignty: Derrida's Declarations of Independence," *Law and Critique* 19, no. 2 (2008): 87–114.

44. Bonnie Honig, "Declarations of Independence: Arendt and Derrida on the Problem of Founding a Republic," *American Political Science Review* 85, no. 1 (1991): 97–113.

45. Costas Douzinas, "The Metaphysics of Jurisdiction," in *Jurisprudence of Jurisdiction*, ed. Shaun McVeigh (Abingdon: Routledge, 2007), 22.

46. Benjamin, "Toward the Critique of Violence," 46.

47. For a lucid illustration of this, see Marianne Constable's reading of Morissette v. United States (1952): Marianne Constable, "Law as Claim to Justice: Legal History and Legal Speech Acts," *UC Irvine Law Review* 1, no. 3 (2011): 637–39.

48. Parker and Sedgwick, "Introduction," 1.

49. Philip Auslander, "Legally Live: Performance in / of the Law," *The Drama Review* 41, no. 2 (1997): 9–29; Kathryn Leader, "Closed-Circuit Television Testimony: Liveness and Truth-Telling," *Law Text Culture* 14, no. 1 (2010): 312–36;

Linda Mulcahy, "The Unbearable Lightness of Being? Shifts towards the Virtual Trial," *Journal of Law and Society* 35, no. 4 (2008): 464–89.

50. Auslander, "Legally Live," 20.

51. Leader, "CCTV Testimony."

52. Cornelia Vismann, *Files: Law and Media Technology*, trans. Geoffrey Winthrop-Young (Stanford, CA: Stanford University Press, 2008); Mayur Suresh, "The 'Paper Case': Evidence and Narrative of a Terrorism Trial in Delhi: The 'Paper Case,'" *Law & Society Review* 53, no. 1 (2019): 173–201.

53. Cornelia Vismann, "Jurisprudence: A Transfer Science," *Law and Critique* 10, no. 3 (1999): 279.

54. Martti Koskenniemi, "Between Impunity and Show Trials," *Max Planck Yearbook of United Nations Law* 6 (2002): 1–35; Costas Douzinas, "History Trials: Can Law Decide History?" *Annual Review of Law and Social Science* 8, no. 1 (2012): 273–89.

55. Robert S. Summers, "Formal Legal Truth and Substantive Truth in Judicial Fact-Finding: Their Justified Divergence in Some Particular Cases," *Law and Philosophy* 18, no. 5 (1999): 498.

56. Sam Roberts, "Figure in Rosenberg Case Admits to Soviet Spying," *New York Times*, 11 September 2008, http://www.nytimes.com/2008/09/12/nyregion/12spy.html; Sam Roberts, "Father Was a Spy, Sons Conclude with Regret," *New York Times*, 26 September 2008, http://www.nytimes.com/2008/09/17/nyregion/17rosenbergs.html.

57. Walter Schneir, *Final Verdict: What Really Happened in the Rosenberg Case* (Brooklyn, NY: Melville House, 2010).

58. Scott Veitch, "Judgment and Calling to Account: Truths, Trials and Reconciliations," in *The Trial on Trial: Judgment and Calling to Account*, ed. Anthony Duff et al., vol. 2 (Oxford: Hart, 2006), 155–71.

59. "Arendt's vision of the trial clearly, then, is thoroughly legalistic in Shklar's sense: a proceeding whose only function is rendering justice—where justice is defined as the scrupulous observance of the rules that define legal form" (Lawrence Douglas, *The Memory of Judgment: Making Law and History in the Trials of the Holocaust* [New Haven: Yale University Press, 2001], 112). Likewise Felman in *The Juridical Unconscious* writes that Arendt has a "conservative legal approach and . . . conservative jurisprudential argument" (Shoshana Felman, *The Juridical Unconscious: Trials and Traumas in the Twentieth Century* [Cambridge, MA: Harvard University Press, 2002], 122).

60. In the first letter she wrote from Jerusalem to Karl Jaspers, she complained about the prosecutor's "overly legalistic" argument, which was "full of nonexistent precedents, on which the prosecutor focuses instead of stressing the unprece-dentedness of the case" (Hannah Arendt and Karl Jaspers, *Correspondence, 1926–1969*, ed. Lotte Köhler and Hans Saner [New York: Harcourt Brace Jovanovich, 1992], 434).

61. Hannah Arendt, *Responsibility and Judgment*, ed. Jerome Kohn (New York: Schocken, 2003), 27.

62. Martha Merrill Umphrey, "Law in Drag: Trials and Legal Performativity," *Columbia Journal of Gender and Law* 21, no. 2 (2011): 120.

63. Felman, *The Scandal*, 14.

64. Ross Charnock, "Overruling as a Speech Act: Performativity and Normative Discourse," *Journal of Pragmatics* 41, no. 3 (2009): 13.

3. Sovereign Infelicities

1. United States v. Dellinger et al., Criminal No. 69-180 (N.D.Ill.).

2. This was an offense under the 1968 Federal Anti-Riot Act, passed in April of that year as a response to inner-city race riots of the mid-1960s.

3. For detailed accounts of the trial, see John Schultz, *The Chicago Conspiracy Trial*, rev. ed. (Chicago: University of Chicago Press, 2009); Pnina Lahav, "Theater in the Courtroom: The Chicago Conspiracy Trial," *Law and Literature* 16, no. 3 (2004): 381–474; Abbie Hoffman, *The Autobiography of Abbie Hoffman* (New York: Four Walls Eight Windows, 2000), 186–209.

4. "Saddam Hussein on Trial: Saddam Hussein Is Too Great to Be Defended Even by Saddam Hussein; I Was Beaten by the Americans," *Memri TV* video, 9:34, archived 27 May 2013, broadcast by *Al-Jazeera TV* in 2005, http://www.memritv.org /clip/en/976.htm.

5. This is part of the Gold (strategic)—Silver (tactical)—Bronze (operational) command structure created by London's Metropolitan Police Service following the Broadwater Farm Riot in 1985. Though the command structure was created for emergencies and has been taken up by other emergency services, the police now use it mainly proactively for policing public events and protests.

6. Michel Foucault, *Discipline and Punish: The Birth of the Prison*, trans. Alan Sheridan, 2nd ed. (New York: Vintage Books, 1995), 9.

7. Leora Bilsky, "Strangers Within: The Barghouti and the Bishara Criminal Trials," in *Law and the Stranger*, ed. Martha Merrill Umphrey, Austin Sarat, and Lawrence Douglas (Stanford, CA: Stanford University Press, 2010), 108.

8. Foucault, *Discipline and Punish*, 48.

9. Otto Kirchheimer, *Political Justice: The Use of Legal Procedure for Political Ends* (Princeton, NJ: Princeton University Press, 1961), 118.

10. Judith Butler, *Excitable Speech: A Politics of the Performative* (New York: Routledge, 1997), 77.

11. Cf. J. L. Austin: "If you are a judge and say 'I hold that . . .' then to say you hold is to hold; with less official persons it is not so clearly so" (J. L. Austin, *How to Do Things with Words*, rev. ed. [1955; Cambridge, MA: Harvard University Press, 1975], 88).

12. Judith Butler, "Performative Agency," *Journal of Cultural Economy* 3, no. 2 (2010): 148.

13. Jacques Derrida, "Signature Event Context," in *Limited Inc* (Evanston, IL: Northwestern University Press, 1988).

14. J. L. Austin, *Philosophical Papers*, 2nd ed. (Oxford: Oxford University Press, 1970), 201.

15. Austin, *How to Do Things with Words*, 7.

16. Nor is Austin to be found in a 1990 essay they published soon after *Gender Trouble*, though here Butler provides an intriguing and itinerant genealogy to the notion of performativity, mentioning John Searle in passim, but drawing mainly on the phenomenological theory of acts (Marleau-Ponty, Husserl) and its feminist uptake by Simone de Beauvoir (Judith Butler, "Performative Acts and Gender Constitution: An Essay in Phenomenology and Feminist Theory," in *Performing Feminisms: Feminist Critical Theory and Theatre*, ed. Sue-Ellen Case [Baltimore: Johns Hopkins University Press, 1990]). Austin gets a brief mention in a short conference response (Judith Butler, "Deconstruction and the Possibility of Justice: Comments on Bernasconi, Cornell, Miller, Weber," *Cardozo Law Review* 11, no. 5–6 [1990]: 1715–18) published the same year, and finally surfaces in Butler's oeuvre more fully, first toward the end of *Bodies That Matter* (New York: Routledge, 1993), and later more extensively in *Excitable Speech* (1997).

17. Eve Kosofsky Sedgwick, *Touching Feeling: Affect, Pedagogy, Performativity* (Durham, NC: Duke University Press, 2003), 8.

18. Seyla Benhabib, "Feminism and Postmodernism: An Uneasy Alliance," in *Feminist Contentions: A Philosophical Exchange*, by Seyla Benhabib et al. (New York: Routledge, 1995), 21. In a later essay included in the same volume, Benhabib admits to having overlooked the speech act theory signification of Butler's usage of performativity (Seyla Benhabib, "Subjectivity, Historiography, and Politics: Reflections on the Feminism/Postmodernism Exchange," in *Feminist Contentions*, 109).

19. Susie Orbach, *Bodies* (London: Profile Books, 2009), 74.

20. J. H. Miller, "Performativity as Performance/Performativity as Speech Act: Derrida's Special Theory of Performativity," *South Atlantic Quarterly* 106, no. 2 (April 1, 2007): 225.

21. Derrida, "Signature Event Context," 7.

22. Austin, *How to Do Things with Words*, 21–22.

23. Derrida, *Limited Inc*, 16.

24. Stanley Cavell, *A Pitch of Philosophy: Autobiographical Exercises* (Cambridge, MA: Harvard University Press, 1994), 85–88.

25. Derrida, *Limited Inc*, 15.

26. Shoshana Felman, *The Scandal of the Speaking Body: Don Juan with J. L. Austin, or Seduction in Two Languages* (Stanford, CA: Stanford University Press, 2003), 43.

27. Derrida, *Limited Inc*, 16.

28. Austin, *Philosophical Papers*, 186.

29. Derrida, *Limited Inc*, 17.

30. Austin, *How to Do Things with Words*, 15.

31. Ibid., 10.

32. Émile Benveniste, *Problems in General Linguistics*, trans. Mary Elizabeth Meek (Coral Gables, FL: University of Miami Press, 1971), 234.

33. For a succinct and thorough account of Benveniste's revision of Austin, see Felman, *The Scandal*, 9–11.

34. Barbara Cassin, "Sophistics, Rhetorics, and Performance; or, How to Really Do Things with Words," trans. Andrew Goffey, *Philosophy & Rhetoric* 42, no. 4 (2009): 349.

35. J. L. Austin, "Performative-Constative," in *Philosophy and Ordinary Language*, ed. Charles Edwin Caton, trans. G. J. Warnock (Urbana: University of Illinois Press, 1963).

36. Derrida, *Limited Inc*, 17, 18, 19.

37. Benveniste, *Problems*, 236.

38. Derrida, *Limited Inc*, 15.

39. Benveniste, *Problems*, 236.

40. Derrida, *Limited Inc*, 18.

41. Cf. Elena Loizidou, *Judith Butler: Ethics, Law, Politics* (Abingdon: Routledge-Cavendish, 2007), 34–35.

42. Judith Butler, "For a Careful Reading," in *Feminist Contentions: A Philosophical Exchange*, by Seyla Benhabib et al. (New York: Routledge, 1995), 134; cf. Derrida "the category of intention will not disappear; it will have its place, but from that place it will no longer be able to govern the entire scene and system of utterance" (*Limited Inc*, 18).

43. Butler, *Excitable Speech*, 141.

44. Derrida, "Limited Inc a b c . . . ," in *Limited Inc*, 75.

45. Felman, *The Scandal*, 65.

46. Similarly for Stanley Cavell the endless failures to which human action is exposed have to do with the body (*A Pitch*, 87).

47. Felman, *The Scandal*, 67.

48. Jacques Derrida, "Force of Law: 'The Mystical Foundation of Authority,'" in *Acts of Religion*, ed. Gil Anidjar, trans. Mary Quaintance (New York: Routledge, 2002)," 252.

49. Butler, *Excitable Speech*, 157.

50. Schultz, *Chicago Conspiracy Trial*, 58.

51. United States v. Seale, 461 F.2d 345, 378 (7th Cir. 1972), LexisNexis.

52. Ibid., 381.

53. Butler, *Excitable Speech*, 146.

54. United States ex re. Allen v. State of Illinois, 413 F.2d 232 (7th Cir. 1969), LexisNexis. Here the Court of Appeals had ruled that despite his "disruptive and disrespectful conduct" the defendant should not have been excluded from the courtroom, but that the "proper course for the trial judge was to have restrained the defendant by whatever means necessary, even if those means included his being shackled and gagged" (at 235).

55. US v. Seale, 383.

4. Ghosts in the Courtroom: The Trial of Soghomon Tehlirian

1. Zoryan Institute, ed., *The Case of Soghomon Tehlirian*, trans. Vartkes Yeghiayan (Los Angeles: A. R. F. Varantian Gomideh, 1985), 33. This is the English translation of the original stenographic record of the trial (Der Prozess Talaat Pascha, C.J. 22/21, LG Berlin 1921) by the Armenian Revolutionary Federation (Dashnaktsutyun), hereafter referenced in text as *ST*.

2. A 22-cm-long cut running from the crown of his head to his jaw, according to a newspaper report: "Die Ermordung Talaat Paschas," *Deutsche Tageszeitung*, 16 March 1921.

3. "Das Geständnis des Mörders Talaat Paschas: Vernehmung im Polizeipräsidium," *Berliner Tageblatt*, 16 March 1921.

4. A constitution was first adopted in 1876, only to be shelved by Sultan Abdülhamid in 1878.

5. M. Şükrü Hanioğlu, *Preparation for a Revolution: The Young Turks, 1902–1908* (Oxford: Oxford University Press, 2001), 280.

6. Feroz Ahmad, *The Young Turks: The Committee of Union and Progress in Turkish Politics, 1908–1914* (London: Hurst, 2010), 214.

7. Henry Morgenthau, *Ambassador Morgenthau's Story* (London: Hodder & Stoughton, 1918), 94.

8. "Die Ermordung Talaat Paschas," *Kölnische Volkszeitung*, 16 March 1921.

9. Vahakn N. Dadrian and Taner Akçam, eds., *Judgment at Istanbul: The Armenian Genocide Trials* (New York: Berghahn Books, 2011), 24; Taner Akçam, *A Shameful Act: The Armenian Genocide and the Question of Turkish Responsibility* (New York: Henry Holt, 2007), 269.

10. Ayhan Aktar, "Debating the Armenian Massacres in the Last Ottoman Parliament, November–December 1918," *History Workshop Journal* 64, no. 1 (2007): 240–70; Akçam, *A Shameful Act*, 257–302; Dadrian and Akçam, *Judgment at Istanbul*, 23–52.

11. Dadrian and Akçam, *Judgment at Istanbul*, 202.

12. Ibid., 71n24.

13. Quoted ibid., 25.

14. "Die Ermordung Talaat Paschas: Die Tat Eines Armeniers," *Vossische Zeitung*, 16 March 1921.

15. Tessa Hofmann, "New Aspects of the Talat Pasha Court Case," *Armenian Review* 42, no. 4 (1989): 44.

16. Section 243 is still in force today in its original form, except for the addition of one subsection which is not relevant to the discussion here.

17. As during the rest of the proceedings, the role of the judge here is not that of an umpire between prosecution and defense, but is inquisitorial in character: The judge has to actively conduct and participate in the trial with an independent obligation to seek and elicit the truth (Douglas G. Morris, *Justice Imperiled: The*

Anti-Nazi Lawyer Max Hirschberg in Weimar, Germany [Ann Arbor: University of Michigan Press, 2005], 208).

18. Although Tehlirian had admitted to premeditation in his initial interrogation by the police, he had the right at this stage to contradict his earlier confession. See, however, Section 254 (still in effect) of the German Code of Criminal Procedure, which allows for the transcript of the police interrogation to be read during the trial when there is a contradiction between statements made to the police and trial testimony. For a brief discussion of how a judge should handle such a contradiction, see Eberhard Schmidt, Introduction to *The German Code of Criminal Procedure*, trans. Manfred A. Pfeiffer (London: Sweet & Maxwell, 1965), 14.

19. According to one particularly embellished account published as the trial was underway: "This is the trial of tortured Armenian people and the gates of the courtroom are besieged by beautifully dark people who stand by the killer with burning hopes" ("Die Ermordung Talaat Paschas," *Vossische Zeitung*, 2 June 1921).

20. Note that the judge's supplement does not function as a suggestion that is meant to trap Tehlirian into admitting a political motive in addition to a personal vendetta. According to the transcript, he does not wait for Tehlirian's response to his supplement before going on to ask another question.

21. The English translation of the transcript, the Armenian Revolutionary Federation edition, has "Talat" in place of "Enver" in this passage. Even though that may be dramaturgically more desirable, Terzibashian says "Enver" according to the original German transcript.

22. Dr. Johannes Lepsius established the German Oriental mission in 1895, had been in the Ottoman Empire through the 1895–96 Armenian massacres, and had raised funds to build orphanages for children who had lost their parents. He went again in 1915 to investigate the Armenian situation on behalf of German missionary interests.

23. Ronald Grigor Suny, "Writing Genocide: The Fate of the Ottoman Armenians," in *A Question of Genocide: Armenians and Turks at the End of the Ottoman Empire*, ed. Ronald Grigor Suny, Fatma Müge Göçek, and Norman M. Naimark (Oxford: Oxford University Press, 2011), 15–41.

24. Taner Akçam, *Killing Orders: Talat Pasha's Telegrams and the Armenian Genocide* (London: Palgrave Macmillan, 2018), 44.

25. Ibid., 240–41.

26. Quoted ibid., 44.

27. Avery Gordon, *Ghostly Matters: Haunting and the Sociological Imagination* (Minneapolis: University of Minnesota Press, 2008), 63.

28. "Die Ermordung Talaat Paschas," *Vossische Zeitung*, 2 June 1921.

29. "Says Mother's Ghost Ordered Him to Kill," *New York Times*, 2 June 1921.

30. Hofmann, "New Aspects," 43.

31. L. van der Horst, "Affective Epilepsy," *Journal of Neurology, Neurosurgery & Psychiatry* 16, no. 1 (1953): 25.

32. In this sense the trial experts' distinction between real epilepsy and affective epilepsy is very similar to the distinction Freud made in his 1928 essay on Dostoevsky: "It is therefore quite right to distinguish between an organic and an 'affective' epilepsy. The practical significance of this is that a person who suffers from the first kind has a disease of the brain, while a person who suffers from the second kind is a neurotic" (Sigmund Freud, "Dostoevsky and Parricide," in The Future of an Illusion, Civilization and Its Discontents, and Other Works, ed. James Strachey, The Standard Edition of the Complete Psychological Works of Sigmund Freud, vol. XXII [London: Hogarth Press, 1961], 181). However, the trial experts identify Tehlirian as a psychotic rather than a neurotic.

33. Quoted in Sigmund Freud, "The 'Uncanny,'" in An Infantile Neurosis and Other Works, ed. James Strachey, The Standard Edition of the Complete Psychological Works of Sigmund Freud, vol. XVII (London: Hogarth Press, 1955), 226.

34. Freud, "Dostoevsky and Parricide," 179.

35. In the English trial transcript this is inaccurately translated as "compulsive precept." Liepmann had served as an assistant to Carl Wernicke, the originator of this doctrine of "over-valued ideas." The doctrine still seems to have currency in psychiatric discourse. For a comparison between its early European and contemporary American definitions, see David Veale, "Over-Valued Ideas: A Conceptual Analysis," Behaviour Research and Therapy 40, no. 4 (2002): 384–86.

36. Edmund Forster also happened to be the neuropsychiatrist who cured Adolf Hitler of his "hysterical blindness" at the front during World War I, see David Lewis, The Man Who Invented Hitler (London: Headline, 2003).

37. Richard F. Wetzell, Inventing the Criminal: A History of German Criminology, 1880–1945 (Chapel Hill: University of North Carolina Press, 2000), 143.

38. Freud's ground-breaking Beyond the Pleasure Principle was published in 1920.

39. Dr. Störmer, for example, says about the ghost, "I certainly had to ask myself if this was not a delusion of the senses. But after a detailed cross-examination, I was able to verify that what the defendant experienced was not a delusion of the senses, but a living mental picture. He does actually see his mother in her physical form. He not only sees her in his dreams but even while he is awake" (ST 96).

40. The verdict was not accompanied by any explanation as to why they decided to relieve Tehlirian of any responsibility for his act, as such justification was not required by German criminal procedure.

41. "Das Geständnis des Mörders Talaat Paschas: Vernehmung im Polizeipräsidium," Berliner Tageblatt, 16 March 1921.

42. Soghomon Tehlirian, Verhisumner (Talaati Ahabekume) (Cairo: Husaber, 1956).

43. Sarkis Atamian, "Soghomon Tehlirian," Armenian Review 13, no. 3 (1960): 41–51; 14, no. 1 (1961): 11–21; 14, no. 2 (1961): 16–36; 14, no. 3 (1961): 44–49.

44. Lindy V. Avakian, The Cross and the Crescent (Phoenix, AZ: USC Press, 1989).

45. In the Introduction, the only part of the book where Avakian inhabits his own voice, he explains that his father, a figure in the Dashnak community of the United

States, had befriended Tehlirian, thus: "My recollections are deeply etched with the inspiring memory of countless discussions with or about Tehlirian, held in the old-fashioned parlor of our home at 422 South Fulton Street in Fresno by representatives of the Armenian Revolutionary Federation and my father" (ibid., 12).

46. Avakian stretches the two-day trial over fifteen days, introduces fictional witnesses and entirely new conflicts into the proceedings, jettisons Tehlirian's testimony along with every other indication that reflects on Tehlirian as less than the manly, muscular, chauvinist hero fantasized throughout the narrative. Further, in Avakian's version, the trial is recast as adversarial, which though much more suitable to the courtroom drama genre that the author was clearly after, had obviously nothing to do with the actual proceedings, which.were inquisitorial.

47. Edward Alexander, *A Crime of Vengeance: An Armenian Struggle for Justice* (Lincoln, NE: iUniverse, 2000).

48. Jacques Derogy, *Resistance and Revenge: The Armenian Assassination of Turkish Leaders Responsible for the 1915 Massacres and Deportations*, trans. A. M. Berrett (New Brunswick, NJ: Transaction Publishers, 1990).

49. Eric Bogosian, *Operation Nemesis: The Assassination Plot That Avenged the Armenian Genocide* (New York: Back Bay Books, 2015).

50. Armen Garo was the nom de guerre of Karekin Pastermadjian, a key ARF leader.

51. An Armenian, Mugerditchian was considered a collaborator and deemed responsible for facilitating the 24 April 1915, apprehension and massacre of Istanbul's Armenian leaders and intellectuals, by handing the government a "black list."

52. Marian Mesrobian Maccurdy, *Sacred Justice: The Voices and Legacy of the Armenian Operation Nemesis* (London: Routledge, 2016).

53. Tim Neshitov, "Der Adler," *Süddeutsche Zeitung*, 19 April 2015, http://www
.sueddeutsche.de/politik/voelkermord-der-adler-1.2442261; Robert Fisk, "My Conversation with the Son of Soghomon Tehlirian, the Man who Assassinated the Organiser of the Armenian Genocide," *The Independent*, 20 June 2016, https://www
.independent.co.uk/voices/robert-fisk-armenian-genocide-conversation-son-of
-soghomon-tehlirian-mehmet-talaat-pasha-assasination-a7091951.html.

54. The discrepancy between this account and Tehlirian's trial testimony was discovered by Turkish newspapers very belatedly, on the occasion of the publication of a book in 2005 in Germany about Operation Nemesis, and it produced headlines such as "Armenian Murderer Told Fairy Tales," which proclaimed that Tehlirian did not actually lose his family in the death marches—see, for example, Celal Özcan, "Katil Ermeni Masal Anlatmış," *Hürriyet*, 27 March 2005, http://hurarsiv.hurriyet
.com.tr/goster/haber.aspx?id=306974. There is some distortion here: Tehlirian's father and brothers remained in Serbia through the war, but he did lose family members who remained behind, including his mother and a brother.

55. All other items on the arrival registry (height, complexion, color of hair, color of eyes, "whether going to join a relative or friend, and if so, his name and complete address," "the name and complete address of nearest relative or friend in country

whence alien came," etc.) also match between the two records. The arrival records are available on http://www.ellisisland.org.

56. Dori Laub, "An Event without a Witness: Truth, Testimony and Survival," in *Testimony: Crises of Witnessing in Literature, Psychoanalysis, and History*, by Shoshana Felman and Dori Laub (New York: Routledge, 1992), 76

57. Gordon, *Ghostly Matters*, 97.

58. Ross Poole, "Two Ghosts and an Angel: Memory and Forgetting in *Hamlet*, *Beloved*, and *The Book of Laughter and Forgetting*," *Constellations* 16, no. 1 (2009): 146n13, 129.

59. Freud, "The 'Uncanny,'" 242.

60. Colin Dayan, *The Law Is a White Dog: How Legal Rituals Make and Unmake Persons* (Princeton, NJ: Princeton University Press, 2011), 9.

61. Gordon, *Ghostly Matters*, 207.

62. Begoña Aretxaga, *States of Terror: Begoña Aretxaga's Essays*, ed. Joseba Zulaika (Reno: Center for Basque Studies, University of Nevada, Reno, 2005), 227.

63. In a study of the pretrial records of Tehlirian's case (four files that resurfaced in East German archives containing case records created by the German police, the state prosecutor, the Ministry of Justice, and the German Foreign Office) Osik Moses identifies that this shift of testimony occurred on 26 March 1921, eleven days after the assassination and more than two months before the trial. On this date, the investigating judge conducted the last hearing of the preliminary investigation, during which Tehlirian gave the version of his story that he reiterated in his trial, even though it contradicted his initial confessions to the police. (Osik Moses, "The Assassination of Talaat Pasha in 1921 in Berlin: A Case Study of Judicial Practices in the Weimar Republic," MA thesis, Northridge, California State University, 2013, http://hdl.handle.net/10211.2/1564.)

64. Atamian, "Soghomon Tehlirian," 19–21; Alexander, *A Crime of Vengeance*, 20, 28.

65. Even during the troubled early years of the Weimar Republic when political assassinations were rife, the largest category of death sentences passed between 1919 and 1925 involved the murder of victims closely related to the offender (Richard J. Evans, *Rituals of Retribution: Capital Punishment in Germany, 1600–1987* [Oxford: Oxford University Press, 1996], 525). One possibility is that the fellow prisoner who advised Tehlirian at the time might have had in mind the political makeup of the German judiciary. Remnants of the previous monarchical regime, judges of the Weimar Republic were famously conservative as they had been selected under Wilhelm II for their political reliability. Statistician Emil Gumbel's study of the adjudication of political crimes between late 1918 and the summer of 1922 revealed that 54 murders committed by rightists resulted in no death sentences, 1 life sentence, a total of 90 years and 2 months in prison and 326 unpunished perpetrators; whereas 22 murders committed by leftists in this period resulted in 10 death sentences, 3 life sentences, a total of 248 years and 9 months in prison, and 4 unpunished perpetrators (Morris, *Justice Imperiled*, 1). This kind of pervasive judicial right-wing

bias could have resulted in a harsh condemnation of the assassin of Talat, an ally of the Kaiser, but that might be an argument stretched too thin.

66. Quoted in Hofmann, "New Aspects of the Talat Pasha Court Case," 44.

67. Eric D. Weitz, "Germany and the Young Turks: Revolutionaries into Statesmen," in *A Question of Genocide: Armenians and Turks at the End of the Ottoman Empire*, ed. Ronald Grigor Suny, Fatma Müge Göçek, and Norman M. Naimark (Oxford: Oxford University Press, 2011), 176–77.

68. Donald Bloxham, *The Great Game of Genocide: Imperialism, Nationalism, and the Destruction of the Ottoman Armenians* (Oxford: Oxford University Press, 2005), 129–30.

69. Lepsius was in fact the perfect candidate for helping prove Germany's innocence, as he had already done much to absolve Germany of complicity. As Moses puts it, "The renowned Armenophile . . . was first and foremost a German nationalist" (Moses, "The Assassination of Talaat Pasha," 16).

5. Spectral Legacies: Legal Aftermaths of the Armenian Genocide

1. See, for example, Emilios A. Christodoulidis, "Law's Immemorial," in *Lethe's Law: Justice, Law and Ethics in Reconciliation*, ed. Emilios A. Christodoulidis and Scott Veitch (Oxford: Hart Publishing, 2001), 207–27; Robert Meister, *After Evil: A Politics of Human Rights*, Columbia Studies in Political Thought/Political History (New York: Columbia University Press, 2011); Stewart Motha and Honni Van Rijswijk, eds., *Law, Memory, Violence: Uncovering the Counter-Archive* (Abingdon: Routledge, 2017); Stewart Motha, *Archiving Sovereignty: Law, History, Violence* (Ann Arbor: University of Michigan Press, 2018); Norman W. Spaulding, "Trauma, Memory, and the Law," in *The Oxford Handbook of Law and Humanities*, ed. Simon Stern, Maksymilian Del Mar, and Bernadette Meyler (New York: Oxford University Press, 2019), 288–316.

2. Jacques Derrida, "Force of Law: 'The Mystical Foundation of Authority,'" in *Acts of Religion*, ed. Gil Anidjar, trans. Mary Quaintance (New York: Routledge, 2002), 242.

3. Jacques Derrida, *Specters of Marx: The State of the Debt, the Work of Mourning and the New International* (New York: Routledge, 2006), 48.

4. Derrida, "Force of Law," 202.

5. Wendy Brown, *Politics Out of History* (Princeton, NJ: Princeton University Press, 2001), 145.

6. Shoshana Felman, *The Juridical Unconscious: Trials and Traumas in the Twentieth Century* (Cambridge, MA: Harvard University Press, 2002), 61.

7. Taner Akçam, *Killing Orders: Talat Pasha's Telegrams and the Armenian Genocide* (London: Palgrave Macmillan, 2018), 8.

8. The most comprehensive study of the tribunal is Vahakn N. Dadrian and Taner Akçam, *Judgment at Istanbul: The Armenian Genocide Trials* (New York: Berghahn Books, 2011).

9. See, for example, Feridun Ata, *İşgal İstanbul'unda Tehcir Yargılamaları* (Ankara: Türk Tarih Kurumu, 2005).

10. One account that risks such a misrecognition is Gary J. Bass's discussion in *Stay the Hand of Vengeance: The Politics of War Crimes Tribunals* (Princeton, NJ: Princeton University Press, 2000), 106–46. His account is valuable for placing the "Constantinople" trials within a historical context of attempted and actual war crimes tribunals from St. Helena to The Hague, thus revising the Nuremberg-centered narrative. However, because Bass chooses to frame the Ottoman trials mainly as an issue for British politics, reconstructing the history principally through British military and diplomatic exchanges, he makes a number of conclusions that end up partaking in the self-centered confusions of British imperialism at that time. For example, Bass claims that the Ottoman court-martial was "created under massive British pressure" (106) and dates the beginning of this pressure to January 1919 (119), which of course, fails to explain the existence of two Ottoman parliamentary commissions investigating the Armenian massacres from as early on as November 1918, a fact that Bass himself notes (ibid.). Bass also blames the failure of the Ottoman tribunals and the frustration of the later international tribunal attempts at Malta on British "legalism" (107), but see Taner Akçam, *A Shameful Act: The Armenian Genocide and the Question of Turkish Responsibility* (New York: Henry Holt, 2007), 415–424, for a much more nuanced discussion that instead highlights the role of British colonialism in this failure.

11. Ayhan Aktar, "Debating the Armenian Massacres in the Last Ottoman Parliament, November December 1918," *History Workshop Journal* 64, no. 1 (2007): 240–70.

12. National Congress of Turkey, *The Turco-Armenian Question: The Turkish Point of View* (Constantinople: Société Anonyme de Papeterie et d'Imprimerie, 1919), 83.

13. "Bütün bir kavmin mevcudiyet-i siyaset değil, mevcudiyet-i hayatiyesini imhaya kalkabildiniz." Mehmed Cavid Bey, *Meşrutiyet Ruznâmesi*, ed. Hasan Babacan and Servet Avşar, vol. 3 (Ankara: Türk Tarih Kurumu, 2014), 135. I am grateful to İpek Çalışlar for alerting me to this source.

14. Vahakn N. Dadrian, "The Turkish Military Tribunal's Prosecution of the Authors of the Armenian Genocide: Four Major Court-Martial Series," *Holocaust and Genocide Studies* 11, no. 1 (1997): 28–59; Bass, *Stay the Hand of Vengeance*.

15. Dadrian and Akçam, *Judgment at Istanbul*.

16. An English translation of the full text of the Key Indictment in the trial against the leading Committee of Union and Progress members and wartime cabinet ministers is printed in ibid., 271–290. A summary of the documentary evidence against Talat can be found in Akçam, *A Shameful Act*, 182.

17. Quoted in Akçam, *A Shameful Act*, 2.

18. M. Cherif Bassiouni, *Crimes against Humanity in International Criminal Law*, 2nd rev. ed. (The Hague: Kluwer Law International, 1999), 1.

19. Raphael Lemkin, *Totally Unofficial: The Autobiography of Raphael Lemkin*, ed. Donna-Lee Frieze (New Haven, CT: Yale University Press, 2013), 20. See also

Philippe Sands's *East West Street: On the Origins of "Genocide" and "Crimes against Humanity"* (New York: Alfred A. Knopf, 2016), 146–49, for a narrative account of Lemkin's encounter with Tehlirian's trial.

20. Quoted in Tessa Hofmann, "New Aspects of the Talat Pasha Court Case," *Armenian Review* 42, no. 4 (1989): 51.

21. For a compelling discussion of the significance of biographical directions in the study of international law, see Gerry Simpson, "The Sentimental Lives of International Lawyers," in *The Sentimental Life of International Law: Literature, Language, and Longing in World Politics* (Oxford: Oxford University Press, 2021), 30–54.

22. The title phrase of this section is from Christina Sharpe, *In the Wake: On Blackness and Being* (Durham, NC: Duke University Press, 2016), 5.

23. "Zum Tode Talaat Paschas," *Kölnische Zeitung*, 16 March 1921.

24. Fritz Bronsart von Schellendorf, "Ein Zeugnis für Talaat Pascha," *Deutsche Allgemeine Zeitung*, 24 July 1921.

25. Hannah Arendt, *Eichmann in Jerusalem: A Report on the Banality of Evil* (1963; New York: Penguin, 1994), 264.

26. Roger Berkowitz, "Assassinating Justly: Reflections on Justice and Revenge in the Osama Bin Laden Killing," *Law, Culture and the Humanities* 7, no. 3 (2011): 350.

27. Arendt, *Eichmann in Jerusalem*, 266, emphasis mine.

28. Mim Kemal Öke, *Duvardaki Kan* (Istanbul: Babıali Kültür, 2012). This was originally the script for a TV series broadcast on Turkish national television in the mid-1980s.

29. Lindy V. Avakian, *The Cross and the Crescent* (Phoenix, AZ: USC Press, 1989), 125.

30. Oktay Ekşi, "Berlin'de hakim var mı?" *Hürriyet*, 1 March 2005, http://webarsiv .hurriyet.com.tr/2005/03/01/606954.asp.

31. "A folk hero to most Armenians, [Tehlirian's] name was often cited when Armenian terrorism against Turkish officials was launched again in 1975" (Khachig Tololyan, "Terrorism in Modern Armenian Political Culture," in *Political Parties and Terrorist Groups*, ed. Leonard Weinberg [London: Frank Cass, 1992], 15).

32. Fatma Müge Göçek, *The Transformation of Turkey: Redefining State and Society from the Ottoman Empire to the Modern Era* (London: I. B. Tauris, 2011), 52, emphasis mine.

33. Zoryan Institute, ed., *The Case of Soghomon Tehlirian*, trans. Vartkes Yeghiayan (Los Angeles: A. R. F. Varantian Gomideh, 1985), vii.

34. Fatma Müge Göçek, *Denial of Violence: Ottoman Past, Turkish Present, and Collective Violence against the Armenians, 1789–2009* (Oxford: Oxford University Press, 2015), 46–47.

35. Taner Akçam and Neşe Düzel, "Ermeni olayında Atatürk'ü izleyelim," *Taraf*, 14 March 2012.

36. Kemal Göktaş, *Hrant Dink Cinayeti: Medya, Yargı, Devlet* (Istanbul: Güncel, 2009).

37. Interview with Hakan Bakırcıoğlu, 28 November 2020, Radyo Agos, *Açık Radyo*. Available at https://soundcloud.com/agosweekly/dink-ailesi-avukatlarindan-hakan-bakircioglu-hrant-dink-cinayeti-davasinda-gelinen-asamayi-degerlendirdi.

38. The Armenian "diaspora" generally refers to people of Armenian ethnic origin living outside of Armenia, Turkey, and Iran, and as such does not include the Armenian population of Turkey.

39. The address ends with the well-known formulation: "The strength you shall need exists in the noble blood flowing through your veins."

40. Fethiye Çetin, *Utanç Duyuyorum! Hrant Dink Cinayetinin Yargısı* (İstanbul: Metis, 2013).

41. European Court of Human Rights, "Press Release: Chamber judgment Dink v. Turkey," *HUDOC*, 14 September 2010, http://hudoc.echr.coe.int/eng-press?i=003-3262169-3640194.

42. For a study of the paradoxes of accountability for state violence that this slogan captures and attests to, see Ceylan Begüm Yıldız, "'The Murderer State Will Be Held to Account': The Myth of the State and Its Violence," PhD thesis, Birkbeck, University of London, 2021, https://eprints.bbk.ac.uk/id/eprint/47302/.

43. Fethiye Çetin and Deniz Tuna, "Hrant Dink Suikastı 2. Yıl Raporu" (Hrant Dink Vakfı, 2009).

44. Rahil Dink et al., 'Esas Hakkında Görüş, Istanbul 14th High Criminal Court, Case no: 2007/428, submitted on 5 December 2011, at 48, 52. Available at https://hrantdink.org/attachments/article/318/Hrant-Dink-Cinayeti-Davasi-Esas-Hakkinda-Gorus-ve-Ekleri.pdf.

45. Ibid., 59–72.

46. Cf. Jacques Vergès, *De la Stratégie judiciare* (Paris: Minuit, 1968).

47. Cf. Emilios A. Christodoulidis, "The Objection That Cannot Be Heard: Communication and Legitimacy in the Courtroom," in *The Trial on Trial: Truth and Due Process*, ed. Anthony Duff et al., vol. 1 (Oxford: Hart, 2004), 179–202.

48. Derrida, *Specters of Marx*, 48.

49. *Reservations to the Convention on the Prevention and Punishment of the Crime of Genocide*, Advisory Opinion, [1951] ICJ Rep 15 at 23.

50. Marc Nichanian, *The Historiographic Perversion*, trans. Gil Anidjar (New York: Columbia University Press, 2009), 27.

51. Derrida, "Force of Law," 296.

52. Qtd. in Vahakn N. Dadrian, "Documentation of Armenian Genocide in German Sources," in *Encyclopedia of Genocide*, ed. Israel W. Charny, vol. 1 (Santa Barbara: ABC-CLIO, 1999), 91.

53. Alice von Bieberstein, "Surviving Hrant Dink: Carnal Mourning under the Specter of Senselessness," *Social Analysis* 61, no. 1 (2017).

54. Walter Benjamin, "Toward the Critique of Violence," trans. Julia Ng, in *Toward the Critique of Violence: A Critical Edition*, ed. Peter D. Fenves and Julia Ng (Stanford, CA: Stanford University Press, 2021), 47.

55. Yetvart Danzikyan, "İnkâr Siyasetinde Kırılma: Hrant Dink'in Kendisi ve Öldürülmesi," *Mülkiye Dergisi* 39, no. 1 (2015): 250. My translation.

56. Derrida, "Force of Law," 242.

57. Nichanian, *Historiographic Perversion*, 37.

6. Law of Denial: The Armenian Genocide before the European Court of Human Rights

1. "Fransa'da 'soykırım yapılmadı' derim," *Milliyet*, 9 October 2006, https://www.milliyet.com.tr/siyaset/fransada-soykirim-yapilmadi-derim-173613. In the end, the French draft bill did not come into force because a political decision prevented it from appearing on the Senate's agenda. Later, in 2011, a draft bill criminalizing the denial of genocides "recognized by law" (including the Armenian genocide, officially recognized in France in 2001, with law no. 2001–70) was passed by both the French National Assembly and the Senate, but overturned by the Constitutional Council in February 2012 (decision no. 2012-647). This was repeated more recently with a draft bill, specifically criminalizing the denial of the Armenian genocide, passed in 2016 and overruled by the Constitutional Council in January 2017 (decision no. 2016-745).

2. The political limitations and functions of free speech absolutism have been highlighted in recent high-profile debates, for example, in the aftermath of the Danish cartoon crisis, following the Charlie Hebdo killings. See, respectively, Mahmood Mamdani, "The Political Uses of Free Speech," *Outlook*, 14 February 2006, https://www.outlookindia.com/website/story/the-political-uses-of-free-speech/230211; Nadine El-Enany and Sarah Keenan, "I Am Charlie and I Guard the Master's House," *Critical Legal Thinking*, 13 January 2015, http://criticallegalthinking.com/2015/01/13/charlie-guard-masters-house/.

3. Dink articulated this in numerous interviews at the time. See also a letter to the French daily *Liberation* that he co-signed with eight others, published one week before the draft bill was due to be debated in the National Assembly: "Le travail sur l'histoire sera bloqué en Turquie," *Liberation*, 10 May 2006, 35.

4. At the time, Archbishop Mesrob II Mutafyan, the Armenian Patriarch of Constantinople, stated that "as Turkish Armenians we feel serious pressure in relation to this bill" and called for increased state security to protect churches and minority schools ("Ermeni Patriği: Fransızlar diyaloğu sabote ettiler," *Hürriyet*, 13 October 2006, http://www.hurriyet.com.tr/gundem/ermeni-patrigi-fransizlar-diyalogu-sabote-ettiler-5251443).

5. Immanuel M. Wallerstein, *European Universalism: The Rhetoric of Power* (New York: New Press, 2006).

6. See, for example, Ludovic Hennebel and Thomas Hochmann, eds., *Genocide Denials and the Law* (Oxford: Oxford University Press, 2011); Stiina Löytömäki, *Law and the Politics of Memory: Confronting the Past* (Abingdon: Routledge, 2014);

Uladzislau Belavusau and Aleksandra Gliszczyńska-Grabias, eds., *Law and Memory: Towards Legal Governance of History* (Cambridge: Cambridge University Press, 2017); Emanuela Fronza, *Memory and Punishment: Historical Denialism, Free Speech and the Limits of Criminal Law* (The Hague: T.M.C. Asser Press, 2018).

7. EU Framework Decision 2008/913/JHA of 28 November 2008.

8. Emilios A. Christodoulidis, "Law's Immemorial," in *Lethe's Law: Justice, Law and Ethics in Reconciliation*, ed. Emilios A. Christodoulidis and Scott Veitch (Oxford: Hart Publishing, 2001), 208.

9. Perinçek v. Switzerland, European Court of Human Rights, application no. 27510/08, Chamber Judgment, 17 December 2013. Hereafter, I will cite "*Perinçek* 2013" for the Chamber judgment, and "*Perinçek* 2015 (GC)" for the Grand Chamber judgment.

10. Marc Nichanian, *The Historiographic Perversion*, trans. Gil Anidjar (New York: Columbia University Press, 2009), 29.

11. While some commentators identify this shift as a full about-turn (e.g., Gün Zileli, "41 yıl önceki TİİKP ve bugünkü VP," 14 May 2015, http://www.gunzileli.com /2015/05/15/41-yil-onceki-tiikp-ve-bugunku-vp/), others trace the party's currently amplified strands of ultranationalism, militarism, Kemalism, and statism to its conception of the political in its earlier guises ("Geçmişin 'Aydınlık'ından Dersler," *Birikim*, no. 98 [1997]: 19–30; Suavi Aydın, "'Milli Demokratik Devrim'den 'Ulusal Sol'a Türk Solunda Özgücü Eğilim," *Toplum ve Bilim*, no. 78 [1998]: 59–91). For a discussion of Perinçek's contemporary political position as neo-conservative, neo-nationalist, and neo-Eurasianist, see Necati Polat, "Resistance to Regime Change in the Middle East: A Liberation Theology of the Neo-Con Variety?" *Interventions* 16, no. 5 (2014): 634–54.

12. I explore the bizarre ironies of the Ergenekon process in "The Conspiracy Archive: Turkey's 'Deep State' on Trial," in *Law, Memory, Violence: Uncovering the Counter-Archive*, ed. Stewart Motha and Honni Van Rijswijk (Abingdon: Routledge, 2017), 177–94.

13. See Ergenekon Case (Turkey) Detailed Judgment, 2014, Istanbul 13th Heavy Penal Court, Case no.: 2009/191, Judgment no.: 2013/95. Perinçek and other Ergenekon defendants' convictions were overturned by the Court of Cassation in April 2016 due to its finding of a host of procedural irregularities, and a retrial was ordered, which began in June 2017 and concluded in July 2019 with acquittals for 235 defendants.

14. *Perinçek* 2015 (GC), §22.

15. Özge Eğrikar, 2010, "Milli Menfaat'ten AİHM'ye Gidiyor," *Hürriyet*, 20 January 2010, http://www.hurriyet.com.tr/milli-menfaat-ten-aihm-ye-gidiyor -28004890.

16. My focus here precludes a wider review of the different arguments and strategies historically employed in the service of denying the Armenian genocide. This is the subject of numerous careful studies published over the last few decades,

notably: Richard G. Hovannisian, "Genocide and Denial: The Armenian Case," in *Toward the Understanding and Prevention of Genocide: Proceedings of the International Conference on the Holocaust and Genocide*, ed. Israel W. Charny (Boulder, CO: Westview Press, 1984), 84–99; Richard G. Hovannisian, "Denial of the Armenian Genocide in Comparison with Holocaust Denial," in *Remembrance and Denial: The Case of the Armenian Genocide*, ed. R. G. Hovannisian (Detroit: Wayne State University Press, 1998), 201–36; Israel W. Charny, "The Psychology of Denial of Known Genocides," in *Genocide: A Critical Bibliographic Review*, ed. Israel W. Charny, vol. 2 (London: Mansell, 1991), 3–37. For a monumental undertaking that traces patterns of collective denial across hundreds of Turkish memoirs, see Fatma Müge Göçek, *Denial of Violence: Ottoman Past, Turkish Present, and Collective Violence against the Armenians, 1789–2009* (Oxford: Oxford University Press, 2015).

17. Although see Hovannisian, "Denial of the Armenian Genocide," for numerous commonalities between Holocaust denialism and Armenian genocide denialism.

18. Stanley Cohen, *States of Denial: Knowing about Atrocities and Suffering* (Cambridge: Polity, 2001), 9, 106.

19. *Perinçek* 2013, §79.

20. Under "Count 3: War crimes": "[The defendants] conducted deliberate and systematic genocide, viz., the extermination of racial and national groups, against the civilian populations of certain occupied territories in order to destroy particular races and classes of people and national, racial, or religious groups, particularly Jews, Poles, and Gypsies and others" (IMT Indictment, VIII A).

21. For the idiosyncratic legal history of "genocide" bound up as it was with the tenacious efforts of Raphael Lemkin, see Hilary Earl, "Prosecuting Genocide before the Genocide Convention: Raphael Lemkin and the Nuremberg Trials, 1945–1949," *Journal of Genocide Research* 15, no. 3 (2013): 317–37. See also Philippe Sands, *East West Street: On the Origins of "Genocide" and "Crimes against Humanity"* (New York: Alfred A. Knopf, 2016).

22. Geoffrey Robertson QC, representing Armenia, made this point in the Grand Chamber hearing: Perinçek v. Switzerland (2015) ECtHR. Application no. 27510/08. Webcast of Grand Chamber Hearing, 28 January 2015, https://www.echr.coe.int /Pages/home.aspx?p=hearings&w=2751008_28012015&language=lang&c=&py=2015.

23. For example, historian Taner Akçam draws on a variety of sources in his attempt to prove intent, including testimonies given in the Ottoman Special Military Tribunal which sentenced Talat and others to death for organizing the massacres of Armenians, reports of Talat's discussions with foreign diplomats, and cables sent by Talat in his capacity as Interior Minister in Taner Akçam, *The Young Turks' Crime against Humanity: The Armenian Genocide and Ethnic Cleansing in the Ottoman Empire*, Human Rights and Crimes against Humanity (Princeton, NJ: Princeton University Press, 2012).

24. *Perinçek* 2013, §83.

25. Although see, for an exception: Fatallayev v. Azerbaijan, European Court of Human Rights, application no. 40984/07, Judgment 22 April 2010.

26. Lehideux and Isorni v. France, European Court of Human Rights, application no. 24662/94, Judgment 23 August 1998, §46.

27. Paolo Lobba, "Holocaust Denial before the European Court of Human Rights: Evolution of an Exceptional Regime," *European Journal of International Law* 26, no. 1 (2015): 237–53.

28. Laurent Pech, "The Law of Holocaust Denial in Europe," in *Genocide Denials and the Law*, ed. Ludovic Hennebel and Thomas Hochmann (Oxford: Oxford University Press, 2011), 219. This article by Laurent Pech provides a comprehensive review of criminalization of Holocaust denial in Europe, and offers a critical take on the EU Framework Decision 2008/913/JHA of 28 November 2008, which calls for each member state to ensure that "publicly condoning, denying or grossly trivializing crimes of genocide, crimes against humanity and war crimes" is punishable. Pech had the opportunity to test some of his analyses and arguments as Perinçek's counsel in the ECtHR Grand Chamber hearing on 28 January 2015, see *Perinçek*, Webcast of GC Hearing.

29. *Perinçek* 2013, §99.

30. See, for example, Chauvy v. France, European Court of Human Rights, application no. 64915/01, Judgment 29 June 2004.

31. Pech, "The Law of Holocaust Denial in Europe," 219.

32. Compare this to the infamous Holocaust denier Robert Faurisson, whose language "is that of the positivist; he is endlessly calling for the opening of archives and the engagement of debate" (Jeffrey Mehlman, Foreword to *Assassins of Memory: Essays on the Denial of the Holocaust*, by Pierre Vidal-Naquet [New York: Columbia University Press, 1992], xix).

33. Compare, again, to Faurisson, who Pierre Vidal-Naquet famously identified as a "paper Eichmann": "Eichmann crossed Europe to organize the train transport system. Faurisson does not have trains at his disposal, but paper. P. Guillaume describes him for us: 'a man thoroughly in possession of his subject (200 kilograms of working documents, representing research on several tons of texts)' (Vérité, p. 139)" (Vidal-Naquet, *Assassins of Memory*, 24).

34. Nichanian, *Historiographic Perversion*, 30.

35. Lewis Case (France) High Court of Paris. 21 June 1995: *Juris-Data* no. 044058.

36. *Perinçek* 2015 (GC), §286.

37. In freedom of expression cases at the ECtHR, the profession of the applicant is taken into account, and for good reason (see discussion in Hennebel and Hochmann, Introduction to *Genocide Denials and the Law*, xxviii–xxix). Yet the emphasis on Perinçek's fifty-year-old doctoral qualification when his subsequent career has had nothing to do with legal practice or scholarship is conspicuous.

38. *Perinçek* 2013, §117.

39. See Chapter 1 for an extended discussion of Kirchheimer's and Shklar's frameworks that are alluded to here.

40. *Perinçek* 2013, §99.

41. *Perinçek* 2013, §117.

42. Jean-François Lyotard, *The Differend: Phrases in Dispute* (Manchester: Manchester University Press, 1988), 8–10, 18–19.

43. Nichanian, *Historiographic Perversion*, 39.

44. For an argument in favor of such self-referentiality in memory laws, see David Fraser, "Law's Holocaust Denial: State, Memory, Legality," in *Genocide Denials and the Law*, ed. Ludovic Hennebel and Thomas Hochmann (Oxford: Oxford University Press, 2011), 21–22.

45. Constitutional Council (France) Decision no. 2015-512 QPC of 8 January 2016.

46. Constitutional Council (France) Decision no. 2012-647 DC of 28 February 2012.

47. Christodoulidis, "Law's Immemorial," 218.

48. *Perinçek* 2013, §13.

49. *Perinçek* 2013, §§114–18.

50. *Perinçek* 2013, §118.

51. *Perinçek*, Webcast of GC hearing.

52. *Perinçek*, Webcast of GC hearing.

53. *Perinçek*, Webcast of GC hearing. Though this is somewhat surprising given his own questioning of the soundness of ECtHR's notion of "clearly established historical facts" (Pech, "The Law of Holocaust Denial in Europe").

54. *Perinçek* 2015 (GC), §156.

55. *Perinçek* 2015 (GC), §157.

56. *Perinçek* 2015 (GC), §243, emphasis mine.

57. *Perinçek* 2015 (GC), §244.

58. *Perinçek* 2015 (GC), §245.

59. *Perinçek* 2015 (GC), §208. However, for an important and insightful set of objections to the "nexus argument" mobilized in the *Perinçek* case, whereby a nexus is required between the state enacting the ban on denial and the historical act being denied, see Robert A. Kahn, "Banning Genocide Denial—Should Geography Matter?" in *Law and Memory: Towards Legal Governance of History*, ed. Uladzislau Belavusau and Aleksandra Gliszczyńska-Grabias (Cambridge: Cambridge University Press, 2017), 329–47.

Conclusion

1. Shoshana Felman, *The Juridical Unconscious: Trials and Traumas in the Twentieth Century* (Cambridge, MA: Harvard University Press, 2002), 124.

2. Tom Segev, *The Seventh Million: The Israelis and the Holocaust* (New York: Hill and Wang, 1993); Lawrence Douglas, *The Memory of Judgment: Making Law*

and History in the Trials of the Holocaust (New Haven, CT: Yale University Press, 2001); Jacqueline Rose, *The Last Resistance* (London: Verso, 2007).

3. Felman, *Juridical Unconscious*, 215n13: "It is hard today (in 2002) not to think in this connection of the Palestinian tragedy (ensuing from the Israeli right to justice) and not to recognize the Palestinians' equal right to justice tragically asserted in the violence and in the daily conflicts on Israel's (today's) still more 'unhappy borders.'"

4. See Hannah Arendt and Karl Jaspers, *Correspondence, 1926–1969*, ed. Lotte Köhler and Hans Saner (New York: Harcourt Brace Jovanovich, 1992), 54.

5. Felman, *Juridical Unconscious*, 3.

6. Roger Berkowitz, "Assassinating Justly: Reflections on Justice and Revenge in the Osama Bin Laden Killing," *Law, Culture and the Humanities* 7, no. 3 (2011): 347.

7. For an astute critique of the earlier "war" against terror, see Edward W. Said, "The Essential Terrorist," *The Nation*, 14 June 1986, 828–33.

8. Nasser Hussain, "Hyperlegality," *New Criminal Law Review* 10, no. 4 (2007): 514.

9. Nasser Hussain, "Beyond Norm and Exception: Guantánamo," *Critical Inquiry* 33, no. 4 (2007): 739.

10. For an interesting counter-analysis, see Matteo Tiratelli, "Reclaiming the Everyday: The Situational Dynamics of the 2011 London Riots," *Social Movement Studies* 17, no. 1 (2018): 64–84.

11. In the words of the then Chief Crown Prosecutor for Northwest England Nazir Afzal, quoted in Joe Sim, "'Shock and Awe': Judicial Responses to the Riots," *Criminal Justice Matters* 89, no. 1 (2012): 26.

12. John Paul Ford Rojas, "London Riots: Lidl Water Thief Jailed for Six Months," *Telegraph*, 11 August 2011, https://www.telegraph.co.uk/news/uknews/crime/8695988/London-riots-Lidl-water-thief-jailed-for-six-months.html.

13. Ministry of Justice, *Statistical Bulletin on the Public Disorder of 6th–9th August 2011–September 2012 Update*, 13 September 2012, https://assets.publishing.service.gov.uk/government/uploads/system/uploads/attachment_data/file/219665/august-public-disorder-stats-bulletin-130912.pdf.

14. Carly Lightowlers and Hannah Quirk, "The 2011 English 'Riots': Prosecutorial Zeal and Judicial Abandon," *British Journal of Criminology* 55, no. 1 (2015): 65–85.

15. Matteo Tiratelli, "The London Riots Ten Years On: How a Crackdown on Protest Became Their Main Legacy," *Conversation*, 2 August 2021, https://theconversation.com/the-london-riots-ten-years-on-how-a-crackdown-on-protest-became-their-main-legacy-165048.

16. Tim Newburn, "Disaster Averted But Questions Remain Over Courts' Response to Riots," *Guardian*, 3 July 2012, https://www.theguardian.com/uk/2012/jul/03/questions-remain-court-response-riots.

17. The Movement for Black Lives and CLEAR, *Struggle for Power: The Ongoing Persecution of the Black Movement by the U.S. Government*, 18 August 2021, https://m4bl.org/struggle-for-power.

18. For the text of the petition, see "We Will Not Be a Party to This Crime," *Academics for Peace* website, 10 January 2016, https://barisicinakademisyenler.net /node/63. For an analysis of the indictment, see Judith Butler and Başak Ertür, "Trials Begin in Turkey for Academics for Peace," *Critical Legal Thinking*, 11 December 2017, https://criticallegalthinking.com/2017/12/11/trials-begin-turkey -academics-peace/.

19. For comprehensive reports on the criminalization of solidarity with people on the move in Europe, see Amnesty International, *Punishing Compassion: Solidarity on Trial in Fortress Europe*, 3 March 2020, AI EUR 01/1828/2020, https://www.amnesty.org/en/documents/euro1/1828/2020/en/; and Nandini Archer, Claudia Torrisi, Claire Provost, Alexander Nabert, and Belen Lobos, "Hundreds of Europeans 'Criminalised' for Helping Migrants—As Far Right Aims to Win Big in European Elections," *OpenDemocracy*, 18 May 2019, https://www.opendemocracy .net/en/5050/hundreds-of-europeans-criminalised-for-helping-migrants-new-data -shows-as-far-right-aims-to-win-big-in-european-elections/. See also Rory Carroll, "Eight Activists Helping Migrants Cross Brutal Desert Charged by US Government," *Guardian*, 24 January 2018, https://www.theguardian.com/us-news/2018/jan/24/us -immigration-activists-arizona-no-more-deaths-charged.

20. See Cemre Baytok, "Political Vigilance in Court Rooms: Feminist Interventions in the Field of Law" (MA thesis, Istanbul, Boğaziçi University, 2012); Daniela Alaattinoğlu and Cemre Baytok, "Fighting Femicide in Turkey—Feminist Legal Challenges," in *Contesting Femicide: Feminism and the Power of Law Revisited*, ed. Adrian Howe and Daniela Alaattinoğlu (Oxon: Routledge, 2019), 73–83.

21. Eyal Weizman, "Introduction: Forensis," in *Forensis: The Architecture of Public Truth*, ed. Forensic Architecture (Berlin: Sternberg Press, 2014), 9.

22. For a succinct overview of the WTI process, its context and rationale, see Richard A. Falk, "World Tribunal on Iraq: Truth Law and Justice," in *The Costs of War: International Law, the UN, and World Order after Iraq* (New York: Routledge, 2008), 171–82. For an in-depth ethnography, see Ayça Çubukçu, *For the Love of Humanity: The World Tribunal on Iraq*, Pennsylvania Studies in Human Rights (Philadelphia: University of Pennsylvania Press, 2018). The proceedings of the culminating session are published as Müge Gürsoy Sökmen, ed., *World Tribunal on Iraq: Making the Case against War* (Northampton: Olive Branch Press, 2008), and documented in Zeynep Dadak et al., *For the Record: The World Tribunal on Iraq*, 2006, https://vimeo.com/190482738.

23. See Russell Tribunal on Palestine website, http://www.russelltribunalonpalestine .com/en/.

24. See Giovanni Prete and Christel Cournil, "Staging International Environmental Justice: The International Monsanto Tribunal," *PoLAR: Political and Legal Anthropology Review* 42, no. 2 (2019): 191–209.

25. See Tribunal NSU-Komplex Auflösen website, https://www.nsu-tribunal.de/en/.

26. Chowra Makaremi and Pardis Shafafi, "Introduction," *PoLAR: Political and Legal Anthropology Review* 42, no. 2 (2019): 181–90.

Index

performance studies, 9, 84
performativity: and agency, 9–11, 76–77,
81–96, 100; and failure, 9–11, 14, 23, 54–56,
63, 76–100, 132, 176, 200n8; and law, 5,
37–38, 41, 44–45, 47–49, 50, 57–75, 132,
159, 168–69, 175–78, 184–85; and performance, 4–11, 53, 56, 64–66, 69–75, 76,
84–87, 95–100; gender, 9–10, 52, 57, 65–66,
68, 84–86, 93, 205n16; theories of, 4–5,
9–11, 52–75, 76–77, 81–96, 98, 131, 176
Peters, Julie Stone, 8–9
Petliura, Symon, 138
Pitcher, George, 202n41
PKK, 181
Plato, 10, 192n16
political trials, 21–51, 53, 63, 69–75, 76–81,
84, 95–100, 131–38, 175–85; definition, 1–3,
11, 13, 21–26, 42–43, 70–75, 194n4; didactic,
pedagogic function, 4, 44, 50, 131; historiographic function, 4, 30, 33, 44, 50, 71–72,
116, 165–71; image-making function, 25,
30, 49, 79, 81; instrumentalist accounts,
1–3, 21–23, 76; memorial function, 4, 17,
50, 116–17, 131
political violence, 2–5, 15–17, 100, 104, 130, 131,
133, 139–43, 155, 157–58, 175, 184–85. See also
extralegal violence; legal violence
Poole, Ross, 125–26
positivism (legal), 41, 47, 57, 61–62, 66
Posner, Eric, 50
principle of legality, 32, 43, 73
principle of publicity, 25–26, 79–81
psychoanalysis, psychoanalytic theory, 10,
94, 120, 209n32
Pussy Riot, 73

R v Sussex Justices (1924), 8, 192n9
revisionism. See genocide: denialism
Riviere, Joan, 65
Rivonia Trial, 13
Rosen, Pinchas, 38
Rosenberg, Julius and Ethel: trial, 12, 45, 72,
192n20
Ross, Alf, 58
Rössler, Walter, 113–15
Rubin, Jerry, 77
Russell Tribunal, 184–85
Russo-Ottoman War (1877–78), 149

Sands, Philippe, 39–40
Schwartzbard, Sholem, 138, 140–41, 197n28
Seale, Bobby, 77–78, 96–99

Searle, John R., 52, 56, 59, 94, 205n16
Sedgwick, Eve Kosofksy, 52, 56, 70, 200n13
September 11 attacks, 177–79
Shafafi, Pardis, 185
Shakespeare, William, 23; Hamlet, 125–26
Shklar, Judith, 3, 13, 26, 41–51, 73, 166, 175,
177, 203n59; Legalism: Law, Morals and
Political Trials, 21–23, 41–48
show trials, 2, 21, 34, 70; distinction from
political trials, 25–26; "liberal," 50
Silesian Uprisings (1919–21, Weimar Republic),
128, 139
SITU Research, 184
slavery, 98–99, 197n28
social contract, 59–60, 80
Socrates trial, 11–12, 192n13, 192n16
Solf, Wilhelm, 106
sovereignty, sovereign power, 4, 10, 11, 36–37,
38, 50–51, 63, 76, 79–100, 185
speech act theory, 10, 54–56, 58–59, 63, 81–95,
200n14
Störmer, Robert, 118, 120, 209n39
state of exception, 179
state violence. See extralegal violence; legal
violence; political violence
strategy of rupture, 13, 149, 193n24. See also
defense strategy

Talat Pasha, 4, 15, 103–16, 122–23, 127–29, 132,
134–37, 139, 141–43, 163, 176, 208n21, 212n65,
213n16, 218n23
Talat Pasha Committee, 143, 160–61
Tehlirian, Soghomon, 103, 121–25, 140–43,
197n28, 208n18, 209n45, 209n46, 210n54,
211n63, 211n65, 214n31. See also Tehlirian
trial
Tehlirian trial, 4, 15–16, 103–30, 136, 165, 170,
176, 210n46; legacy, 130, 132–33, 139–43, 155
Terzibashian, Christine, 110, 111, 208n21
theatricality, 5–8, 9–10, 56, 65, 70, 73, 84–87,
93, 191n6, 199n8. See also performativity:
and performance
transitional justice, 3, 46, 49–50, 117, 131
trauma, 104, 118, 120, 153, 209n38
trauma studies, 14–15
Treaty of Lausanne (1923), 137
Treaty of Sevres (1920), 137
Treaty of Versailles (1919), 106, 137
Tribunal Unravelling the NSU-Complex, 185
Truth Justice Memory Center (Turkey), 160,
172
Turkey's Human Rights Association, 160, 172

BAŞAK ERTÜR teaches at the School of Law and co-directs the Centre for Law & the Humanities at Birkbeck, University of London. She is a Research Fellow at Forensic Architecture, Goldsmiths, University of London.

www.ingramcontent.com/pod-product-compliance
Lightning Source LLC
Chambersburg PA
CBHW020251030426
42336CB00010B/713

* 9 7 8 1 5 3 1 5 0 1 8 6 0 *